Abstergo

AN ASSASSIN'S CREED SERIES
TEMPLARS
BLACK CROSS

WRITER
FRED VAN LENTE

ARTIST
DENNIS CALERO

LETTERER
RICHARD STARKINGS AND COMICRAFT'S
JIMMY BETANCOURT

Abstergo

ASSASSIN'S CREED: TEMPLARS VOL. 1: BLACK CROSS
ISBN: 9781782763116

Published by Titan Comics
A division of Titan Publishing Group Ltd.
144 Southwark St.
London
SE1 0UP

A CIP catalogue record for this title is available from the British Library

First edition: November 2016

10 9 8 7 6 5 4 3 2 1

Printed in China.
Titan Comics. 0737

TITAN COMICS

EDITOR **LIZZIE KAYE**
SENIOR DESIGNER **ANDREW LEUNG**

Senior Comics Editor **Andrew James**
Titan Comics Editorial **Tom Williams, Jessica Burton, Amoona Saohin**
Production Supervisions **Jackie Flook, Maria Pearson**
Production Assistant **Peter James**
Production Manager **Obi Onuora**
Art Director **Oz Browne**
Senior Sales Manager **Steve Tothill**
Press Officer **Will O'Mullane**
Direct Sales & Marketing Manager **Ricky Claydon**
Publishing Manager **Darryl Tothill**
Publishing Director **Chris Teather**
Operations Director **Leigh Baulch**
Executive Director **Vivian Cheung**
Publisher **Nick Landau**

WWW.TITAN-COMICS.COM

Follow us on Twitter @ComicsTitan

Visit us at facebook.com/comicstitan

ACKNOWLEDGEMENTS:
Many thanks to Aymar Azaizia, Anouk Bachman, Richard Farrese,
Raphaël Lacoste, Caroline Lamache and Clémence Deleuze.

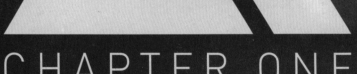

CHAPTER ONE

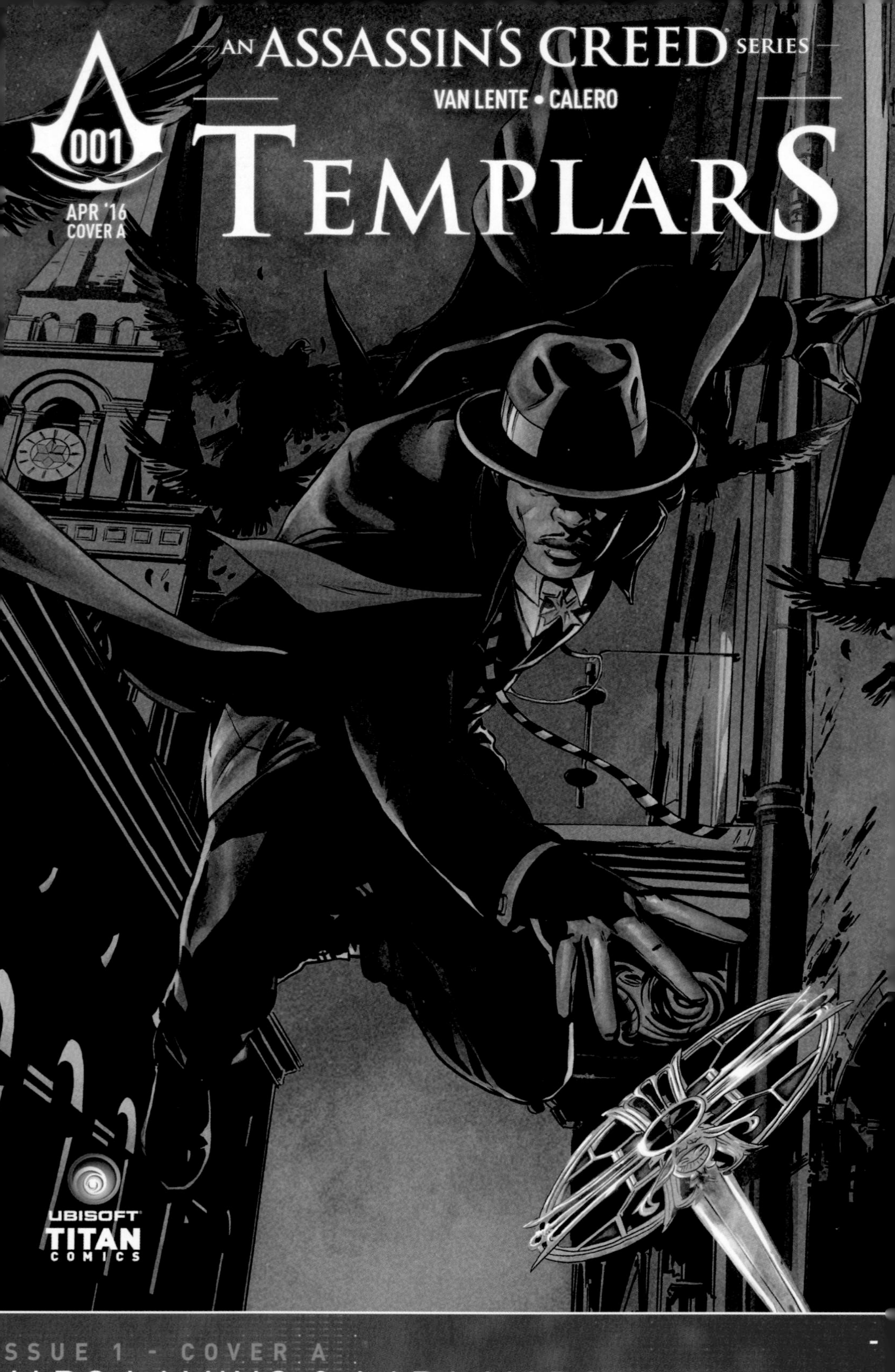
AN ASSASSIN'S CREED SERIES
VAN LENTE • CALERO
001
APR '16
COVER A
TEMPLARS
UBISOFT
TITAN
COMICS

SSUE 1 - COVER A
MARC LAMING & LARA MARGARIDA

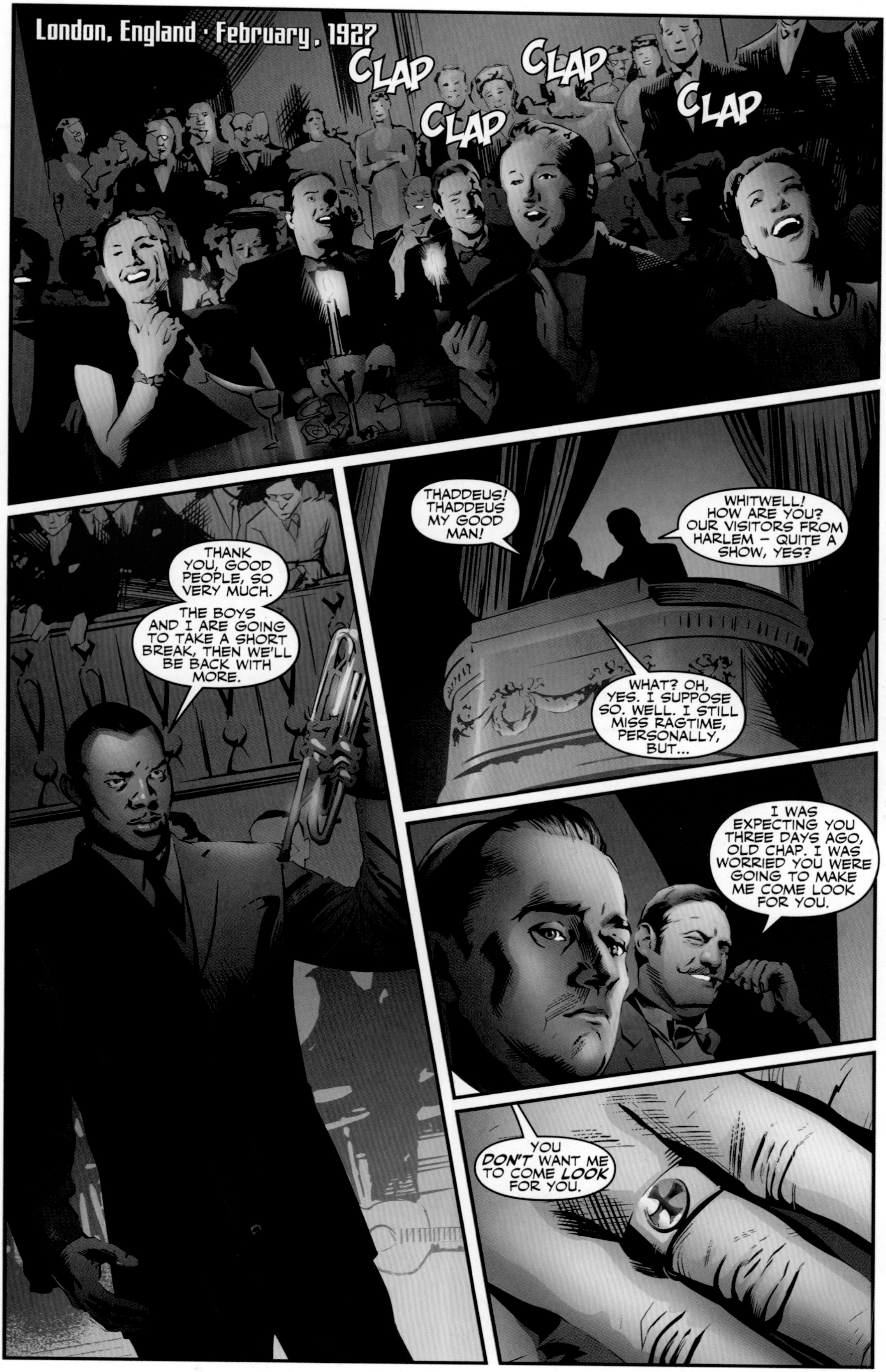
London, England · February, 1927
CLAP
CLAP
CLAP
CLAP
THANK YOU, GOOD PEOPLE, SO VERY MUCH.
THE BOYS AND I ARE GOING TO TAKE A SHORT BREAK, THEN WE'LL BE BACK WITH MORE.
THADDEUS! THADDEUS MY GOOD MAN!
WHITWELL! HOW ARE YOU? OUR VISITORS FROM HARLEM – QUITE A SHOW, YES?
WHAT? OH, YES. I SUPPOSE SO. WELL. I STILL MISS RAGTIME, PERSONALLY, BUT...
I WAS EXPECTING YOU THREE DAYS AGO, OLD CHAP. I WAS WORRIED YOU WERE GOING TO MAKE ME COME LOOK FOR YOU.
YOU *DON'T* WANT ME TO COME *LOOK* FOR YOU.

YES. DAMNEDEST THING. I THOUGHT I COULD HAVE THE MONEY TOGETHER BY NOW, BUT — CURSE THE LUCK — I'M NOT AS... AS LIQUID AS I THOUGHT I WAS --

LIQUID? *LIQUID?*

OLD BOY, YOU *KNOW* WHO I SERVE. YOU DON'T HOLD OUT ON *MY* PEOPLE... ...OR YOU WILL BECOME MORE *LIQUID* THAN YOU COULD POSSIBLY *IMAGINE*--

PLEASE — PLEASE — JUST GIVE ME — FIVE? FIVE BANKING DAYS. THEN I CAN COME UP WITH WHAT I OWE. I PROMISE--

THREE DAYS. AND NOW THE PRINCIPAL IS FIFTEEN PERCENT HIGHER.

AND I WOULD VERY MUCH LIKE TO SPEND SOME TIME WITH YOUR NEW WIFE.

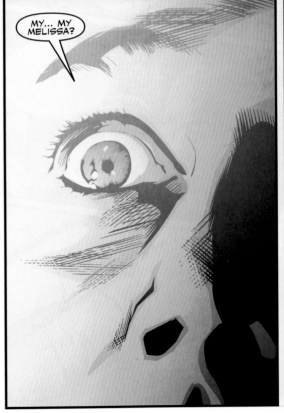

MY... MY MELISSA?

YES. WHY DON'T YOU INTRODUCE US?

THEN PISS OFF FOR THE EVENING?

MR. GIFT? THADDEUS GIFT? I WAS ASKED TO GIVE THIS TO YOU.

I WOULD ACCEPT WHATEVER YOU OFFERED, LOVE...

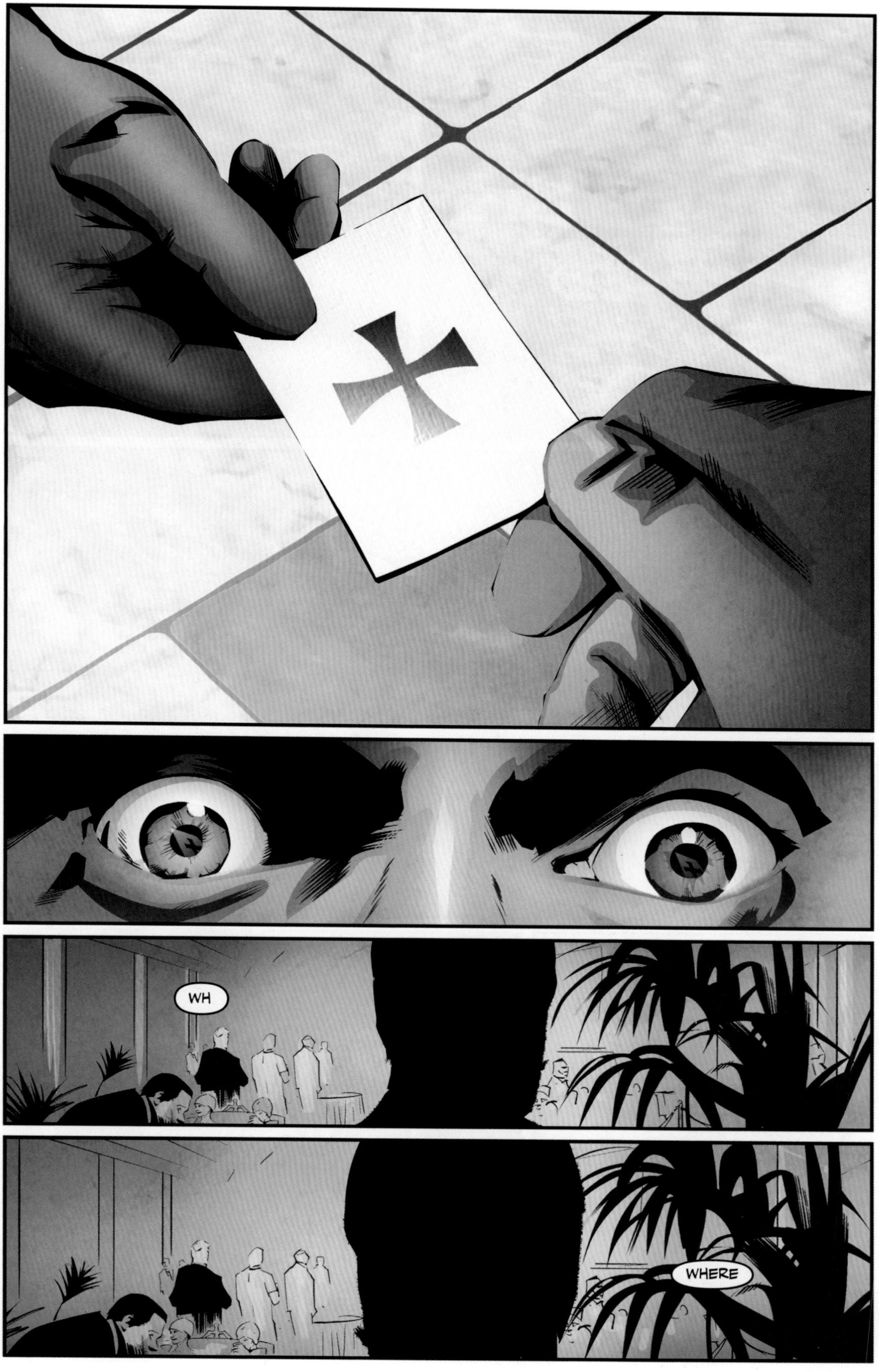
WH
WHERE

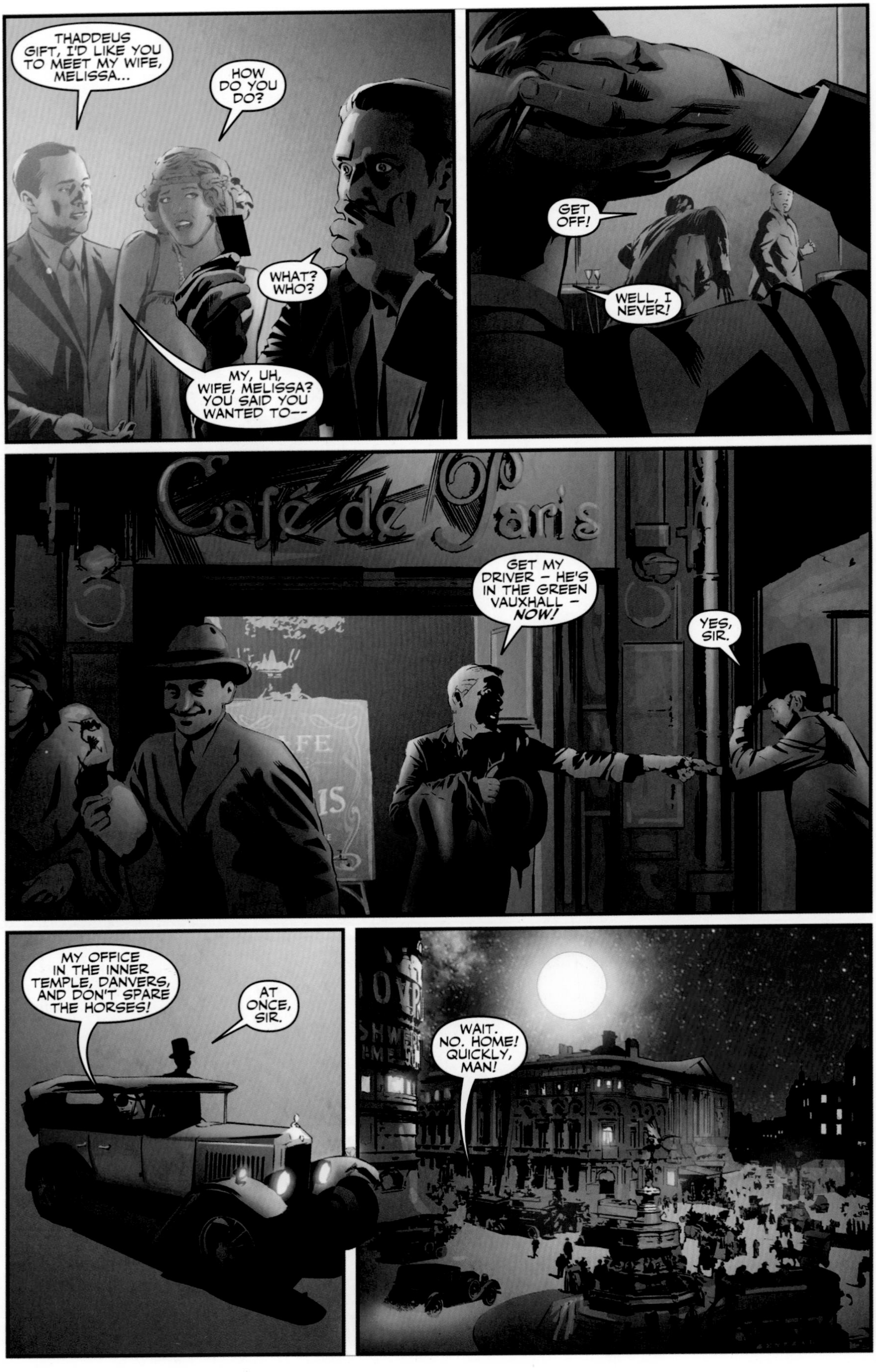
THADDEUS GIFT, I'D LIKE YOU TO MEET MY WIFE, MELISSA...
HOW DO YOU DO?
WHAT? WHO?
MY, UH, WIFE, MELISSA? YOU SAID YOU WANTED TO--
GET OFF!
WELL, I NEVER!
Café de Paris
GET MY DRIVER – HE'S IN THE GREEN VAUXHALL – *NOW!*
YES, SIR.
MY OFFICE IN THE INNER TEMPLE, DANVERS, AND DON'T SPARE THE HORSES!
AT ONCE, SIR.
WAIT. NO. HOME! QUICKLY, MAN!

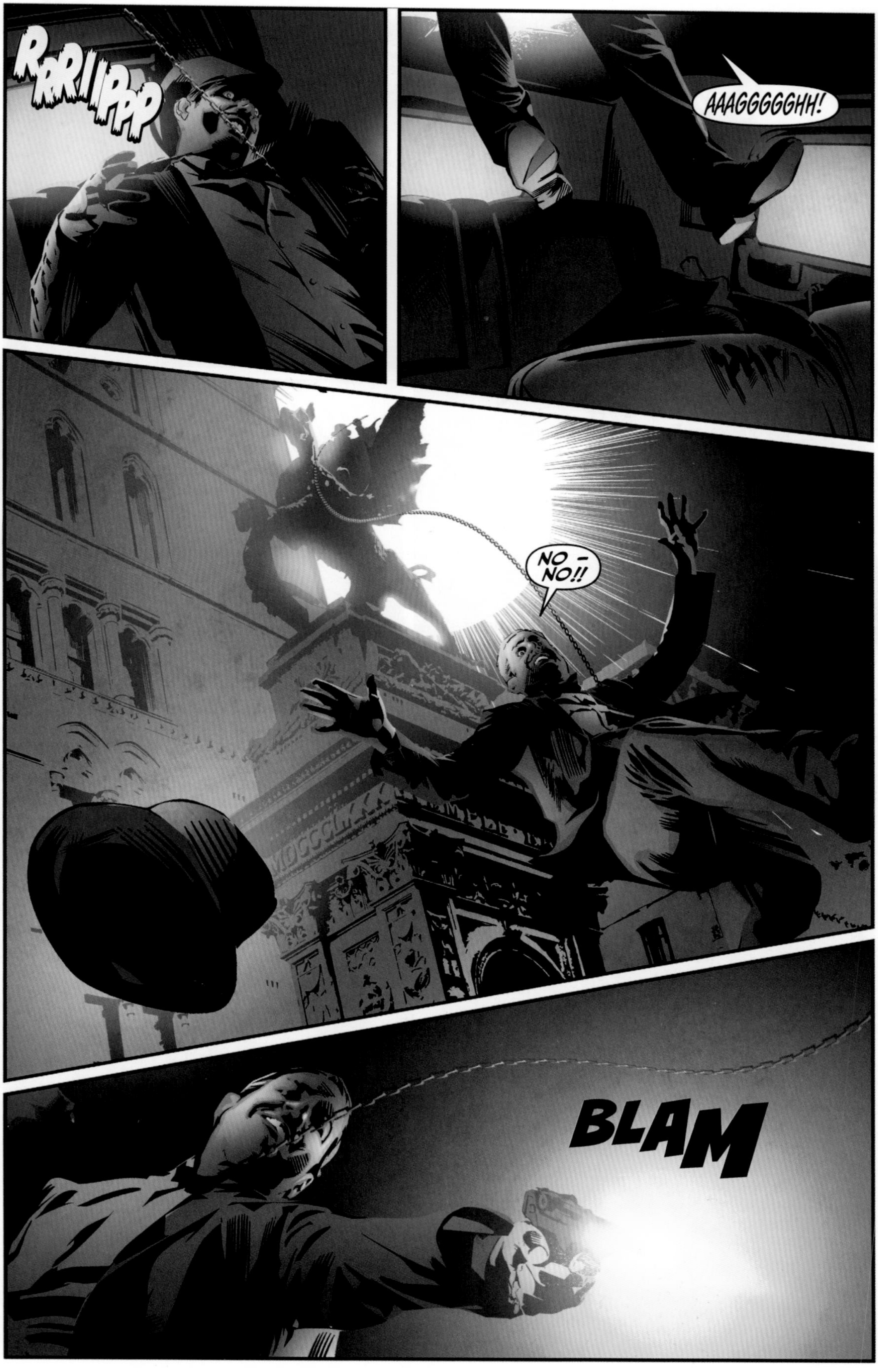
RRRIIPPP
AAAGGGGGHH!
NO – NO!!
BLAM

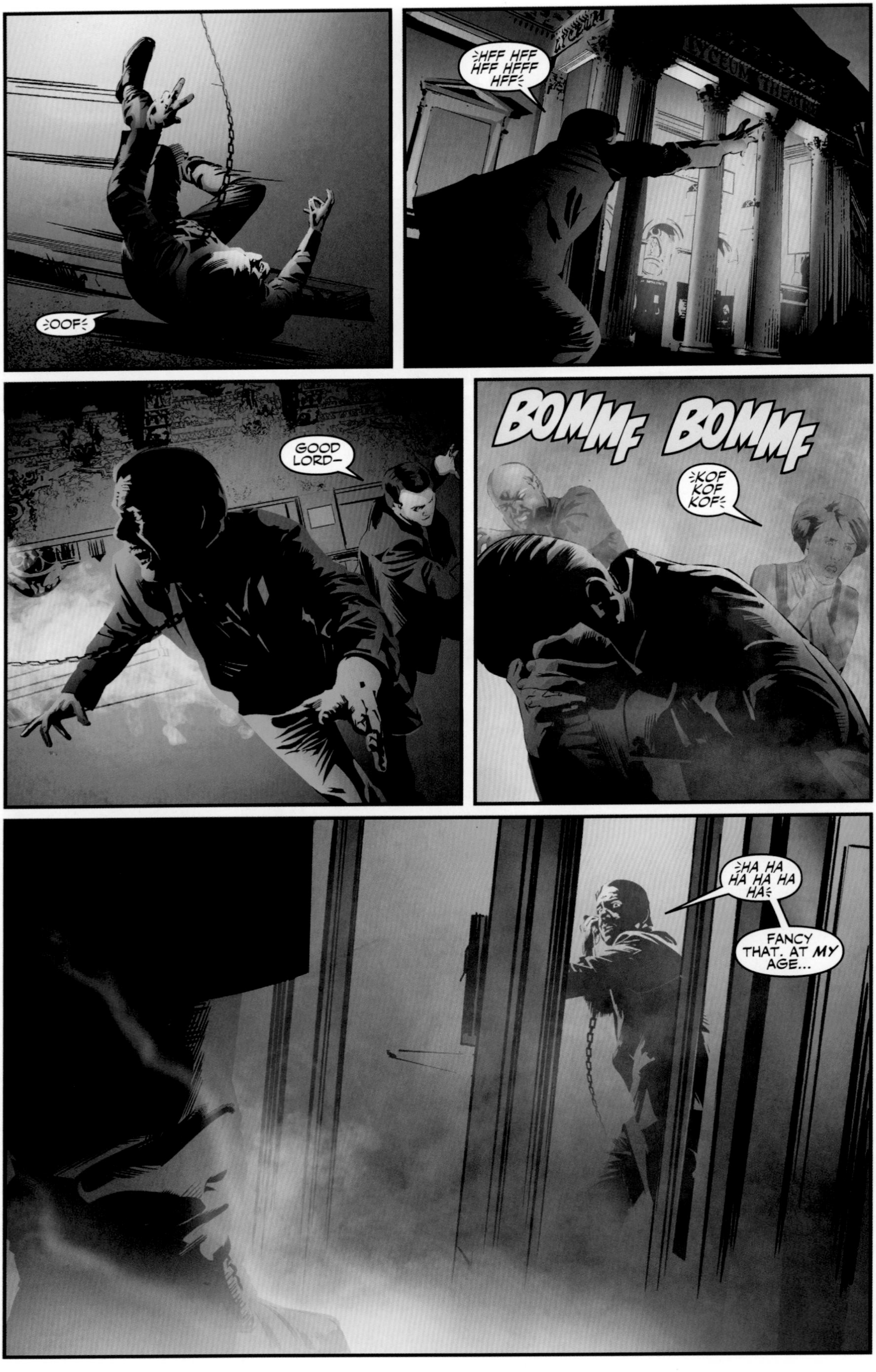
OOF
HFF HFF HFF HFFF HFF
LYCEUM THEATRE
GOOD LORD–
BOMMF BOMMF
KOF KOF KOF
HA HA HA HA HA HA
FANCY THAT. AT *MY* AGE...

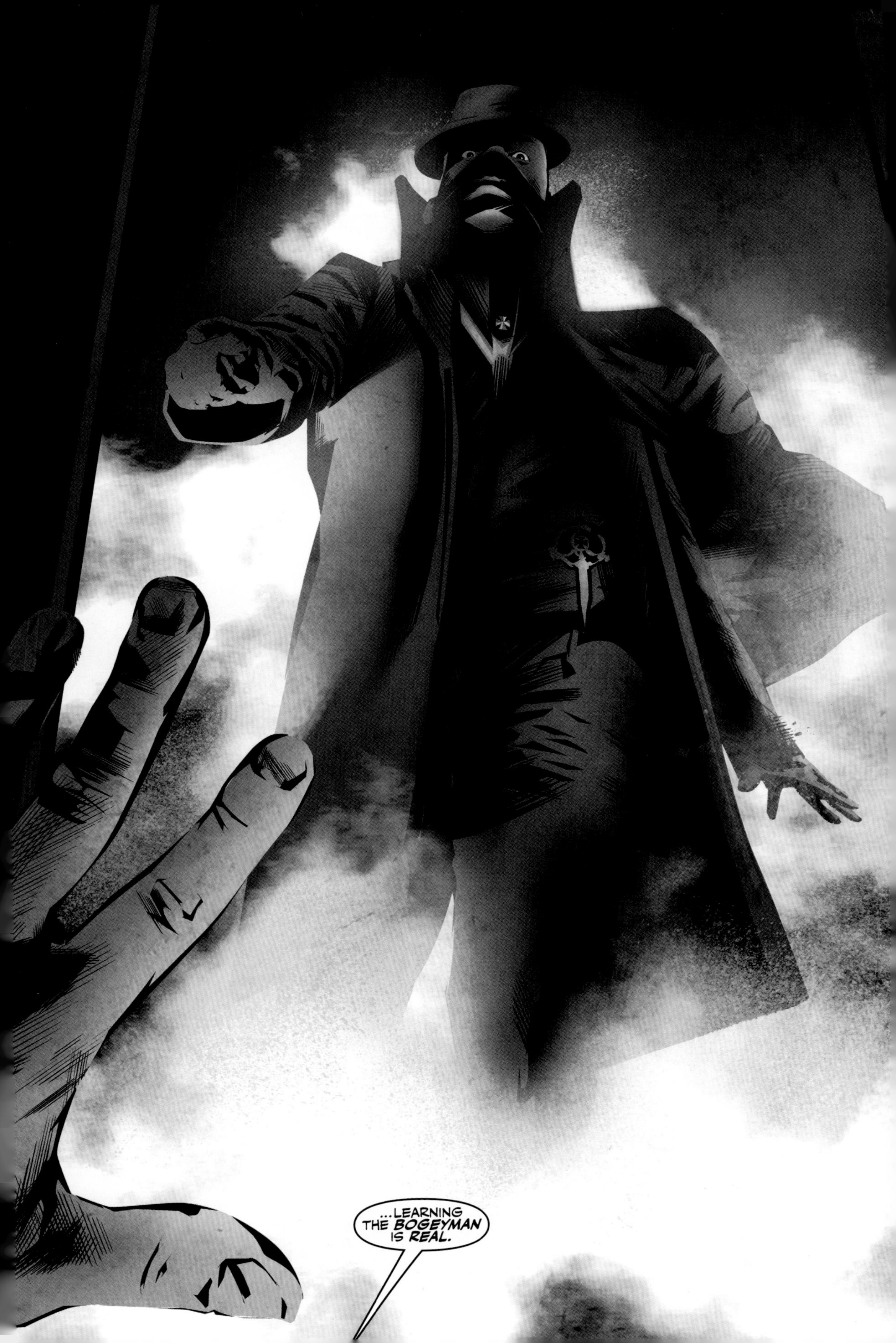
...LEARNING THE BOGEYMAN IS REAL.

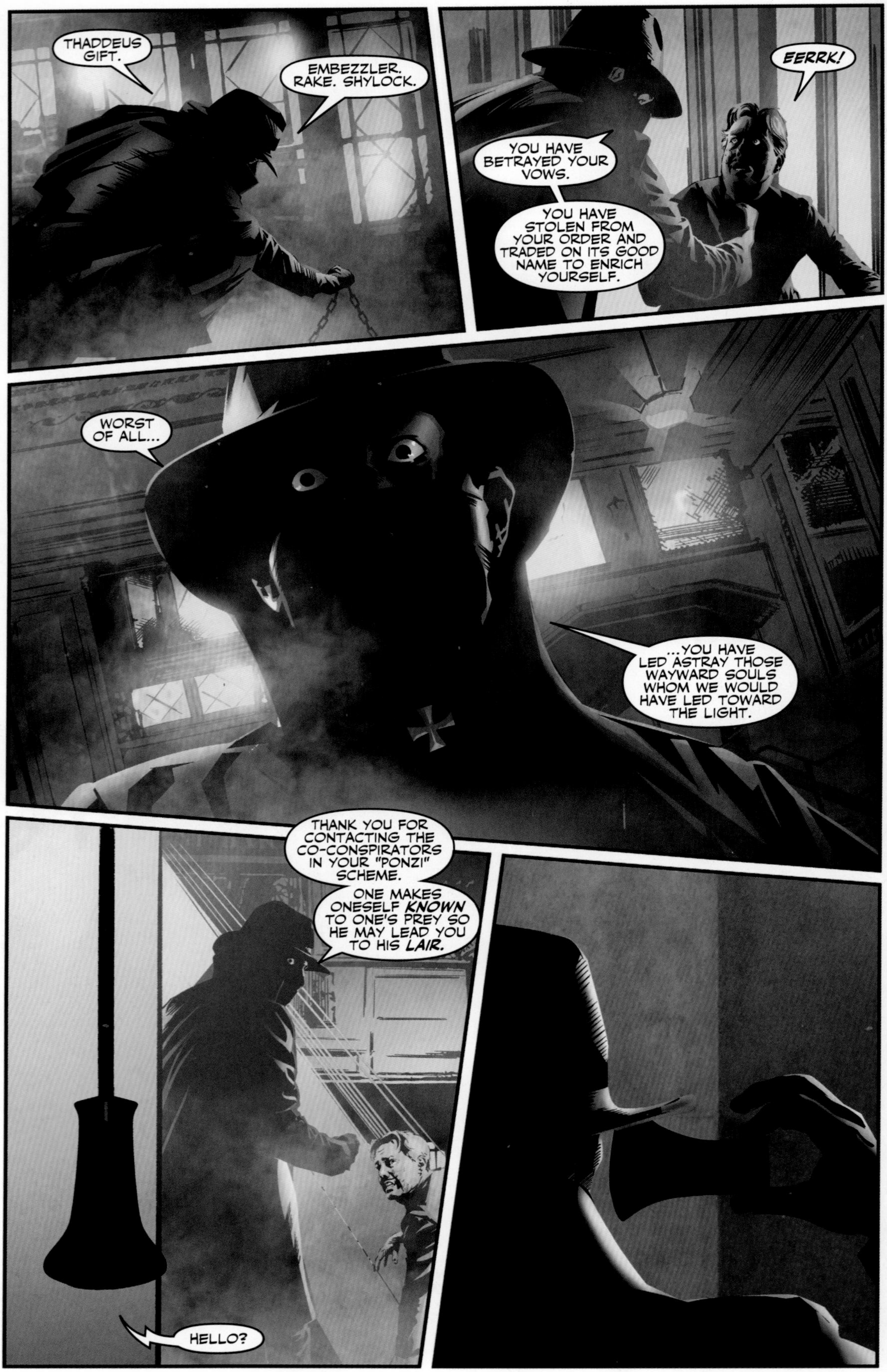
THADDEUS GIFT.
EMBEZZLER. RAKE. SHYLOCK.
EERRK!
YOU HAVE BETRAYED YOUR VOWS.
YOU HAVE STOLEN FROM YOUR ORDER AND TRADED ON ITS GOOD NAME TO ENRICH YOURSELF.
WORST OF ALL...
...YOU HAVE LED ASTRAY THOSE WAYWARD SOULS WHOM WE WOULD HAVE LED TOWARD THE LIGHT.
THANK YOU FOR CONTACTING THE CO-CONSPIRATORS IN YOUR "PONZI" SCHEME.
ONE MAKES ONESELF KNOWN TO ONE'S PREY SO HE MAY LEAD YOU TO HIS LAIR.
HELLO?

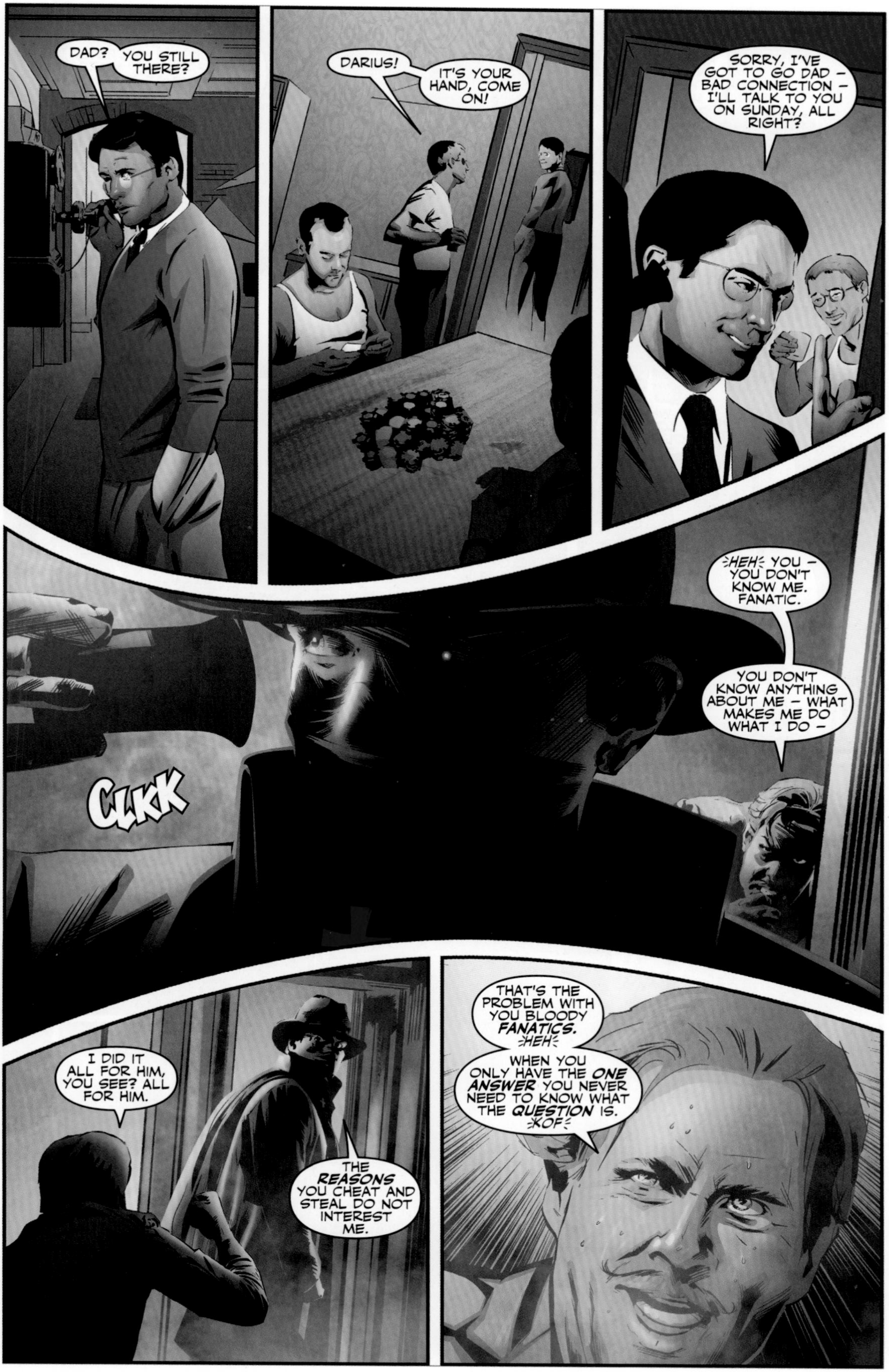
DAD? YOU STILL THERE?
DARIUS! IT'S YOUR HAND, COME ON!
SORRY, I'VE GOT TO GO DAD - BAD CONNECTION - I'LL TALK TO YOU ON SUNDAY, ALL RIGHT?
HEH YOU - YOU DON'T KNOW ME. FANATIC.
YOU DON'T KNOW ANYTHING ABOUT ME - WHAT MAKES ME DO WHAT I DO -
CLKK
I DID IT ALL FOR HIM, YOU SEE? ALL FOR HIM.
THE REASONS YOU CHEAT AND STEAL DO NOT INTEREST ME.
THAT'S THE PROBLEM WITH YOU BLOODY FANATICS. HEH
WHEN YOU ONLY HAVE THE ONE ANSWER YOU NEVER NEED TO KNOW WHAT THE QUESTION IS. KOF

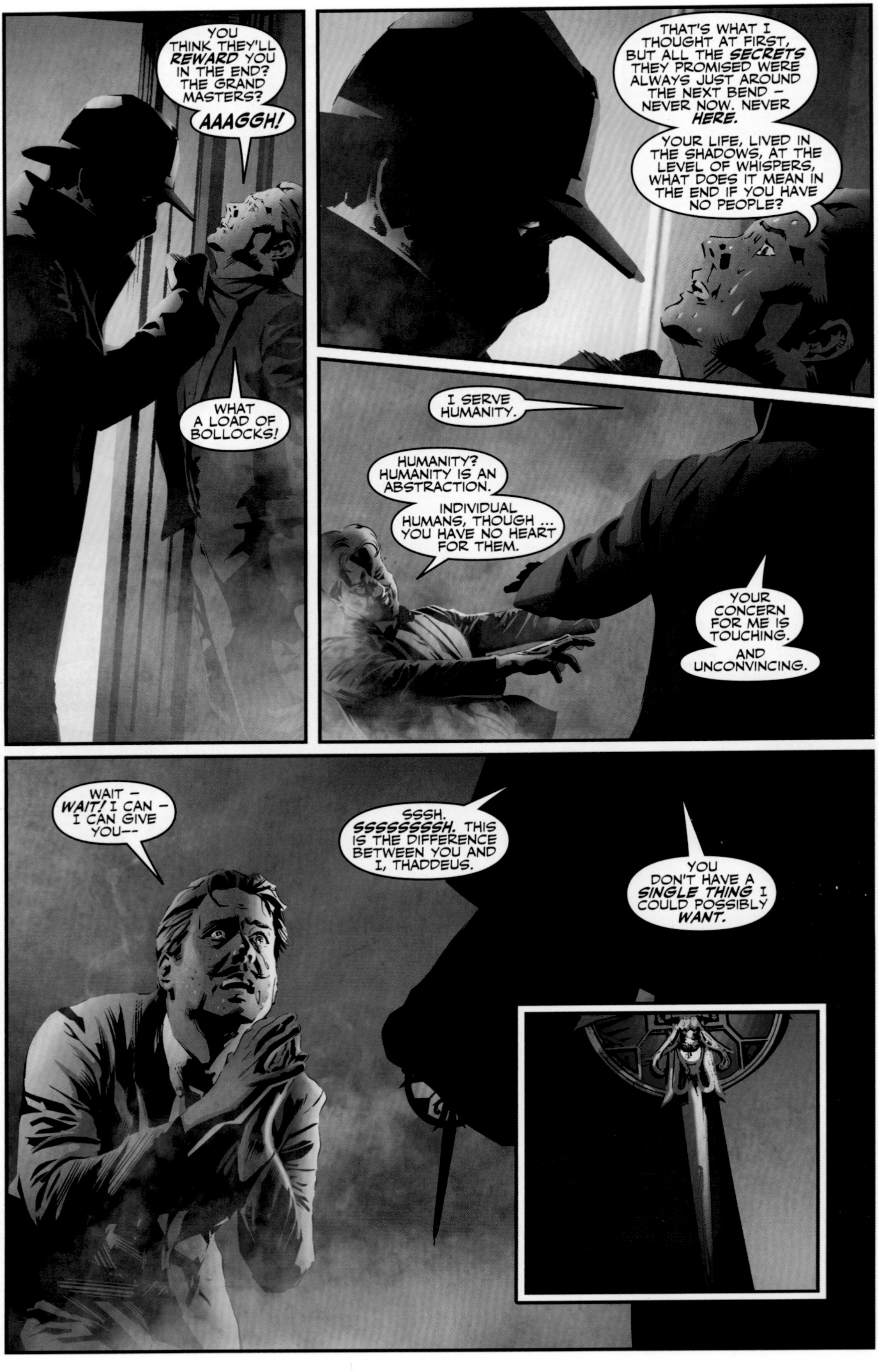
YOU THINK THEY'LL REWARD YOU IN THE END? THE GRAND MASTERS?
AAAGGH!
WHAT A LOAD OF BOLLOCKS!
THAT'S WHAT I THOUGHT AT FIRST, BUT ALL THE SECRETS THEY PROMISED WERE ALWAYS JUST AROUND THE NEXT BEND – NEVER NOW. NEVER HERE.
YOUR LIFE, LIVED IN THE SHADOWS, AT THE LEVEL OF WHISPERS, WHAT DOES IT MEAN IN THE END IF YOU HAVE NO PEOPLE?
I SERVE HUMANITY.
HUMANITY? HUMANITY IS AN ABSTRACTION.
INDIVIDUAL HUMANS, THOUGH ... YOU HAVE NO HEART FOR THEM.
YOUR CONCERN FOR ME IS TOUCHING.
AND UNCONVINCING.
WAIT – WAIT! I CAN – I CAN GIVE YOU--
SSSH. SSSSSSSSH. THIS IS THE DIFFERENCE BETWEEN YOU AND I, THADDEUS.
YOU DON'T HAVE A SINGLE THING I COULD POSSIBLY WANT.

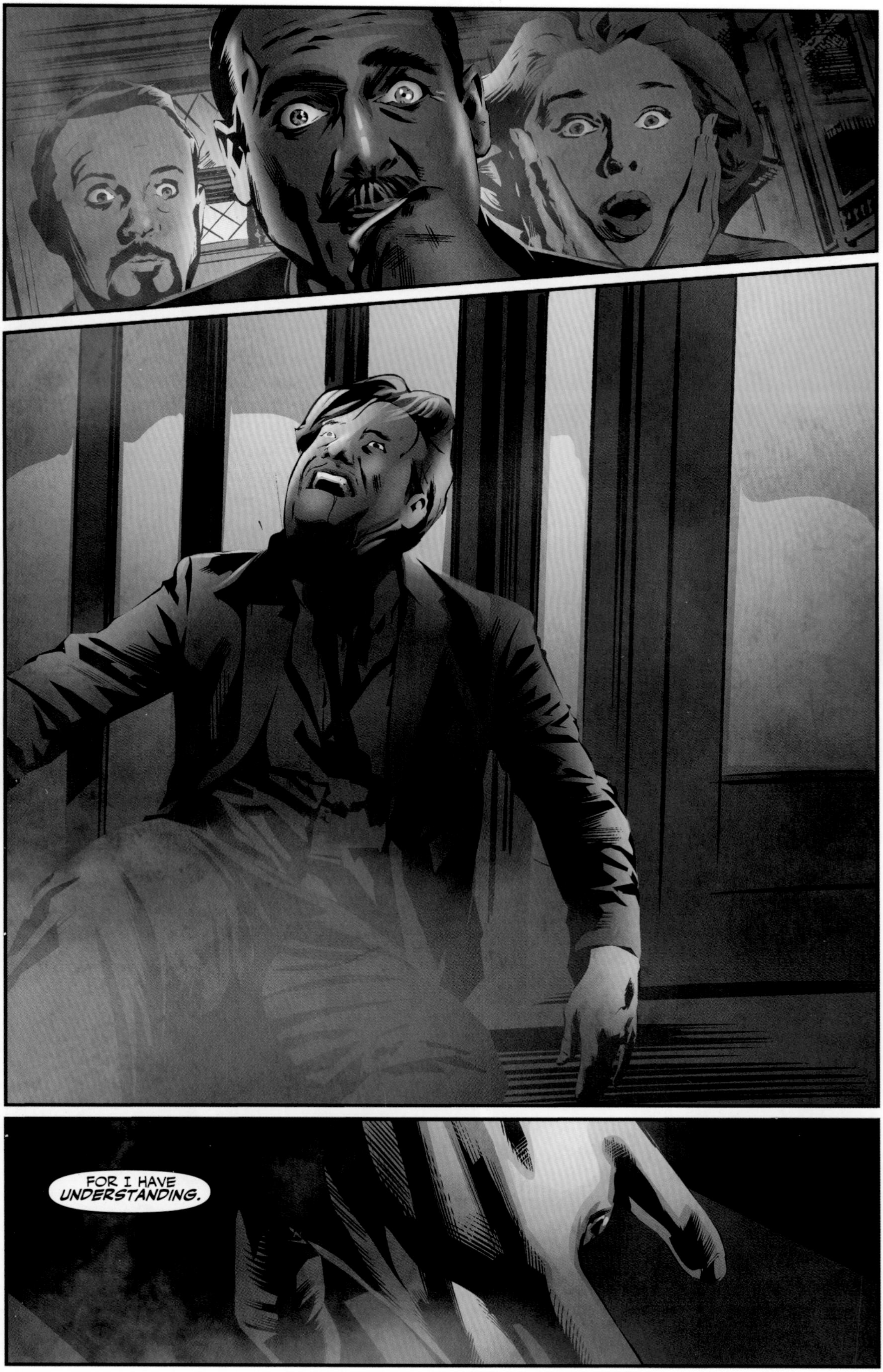
FOR I HAVE UNDERSTANDING.

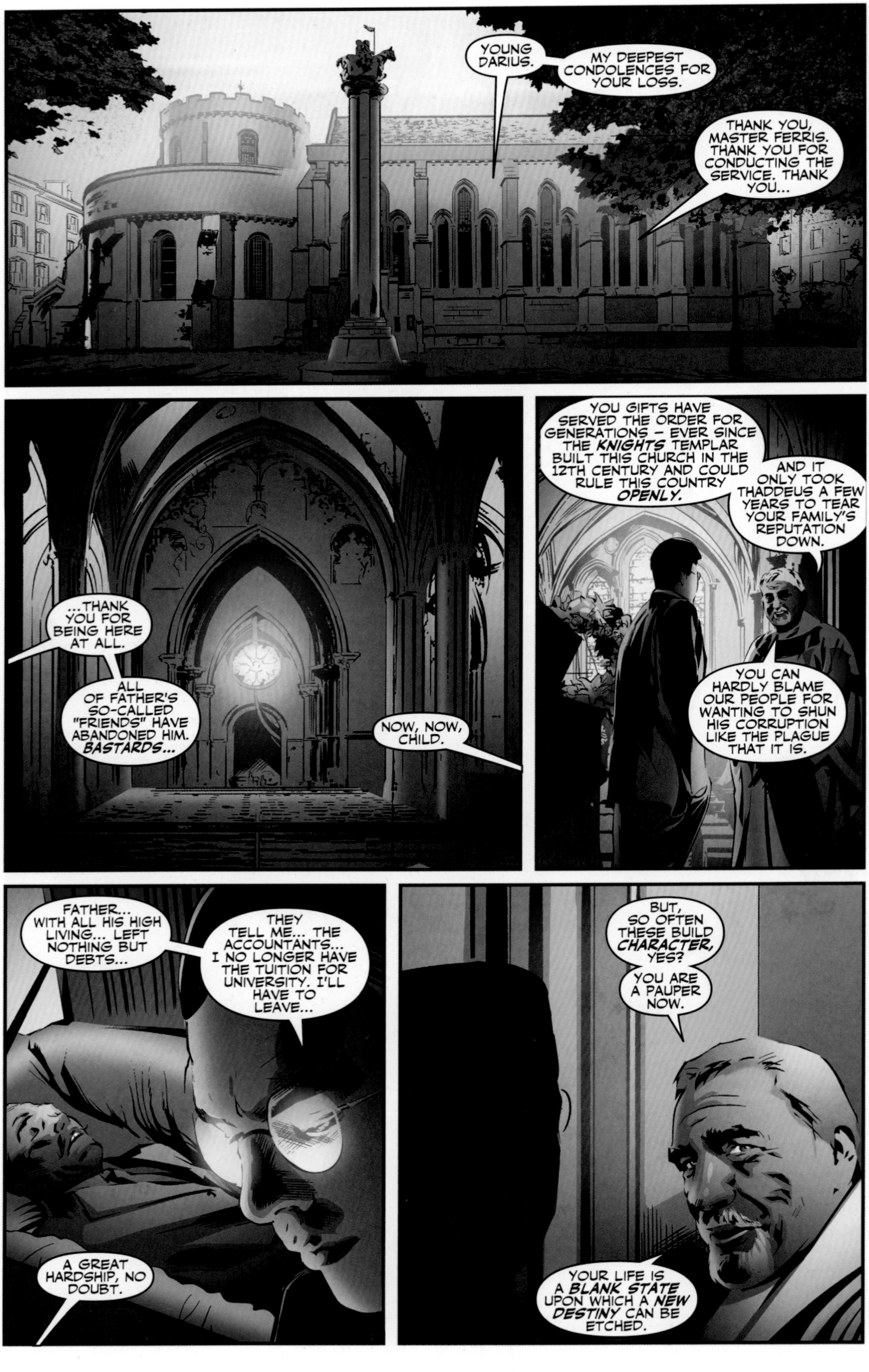
YOUNG DARIUS.
MY DEEPEST CONDOLENCES FOR YOUR LOSS.
THANK YOU, MASTER FERRIS. THANK YOU FOR CONDUCTING THE SERVICE. THANK YOU...
...THANK YOU FOR BEING HERE AT ALL.
ALL OF FATHER'S SO-CALLED "FRIENDS" HAVE ABANDONED HIM. BASTARDS...
NOW, NOW, CHILD.
YOU GIFTS HAVE SERVED THE ORDER FOR GENERATIONS – EVER SINCE THE KNIGHTS TEMPLAR BUILT THIS CHURCH IN THE 12TH CENTURY AND COULD RULE THIS COUNTRY OPENLY.
AND IT ONLY TOOK THADDEUS A FEW YEARS TO TEAR YOUR FAMILY'S REPUTATION DOWN.
YOU CAN HARDLY BLAME OUR PEOPLE FOR WANTING TO SHUN HIS CORRUPTION LIKE THE PLAGUE THAT IT IS.
FATHER... WITH ALL HIS HIGH LIVING... LEFT NOTHING BUT DEBTS...
THEY TELL ME... THE ACCOUNTANTS... I NO LONGER HAVE THE TUITION FOR UNIVERSITY. I'LL HAVE TO LEAVE...
A GREAT HARDSHIP, NO DOUBT.
BUT, SO OFTEN THESE BUILD CHARACTER, YES?
YOU ARE A PAUPER NOW.
YOUR LIFE IS A BLANK STATE UPON WHICH A NEW DESTINY CAN BE ETCHED.

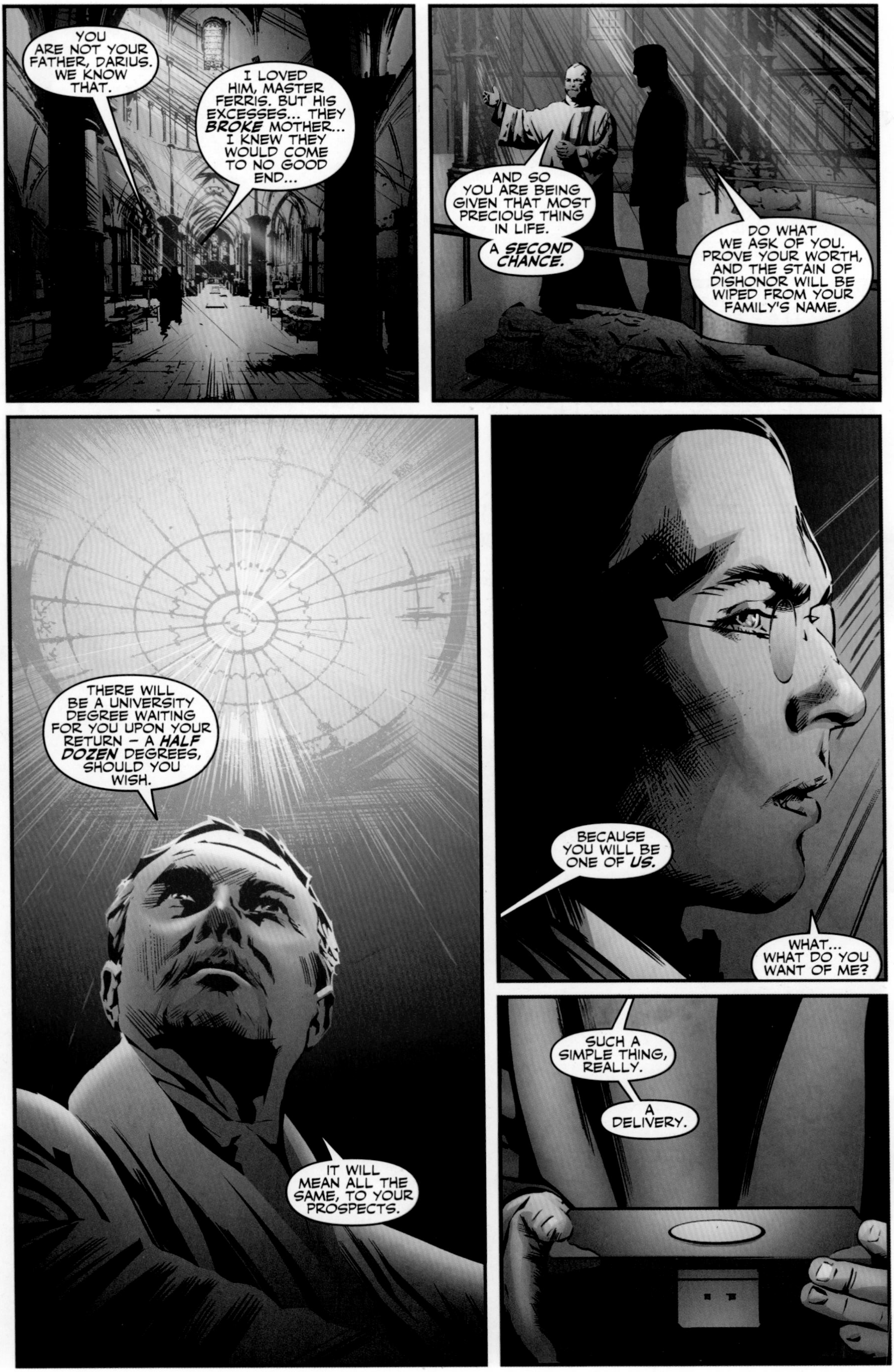
YOU ARE NOT YOUR FATHER, DARIUS. WE KNOW THAT.
I LOVED HIM, MASTER FERRIS. BUT HIS EXCESSES... THEY BROKE MOTHER... I KNEW THEY WOULD COME TO NO GOOD END...
AND SO YOU ARE BEING GIVEN THAT MOST PRECIOUS THING IN LIFE.
A SECOND CHANCE.
DO WHAT WE ASK OF YOU. PROVE YOUR WORTH, AND THE STAIN OF DISHONOR WILL BE WIPED FROM YOUR FAMILY'S NAME.
THERE WILL BE A UNIVERSITY DEGREE WAITING FOR YOU UPON YOUR RETURN – A HALF DOZEN DEGREES, SHOULD YOU WISH.
IT WILL MEAN ALL THE SAME, TO YOUR PROSPECTS.
BECAUSE YOU WILL BE ONE OF US.
WHAT... WHAT DO YOU WANT OF ME?
SUCH A SIMPLE THING, REALLY.
A DELIVERY.

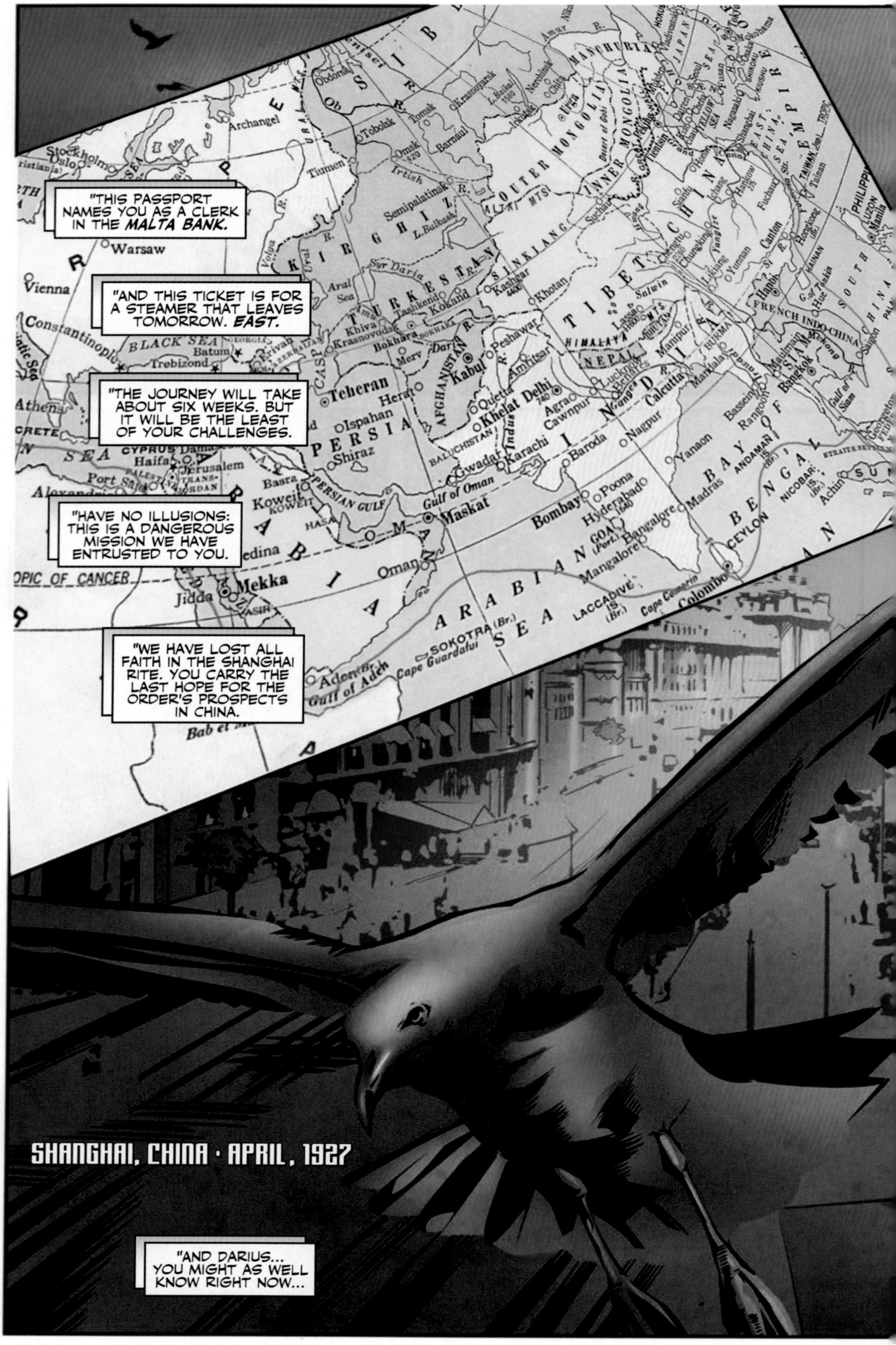

"THIS PASSPORT NAMES YOU AS A CLERK IN THE *MALTA BANK.*
"AND THIS TICKET IS FOR A STEAMER THAT LEAVES TOMORROW. *EAST.*
"THE JOURNEY WILL TAKE ABOUT SIX WEEKS. BUT IT WILL BE THE LEAST OF YOUR CHALLENGES.
"HAVE NO ILLUSIONS: THIS IS A DANGEROUS MISSION WE HAVE ENTRUSTED TO YOU.
"WE HAVE LOST ALL FAITH IN THE SHANGHAI RITE. YOU CARRY THE LAST HOPE FOR THE ORDER'S PROSPECTS IN CHINA.
SHANGHAI, CHINA · APRIL, 1927
"AND DARIUS... YOU MIGHT AS WELL KNOW RIGHT NOW...

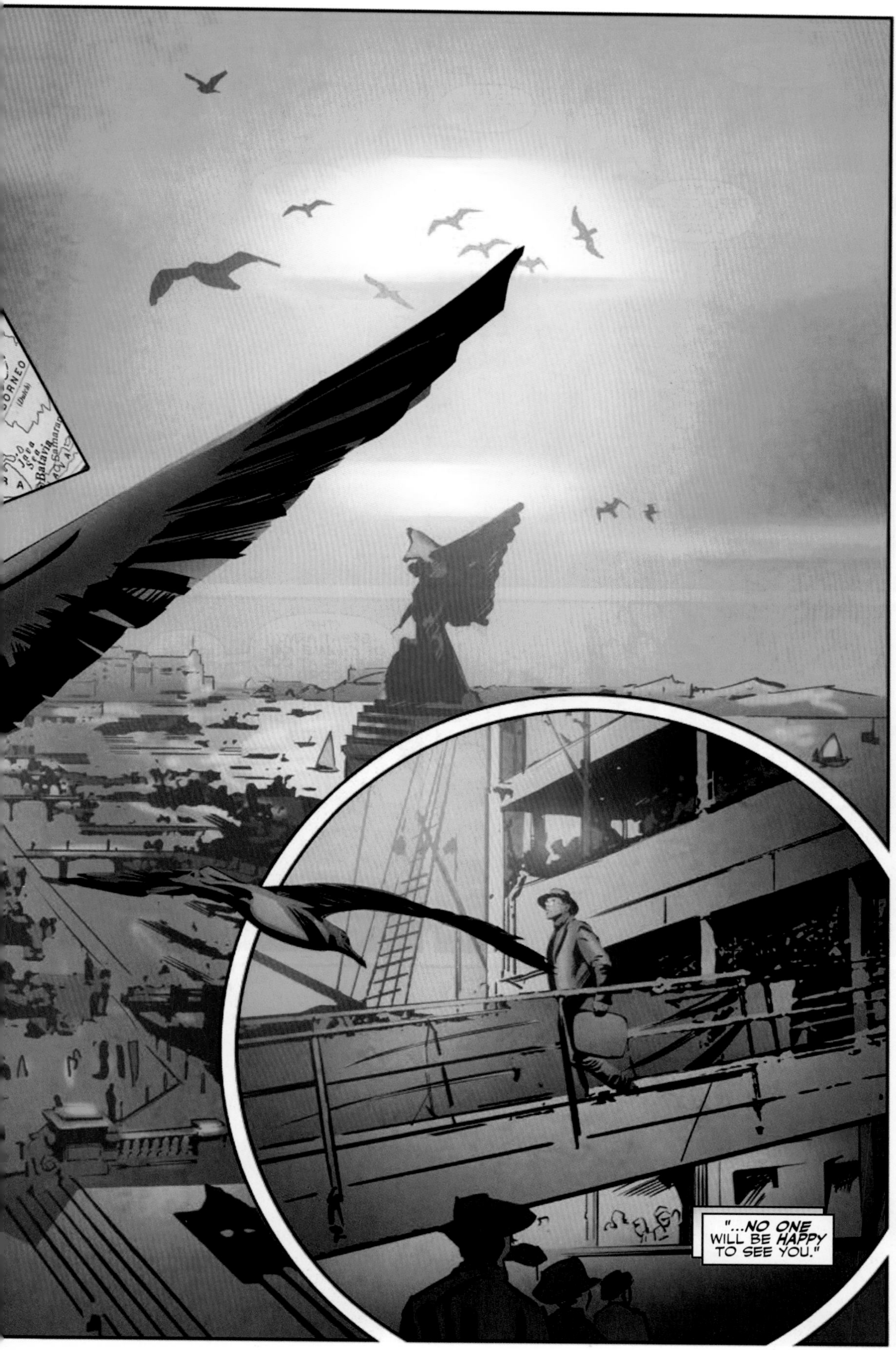
"...NO ONE WILL BE HAPPY TO SEE YOU."

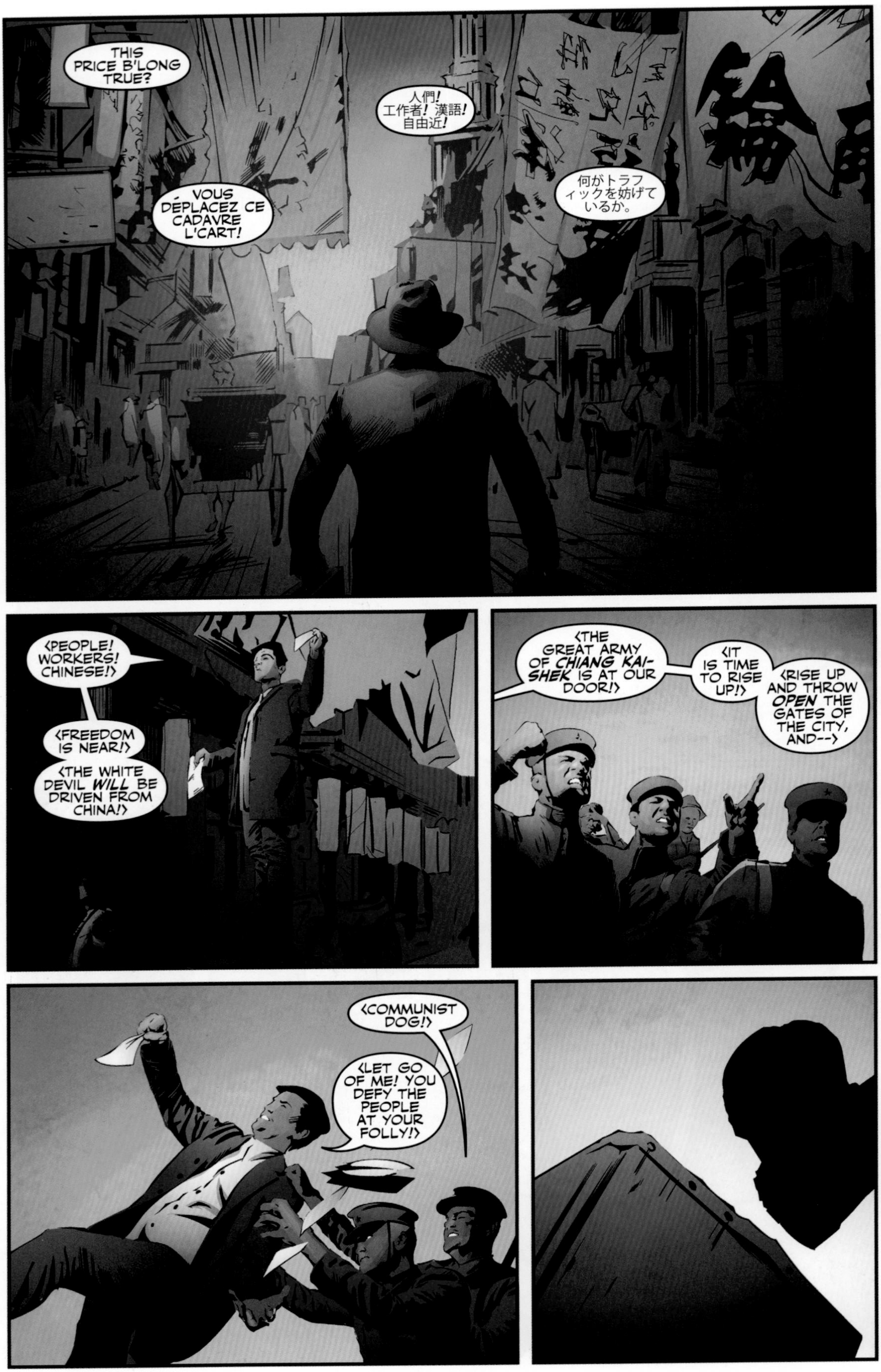
THIS PRICE B'LONG TRUE?
人們! 工作者! 漢語! 自由近!
VOUS DÉPLACEZ CE CADAVRE L'CART!
何がトラフィックを妨げているか。
<PEOPLE! WORKERS! CHINESE!>
<FREEDOM IS NEAR!>
<THE WHITE DEVIL WILL BE DRIVEN FROM CHINA!>
<THE GREAT ARMY OF CHIANG KAI-SHEK IS AT OUR DOOR!>
<IT IS TIME TO RISE UP!>
<RISE UP AND THROW OPEN THE GATES OF THE CITY, AND-->
<COMMUNIST DOG!>
<LET GO OF ME! YOU DEFY THE PEOPLE AT YOUR FOLLY!>

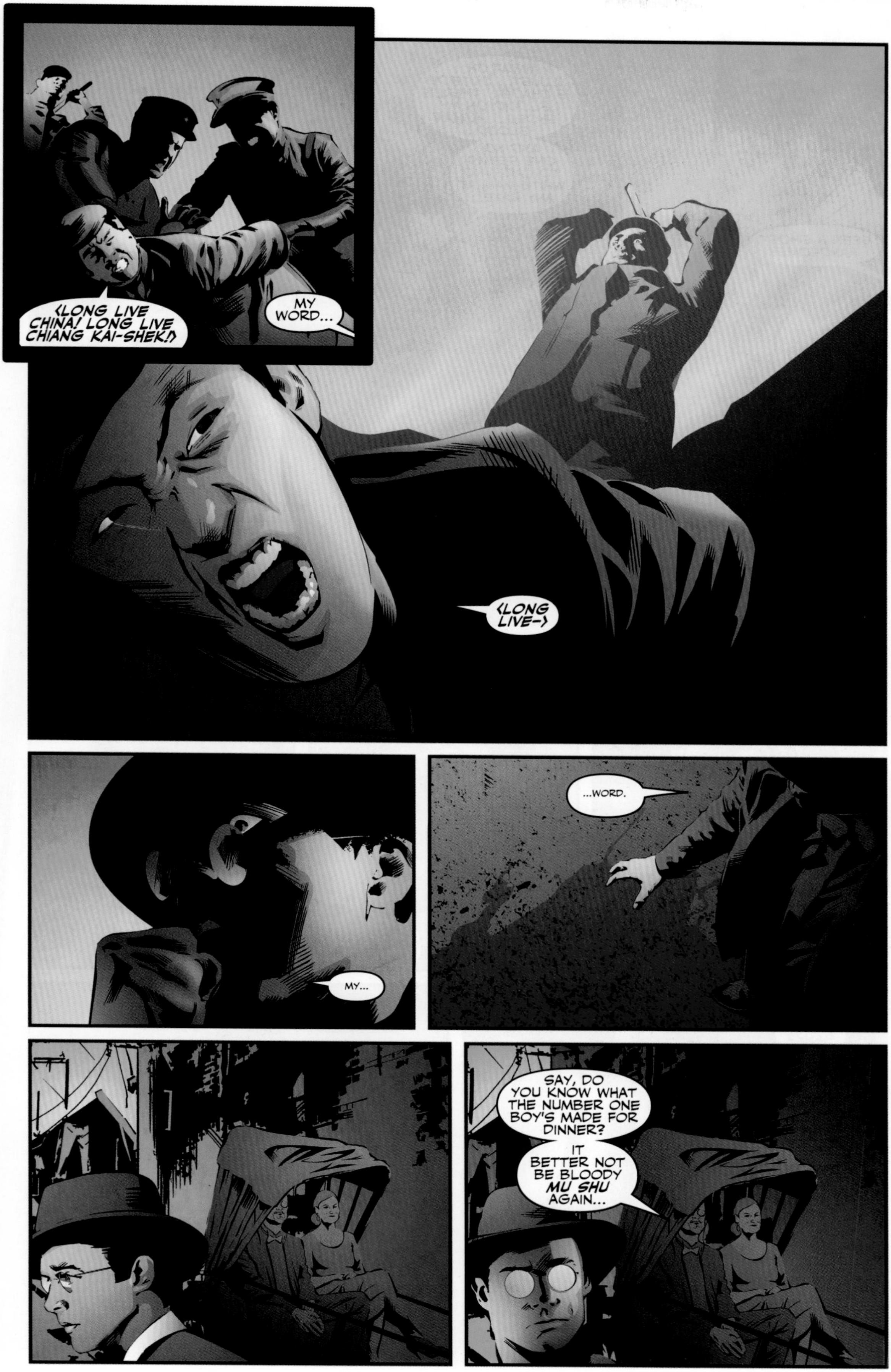
‹LONG LIVE CHINA! LONG LIVE CHIANG KAI-SHEK!›
MY WORD...
‹LONG LIVE-›
MY...
...WORD.
SAY, DO YOU KNOW WHAT THE NUMBER ONE BOY'S MADE FOR DINNER?
IT BETTER NOT BE BLOODY MU SHU AGAIN...

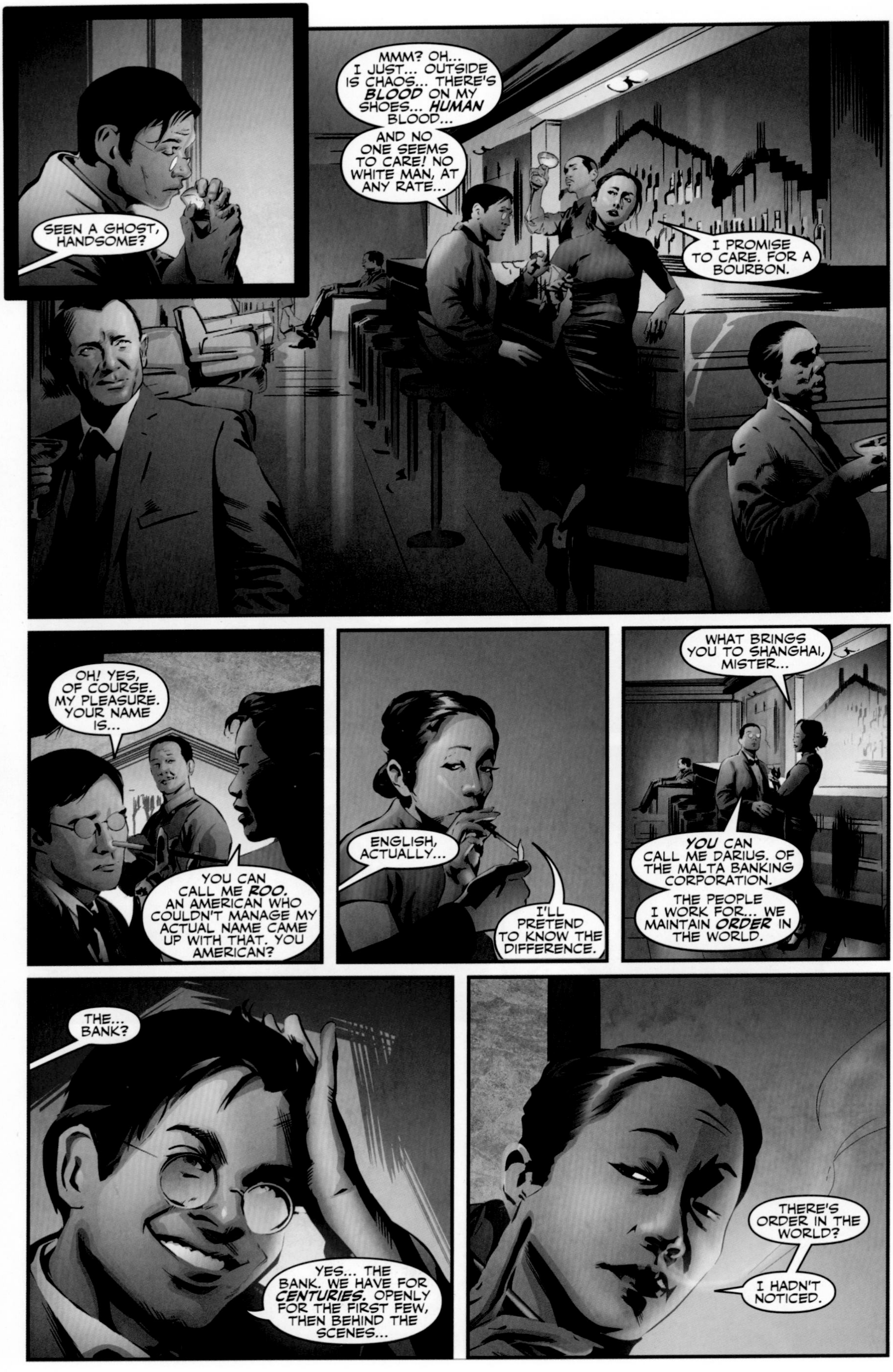
SEEN A GHOST, HANDSOME?
MMM? OH... I JUST... OUTSIDE IS CHAOS... THERE'S BLOOD ON MY SHOES... HUMAN BLOOD...
AND NO ONE SEEMS TO CARE! NO WHITE MAN, AT ANY RATE...
I PROMISE TO CARE. FOR A BOURBON.
OH! YES, OF COURSE. MY PLEASURE. YOUR NAME IS...
YOU CAN CALL ME ROO. AN AMERICAN WHO COULDN'T MANAGE MY ACTUAL NAME CAME UP WITH THAT. YOU AMERICAN?
ENGLISH, ACTUALLY...
I'LL PRETEND TO KNOW THE DIFFERENCE.
WHAT BRINGS YOU TO SHANGHAI, MISTER...
YOU CAN CALL ME DARIUS. OF THE MALTA BANKING CORPORATION.
THE PEOPLE I WORK FOR... WE MAINTAIN ORDER IN THE WORLD.
THE... BANK?
YES... THE BANK. WE HAVE FOR CENTURIES. OPENLY FOR THE FIRST FEW, THEN BEHIND THE SCENES...
THERE'S ORDER IN THE WORLD?
I HADN'T NOTICED.

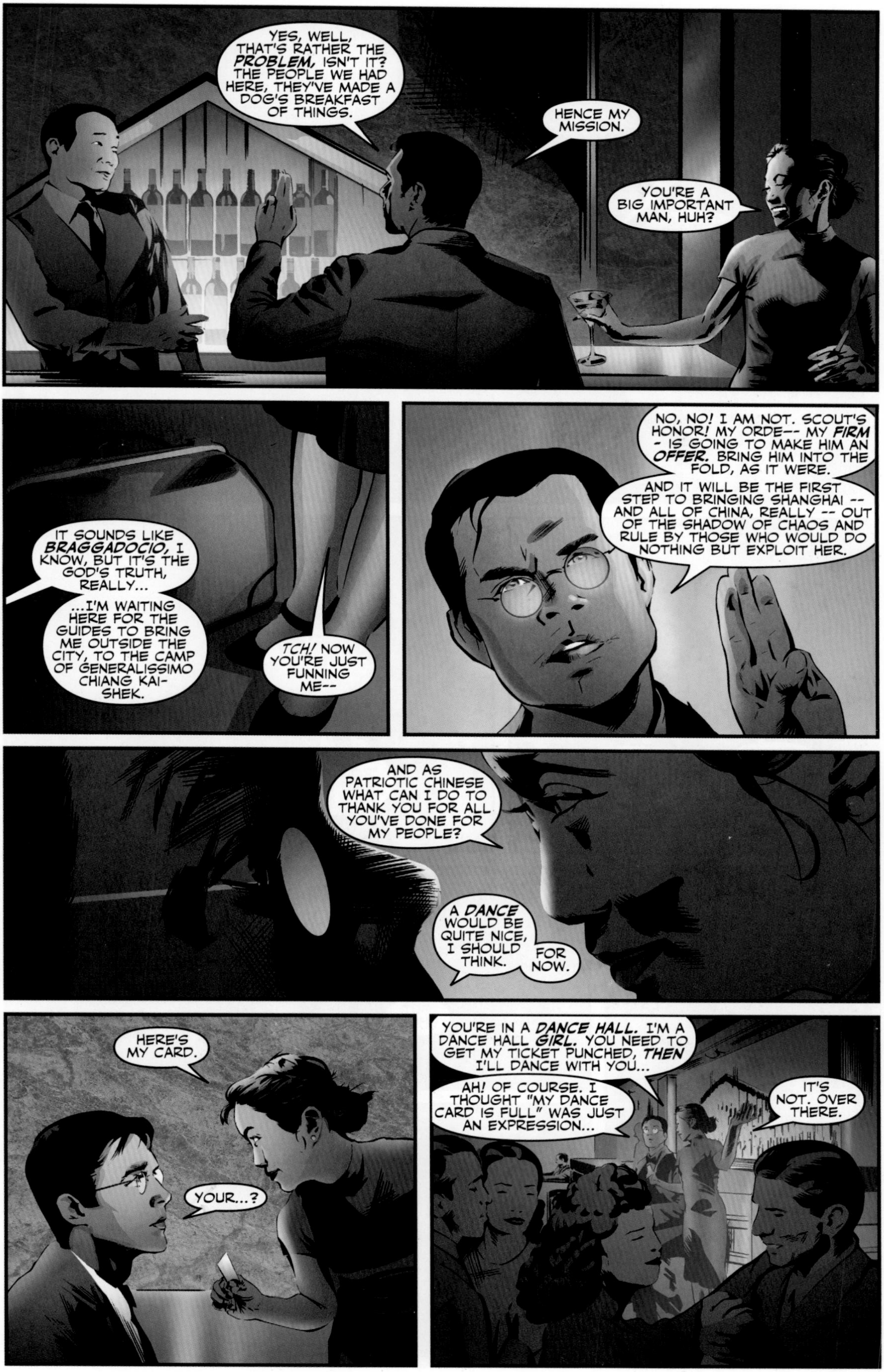
YES, WELL, THAT'S RATHER THE PROBLEM, ISN'T IT? THE PEOPLE WE HAD HERE, THEY'VE MADE A DOG'S BREAKFAST OF THINGS.
HENCE MY MISSION.
YOU'RE A BIG IMPORTANT MAN, HUH?
IT SOUNDS LIKE BRAGGADOCIO, I KNOW, BUT IT'S THE GOD'S TRUTH, REALLY...
...I'M WAITING HERE FOR THE GUIDES TO BRING ME OUTSIDE THE CITY, TO THE CAMP OF GENERALISSIMO CHIANG KAI-SHEK.
TCH! NOW YOU'RE JUST FUNNING ME--
NO, NO! I AM NOT. SCOUT'S HONOR! MY ORDE-- MY FIRM - IS GOING TO MAKE HIM AN OFFER. BRING HIM INTO THE FOLD, AS IT WERE.
AND IT WILL BE THE FIRST STEP TO BRINGING SHANGHAI -- AND ALL OF CHINA, REALLY -- OUT OF THE SHADOW OF CHAOS AND RULE BY THOSE WHO WOULD DO NOTHING BUT EXPLOIT HER.
AND AS PATRIOTIC CHINESE WHAT CAN I DO TO THANK YOU FOR ALL YOU'VE DONE FOR MY PEOPLE?
A DANCE WOULD BE QUITE NICE, I SHOULD THINK.
FOR NOW.
HERE'S MY CARD.
YOUR...?
YOU'RE IN A DANCE HALL. I'M A DANCE HALL GIRL. YOU NEED TO GET MY TICKET PUNCHED, THEN I'LL DANCE WITH YOU...
AH! OF COURSE. I THOUGHT "MY DANCE CARD IS FULL" WAS JUST AN EXPRESSION...
IT'S NOT. OVER THERE.

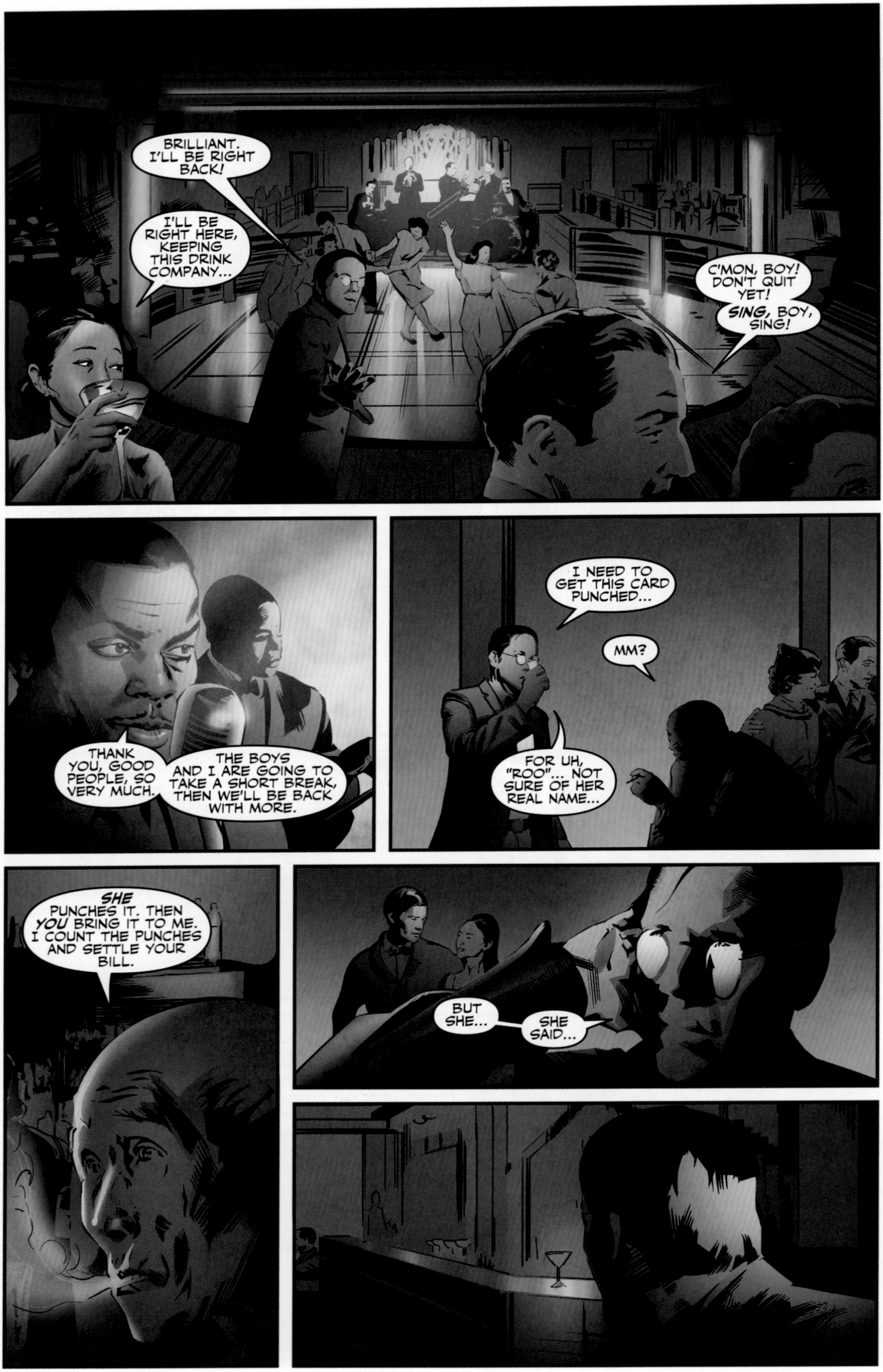
BRILLIANT. I'LL BE RIGHT BACK!
I'LL BE RIGHT HERE, KEEPING THIS DRINK COMPANY...
C'MON, BOY! DON'T QUIT YET! SING, BOY, SING!
THANK YOU, GOOD PEOPLE, SO VERY MUCH.
THE BOYS AND I ARE GOING TO TAKE A SHORT BREAK, THEN WE'LL BE BACK WITH MORE.
I NEED TO GET THIS CARD PUNCHED...
MM?
FOR UH, "ROO"... NOT SURE OF HER REAL NAME...
SHE PUNCHES IT. THEN YOU BRING IT TO ME. I COUNT THE PUNCHES AND SETTLE YOUR BILL.
BUT SHE...
SHE SAID...

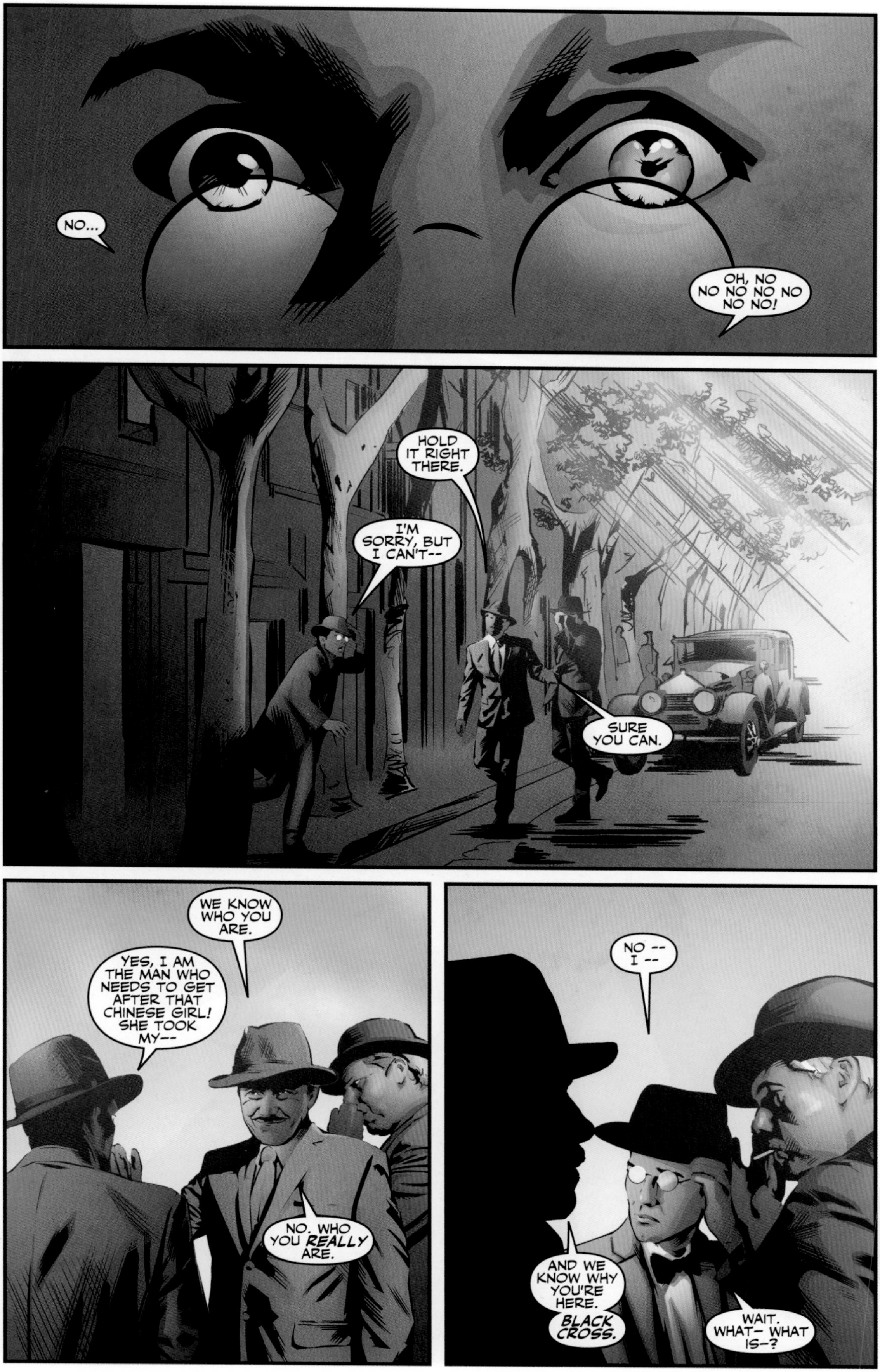
NO...
OH, NO NO NO NO NO NO NO!
HOLD IT RIGHT THERE.
I'M SORRY, BUT I CAN'T--
SURE YOU CAN.
WE KNOW WHO YOU ARE.
YES, I AM THE MAN WHO NEEDS TO GET AFTER THAT CHINESE GIRL! SHE TOOK MY--
NO. WHO YOU *REALLY* ARE.
NO -- I --
AND WE KNOW WHY YOU'RE HERE. *BLACK CROSS.*
WAIT. WHAT- WHAT IS-?

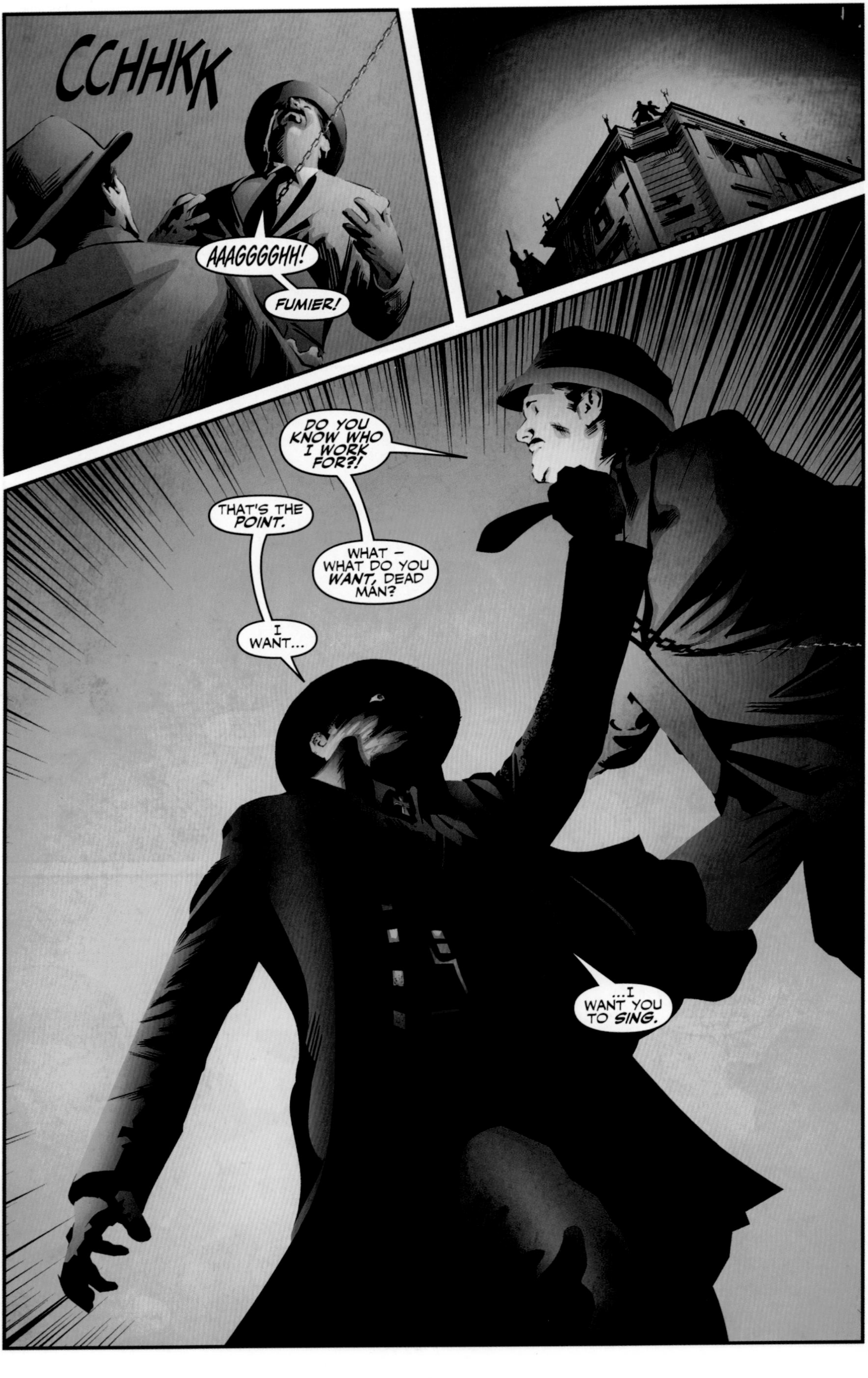
CCHHKK
AAAGGGGHH!
FUMIER!
DO YOU KNOW WHO I WORK FOR?!
THAT'S THE POINT.
WHAT – WHAT DO YOU WANT, DEAD MAN?
I WANT...
...I WANT YOU TO SING.

CHAPTER TWO

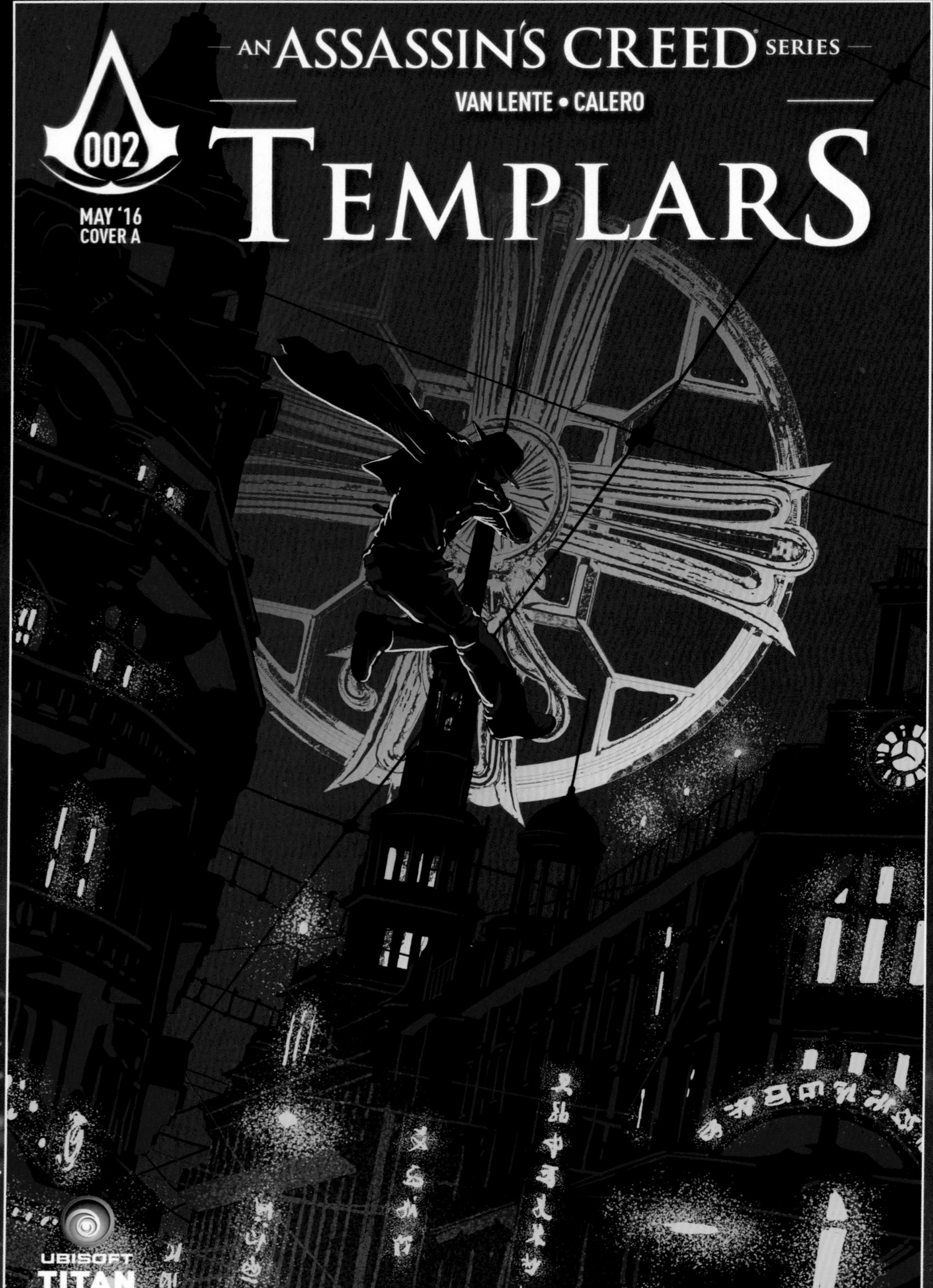
AN ASSASSIN'S CREED SERIES
VAN LENTE • CALERO
002
TEMPLARS
MAY '16
COVER A
UBISOFT
TITAN
COMICS

ISSUE 2 - COVER A

CHRIS THORNLEY

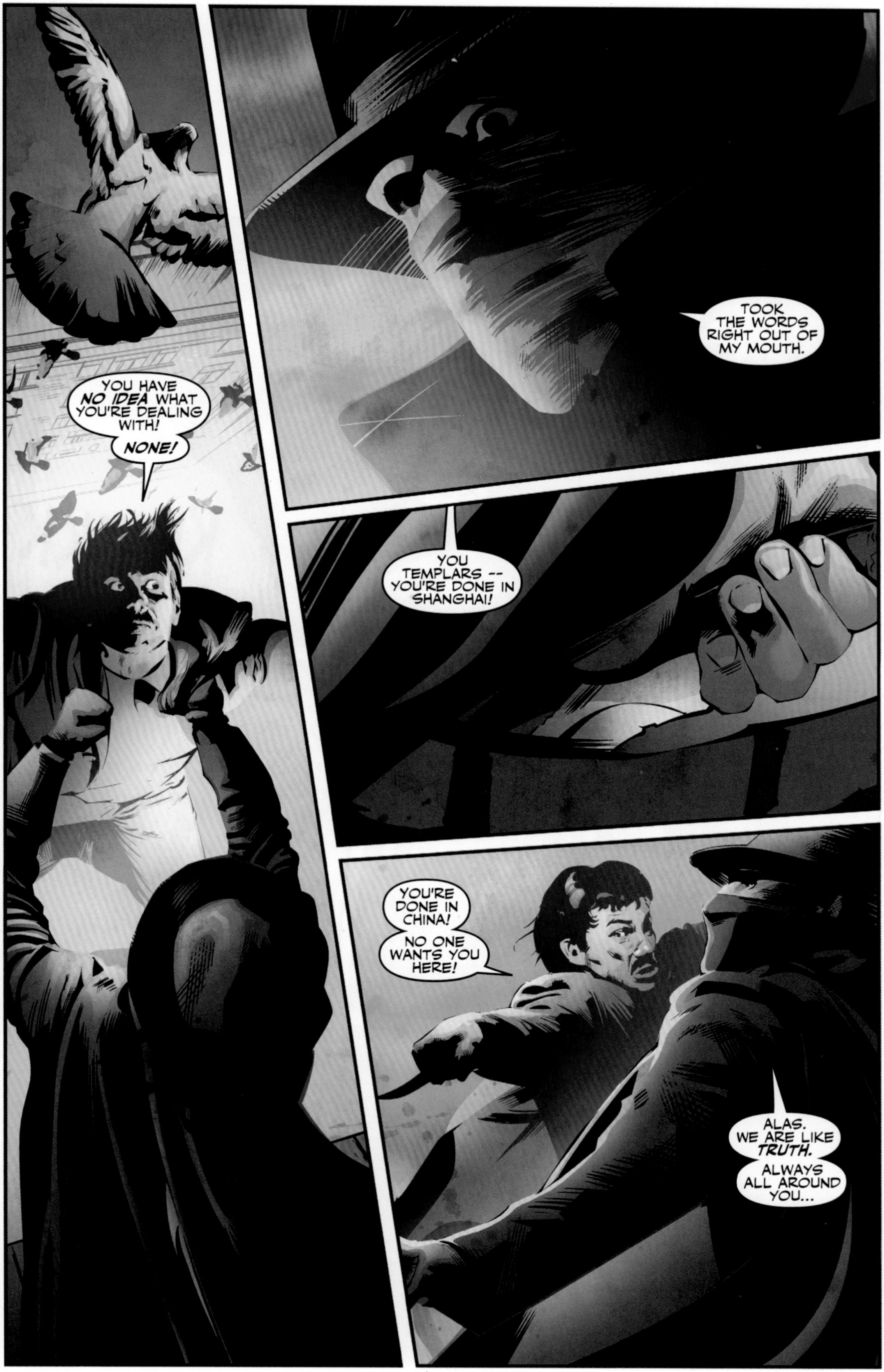

TOOK THE WORDS RIGHT OUT OF MY MOUTH.
YOU HAVE NO IDEA WHAT YOU'RE DEALING WITH!
NONE!
YOU TEMPLARS -- YOU'RE DONE IN SHANGHAI!
YOU'RE DONE IN CHINA!
NO ONE WANTS YOU HERE!
ALAS. WE ARE LIKE TRUTH.
ALWAYS ALL AROUND YOU...

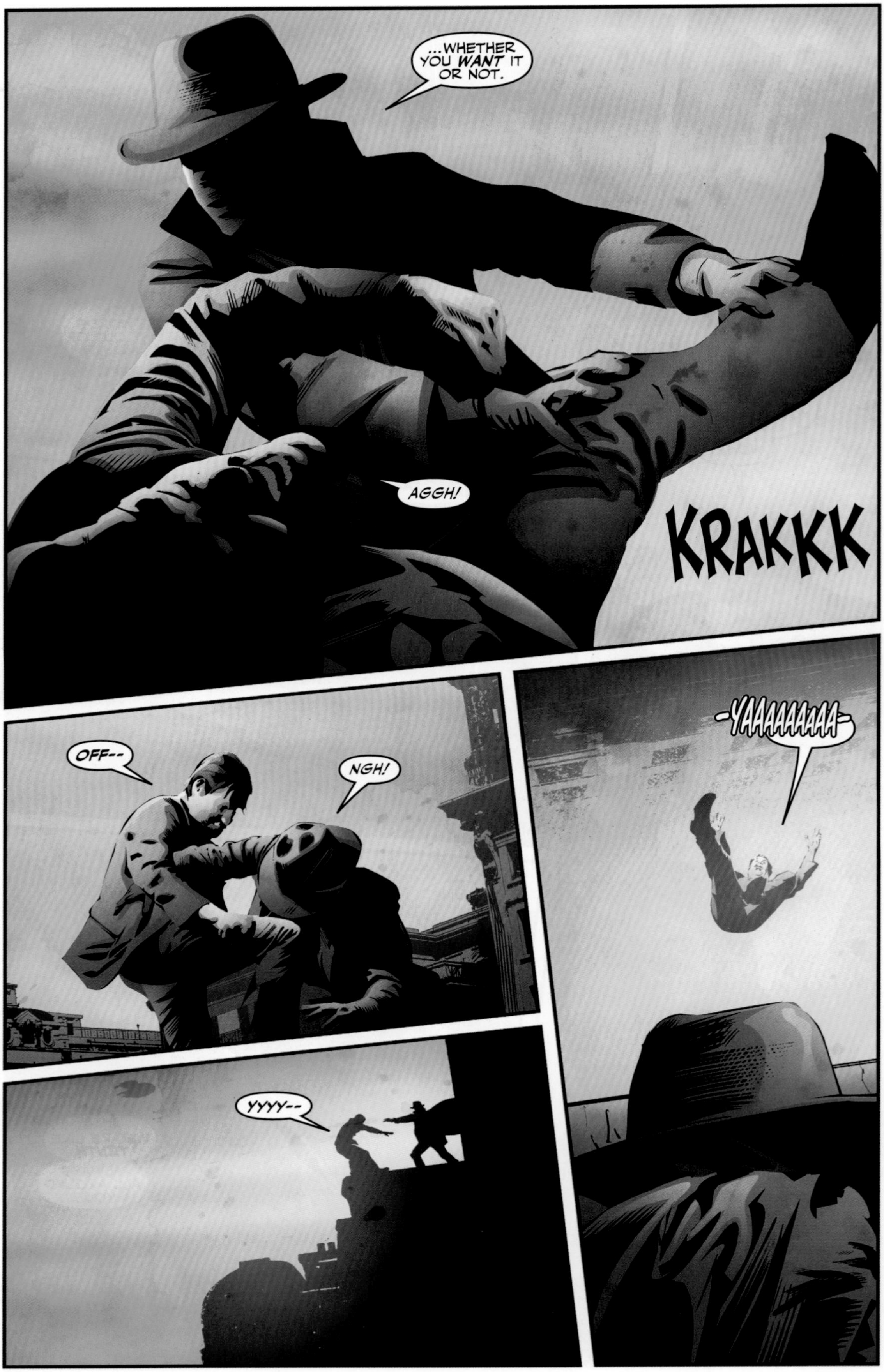
...WHETHER YOU WANT IT OR NOT.
AGGH!
KRAKKK
OFF--
NGH!
-YAAAAAAAAA-
YYYY--

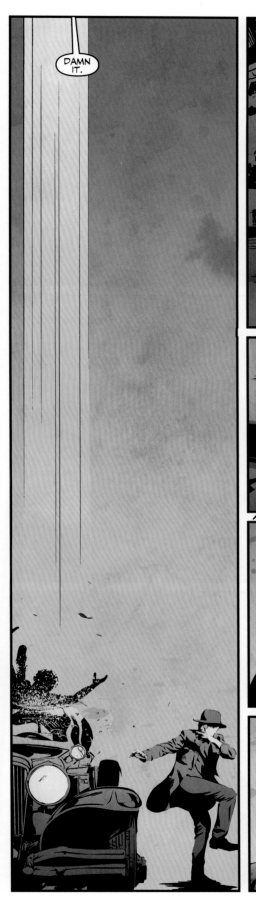

DAMN
IT.

WHERE'S
THE OTHER
ONE?

HE'S --
GONE! MUST
HAVE RUN OFF
WHILE I WAS
WATCHING
YOU.

YOU HAVE
A *PROBLEM*
KEEPING YOUR
EYE ON THINGS,
DON'T YOU?

...

DO YOU --
ARE YOU
FROM THE
ORDER?

I'M THE
ONLY REASON
YOU'RE STILL
ALIVE.

THAT
SHOULD BE
ENOUGH,
YES?

HRM. HENRI MELVILLE.
POLICE INSPECTOR
WITH THE FRENCH
CONCESSION GARDE
MUNICIPALE.

NAUGHTY,
NAUGHTY...

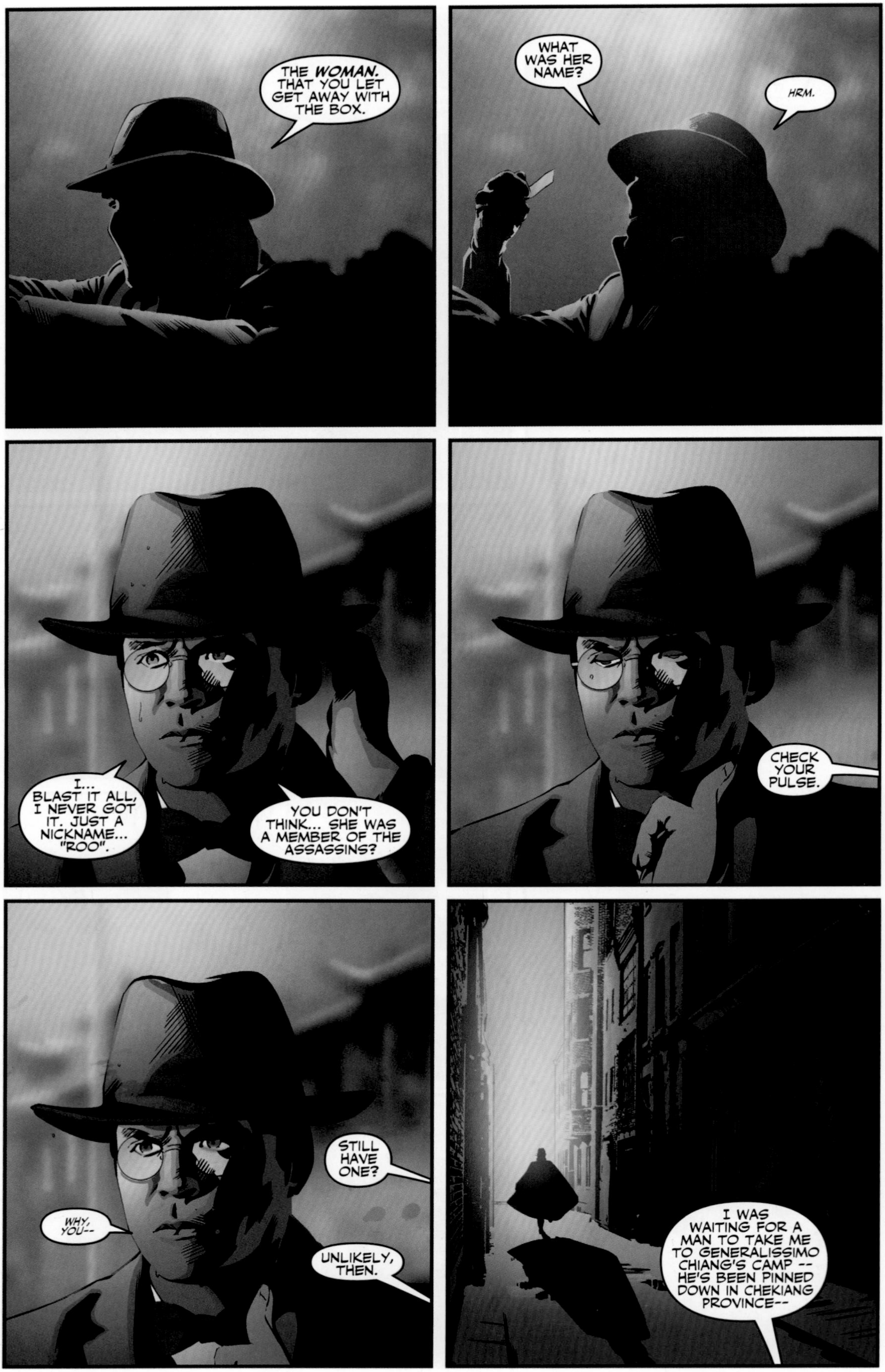
THE WOMAN. THAT YOU LET GET AWAY WITH THE BOX.
WHAT WAS HER NAME?
HRM.
I... BLAST IT ALL, I NEVER GOT IT. JUST A NICKNAME... "ROO".
YOU DON'T THINK... SHE WAS A MEMBER OF THE ASSASSINS?
CHECK YOUR PULSE.
STILL HAVE ONE?
WHY, YOU--
UNLIKELY, THEN.
I WAS WAITING FOR A MAN TO TAKE ME TO GENERALISSIMO CHIANG'S CAMP -- HE'S BEEN PINNED DOWN IN CHEKIANG PROVINCE--

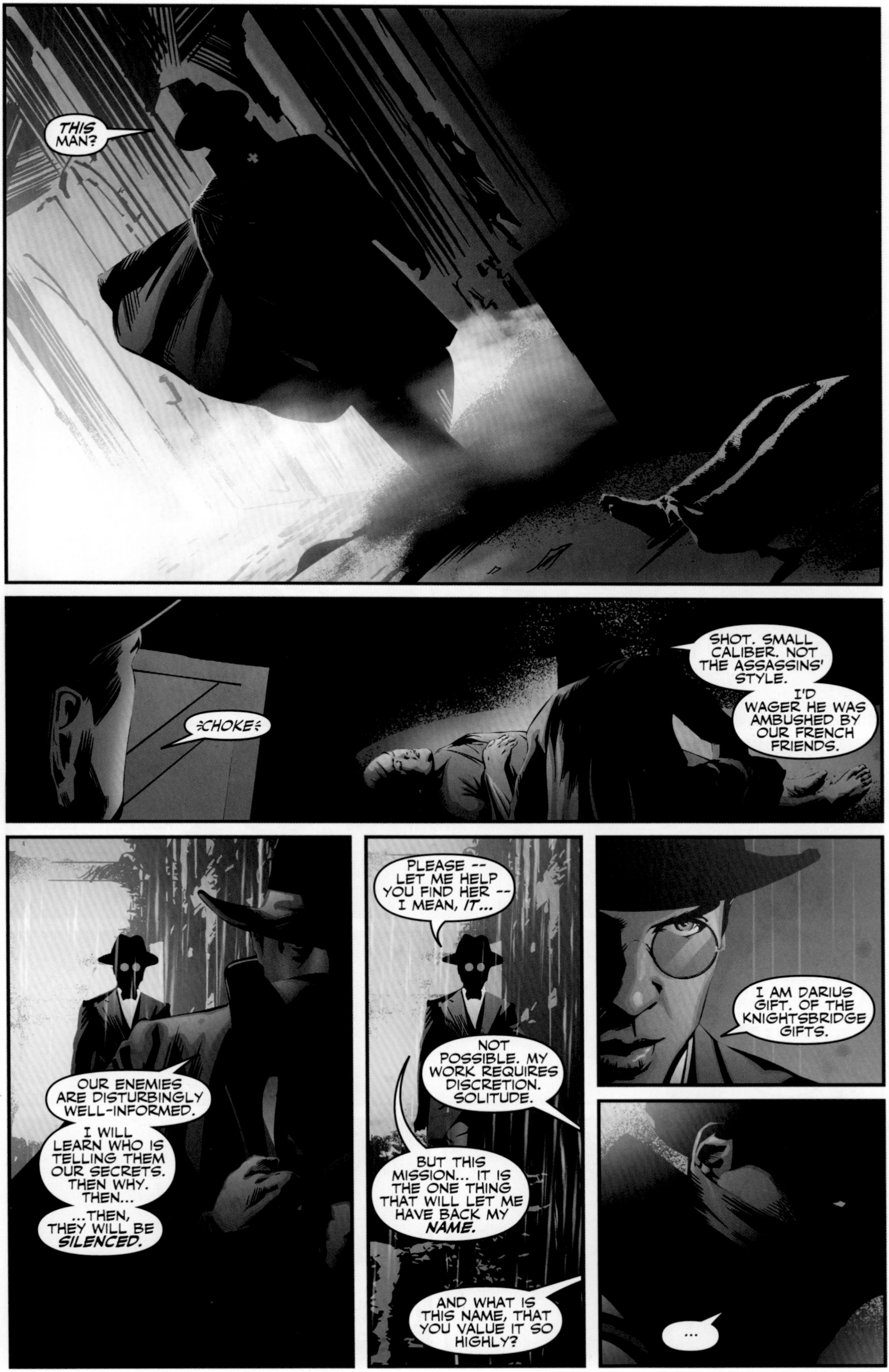
THIS MAN?
SHOT. SMALL CALIBER. NOT THE ASSASSINS' STYLE.
I'D WAGER HE WAS AMBUSHED BY OUR FRENCH FRIENDS.
CHOKE
OUR ENEMIES ARE DISTURBINGLY WELL-INFORMED.
I WILL LEARN WHO IS TELLING THEM OUR SECRETS. THEN WHY. THEN...
...THEN, THEY WILL BE *SILENCED.*
PLEASE -- LET ME HELP YOU FIND HER -- I MEAN, *IT...*
NOT POSSIBLE. MY WORK REQUIRES DISCRETION. SOLITUDE.
BUT THIS MISSION... IT IS THE ONE THING THAT WILL LET ME HAVE BACK MY ***NAME.***
AND WHAT IS THIS NAME, THAT YOU VALUE IT SO HIGHLY?
I AM DARIUS GIFT. OF THE KNIGHTSBRIDGE GIFTS.
...

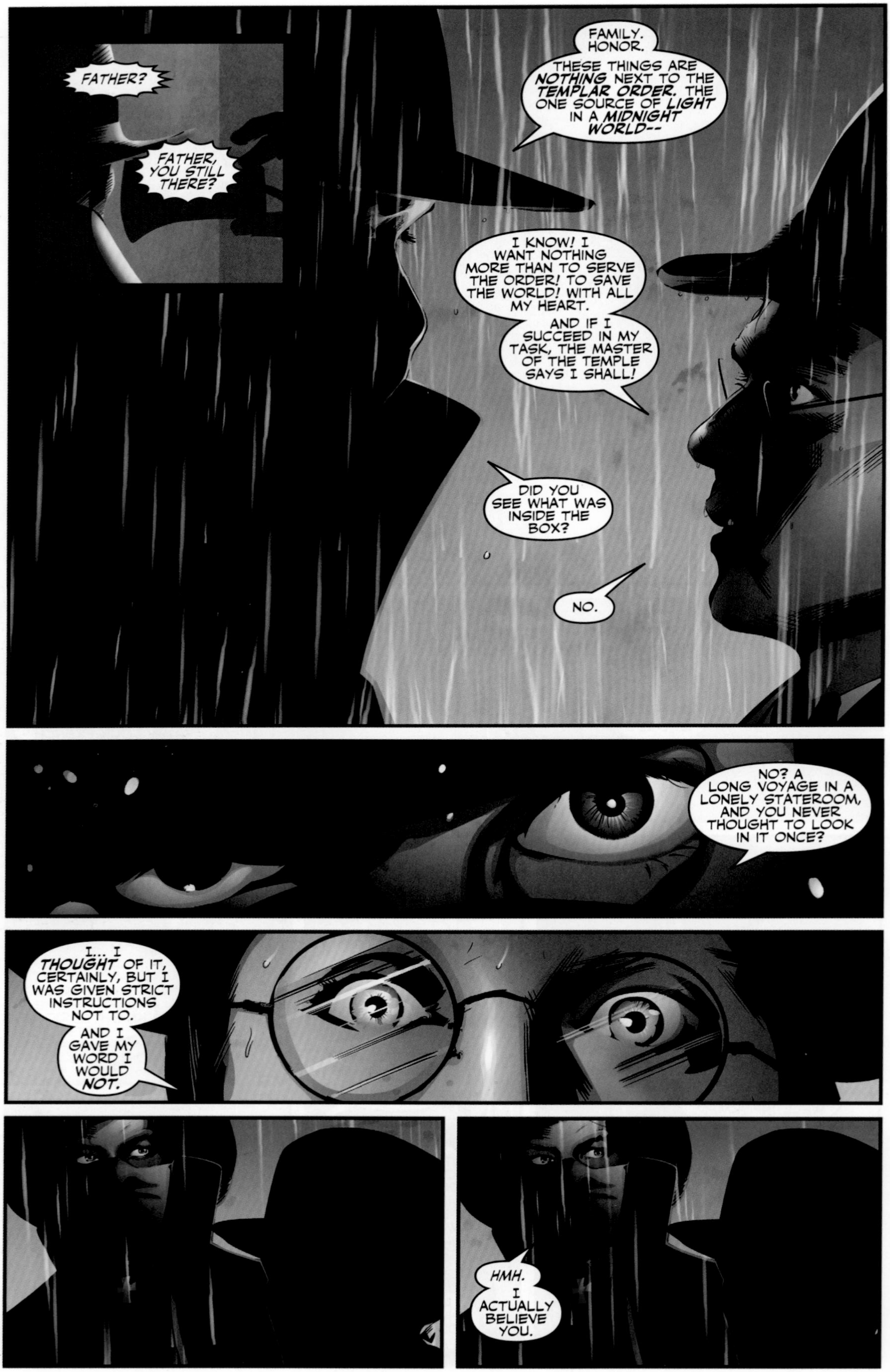
FATHER?
FATHER, YOU STILL THERE?
FAMILY. HONOR.
THESE THINGS ARE *NOTHING* NEXT TO THE *TEMPLAR ORDER.* THE ONE SOURCE OF *LIGHT* IN A *MIDNIGHT WORLD--*
I KNOW! I WANT NOTHING MORE THAN TO SERVE THE ORDER! TO SAVE THE WORLD! WITH ALL MY HEART.
AND IF I SUCCEED IN MY TASK, THE MASTER OF THE TEMPLE SAYS I SHALL!
DID YOU SEE WHAT WAS INSIDE THE BOX?
NO.
NO? A LONG VOYAGE IN A LONELY STATEROOM, AND YOU NEVER THOUGHT TO LOOK IN IT ONCE?
I... I *THOUGHT* OF IT, CERTAINLY, BUT I WAS GIVEN STRICT INSTRUCTIONS NOT TO.
AND I GAVE MY WORD I WOULD *NOT.*
HMH.
I ACTUALLY BELIEVE YOU.

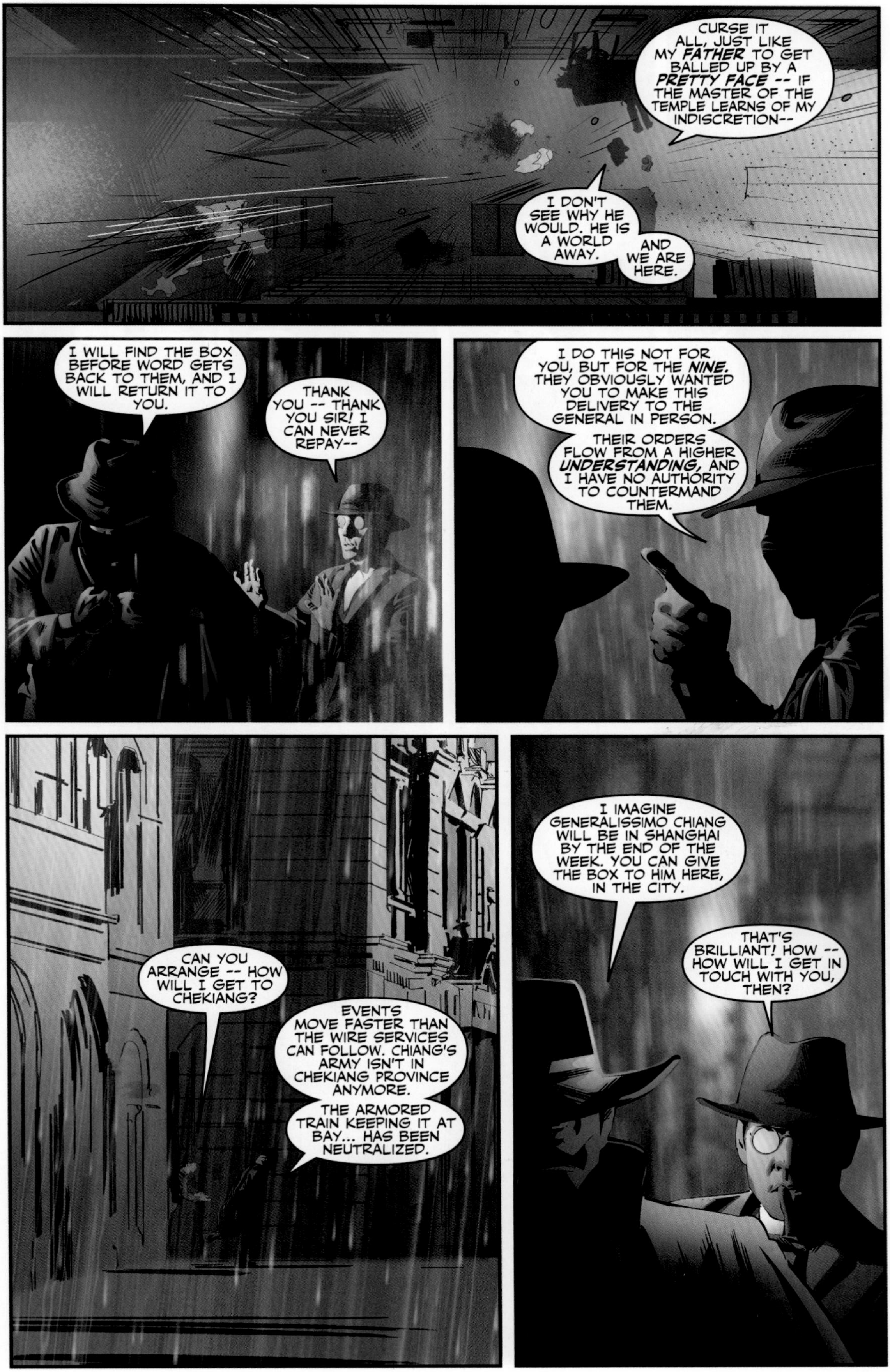
CURSE IT ALL, JUST LIKE MY FATHER TO GET BALLED UP BY A PRETTY FACE -- IF THE MASTER OF THE TEMPLE LEARNS OF MY INDISCRETION--
I DON'T SEE WHY HE WOULD. HE IS A WORLD AWAY.
AND WE ARE HERE.
I WILL FIND THE BOX BEFORE WORD GETS BACK TO THEM, AND I WILL RETURN IT TO YOU.
THANK YOU -- THANK YOU SIR! I CAN NEVER REPAY--
I DO THIS NOT FOR YOU, BUT FOR THE NINE. THEY OBVIOUSLY WANTED YOU TO MAKE THIS DELIVERY TO THE GENERAL IN PERSON.
THEIR ORDERS FLOW FROM A HIGHER UNDERSTANDING, AND I HAVE NO AUTHORITY TO COUNTERMAND THEM.
CAN YOU ARRANGE -- HOW WILL I GET TO CHEKIANG?
EVENTS MOVE FASTER THAN THE WIRE SERVICES CAN FOLLOW. CHIANG'S ARMY ISN'T IN CHEKIANG PROVINCE ANYMORE.
THE ARMORED TRAIN KEEPING IT AT BAY... HAS BEEN NEUTRALIZED.
I IMAGINE GENERALISSIMO CHIANG WILL BE IN SHANGHAI BY THE END OF THE WEEK. YOU CAN GIVE THE BOX TO HIM HERE, IN THE CITY.
THAT'S BRILLIANT! HOW -- HOW WILL I GET IN TOUCH WITH YOU, THEN?

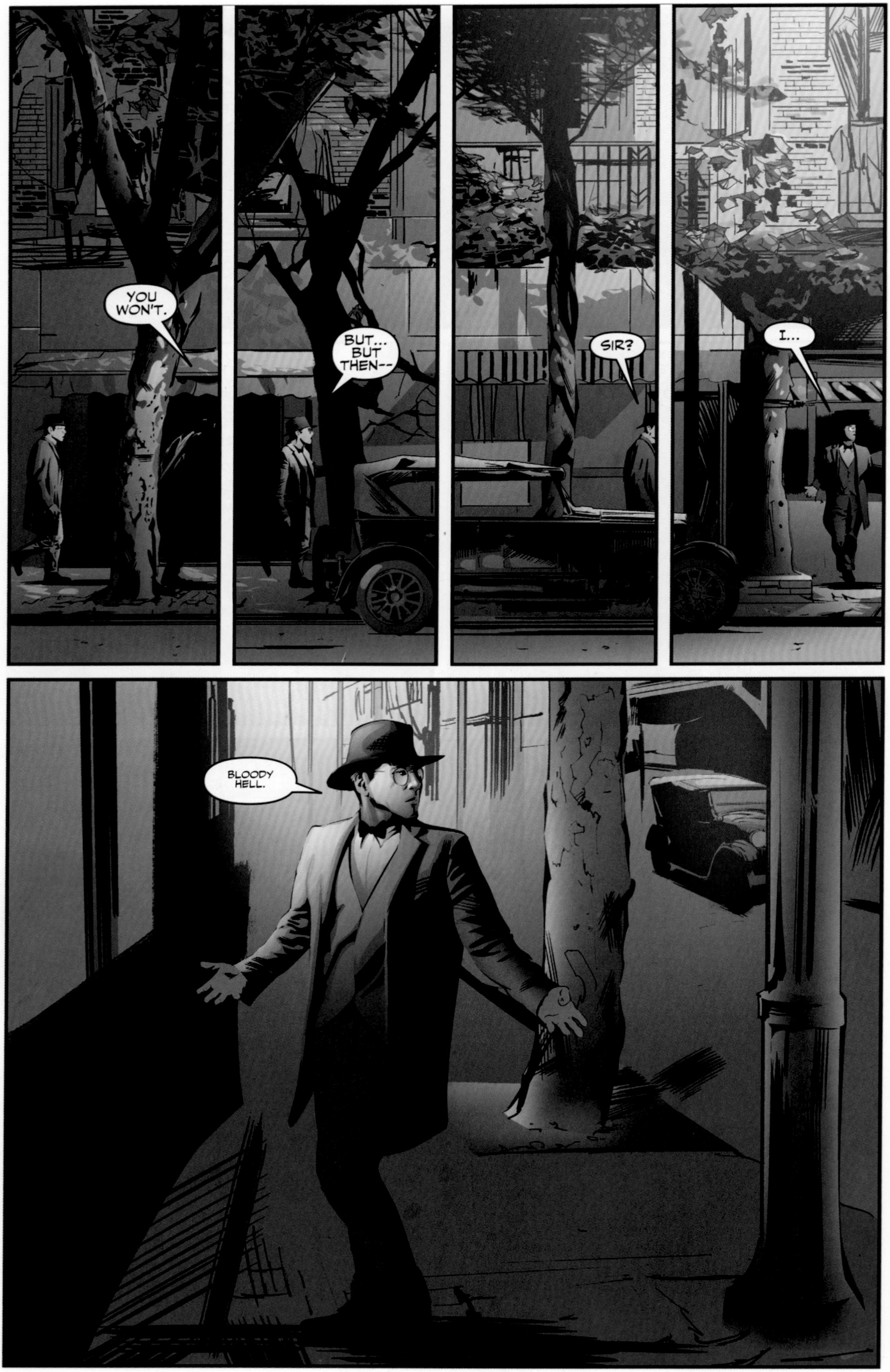
YOU WON'T.
BUT... BUT THEN--
SIR?
I...
BLOODY HELL.

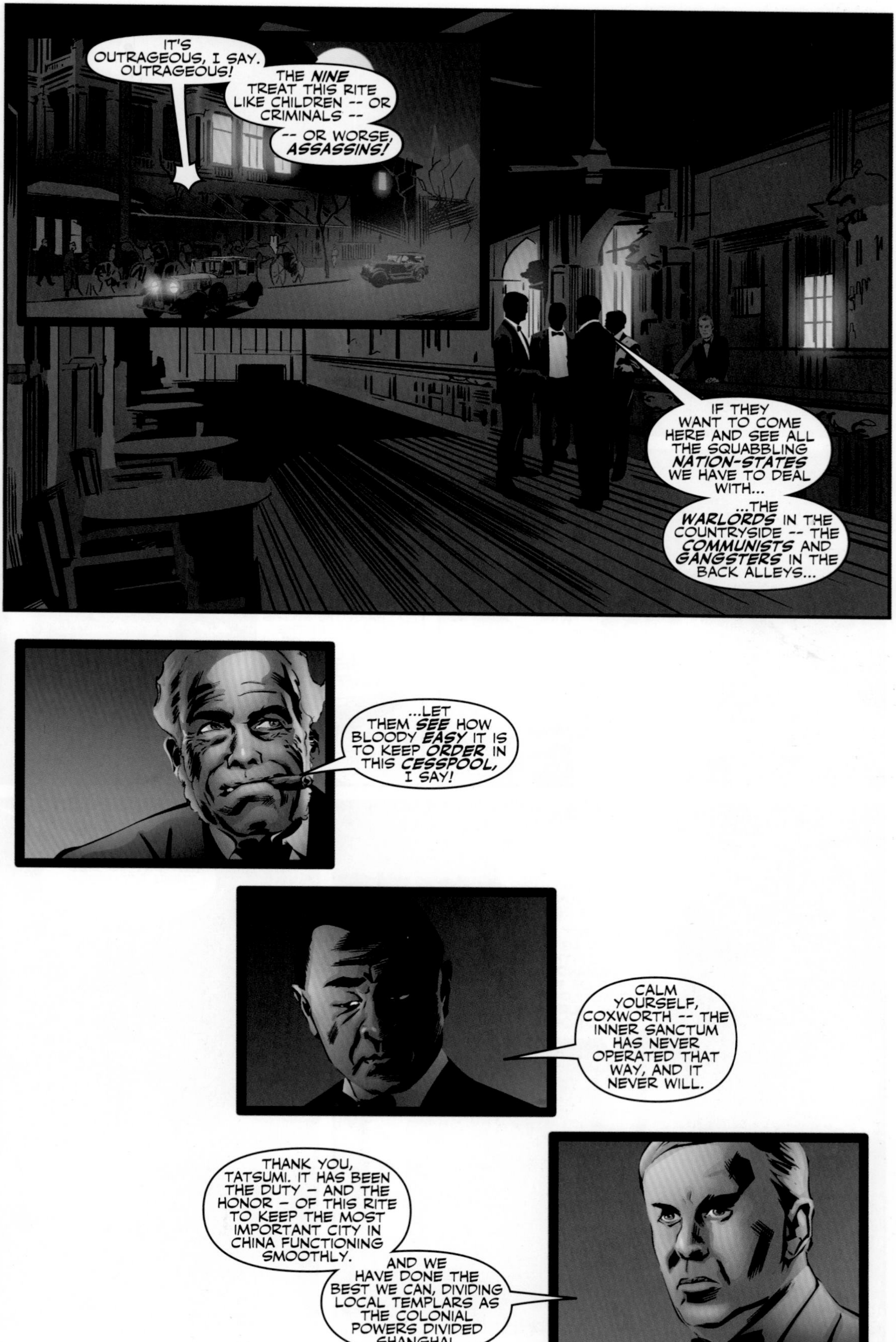

IT'S OUTRAGEOUS, I SAY. OUTRAGEOUS!
THE NINE TREAT THIS RITE LIKE CHILDREN -- OR CRIMINALS --
-- OR WORSE, ASSASSINS!
IF THEY WANT TO COME HERE AND SEE ALL THE SQUABBLING NATION-STATES WE HAVE TO DEAL WITH...
...THE WARLORDS IN THE COUNTRYSIDE -- THE COMMUNISTS AND GANGSTERS IN THE BACK ALLEYS...
...LET THEM SEE HOW BLOODY EASY IT IS TO KEEP ORDER IN THIS CESSPOOL, I SAY!
CALM YOURSELF, COXWORTH -- THE INNER SANCTUM HAS NEVER OPERATED THAT WAY, AND IT NEVER WILL.
THANK YOU, TATSUMI. IT HAS BEEN THE DUTY – AND THE HONOR – OF THIS RITE TO KEEP THE MOST IMPORTANT CITY IN CHINA FUNCTIONING SMOOTHLY.
AND WE HAVE DONE THE BEST WE CAN, DIVIDING LOCAL TEMPLARS AS THE COLONIAL POWERS DIVIDED SHANGHAI.

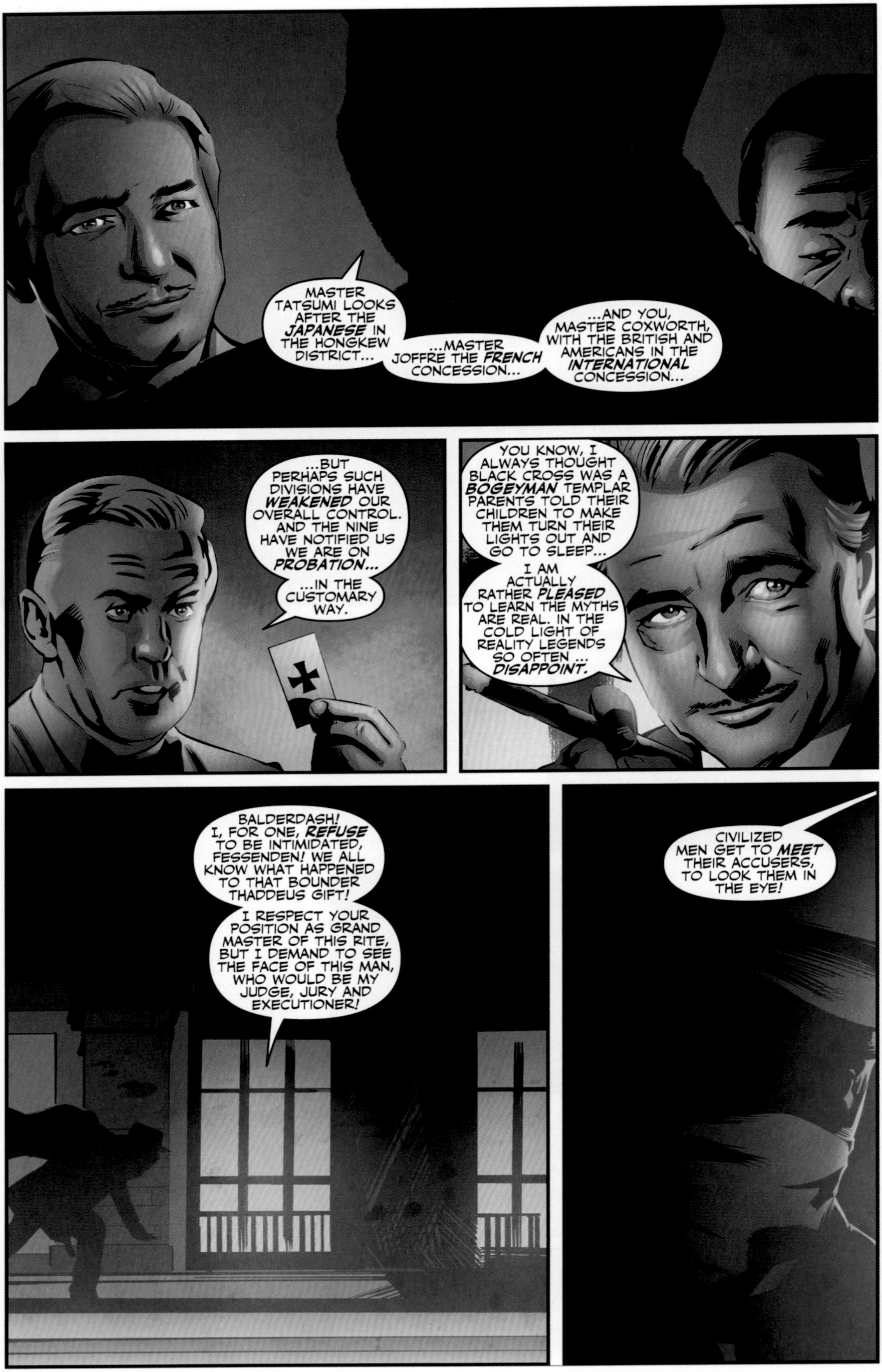
MASTER TATSUMI LOOKS AFTER THE JAPANESE IN THE HONGKEW DISTRICT...
...MASTER JOFFRE THE FRENCH CONCESSION...
...AND YOU, MASTER COXWORTH, WITH THE BRITISH AND AMERICANS IN THE INTERNATIONAL CONCESSION...
...BUT PERHAPS SUCH DIVISIONS HAVE WEAKENED OUR OVERALL CONTROL. AND THE NINE HAVE NOTIFIED US WE ARE ON PROBATION...
...IN THE CUSTOMARY WAY.
YOU KNOW, I ALWAYS THOUGHT BLACK CROSS WAS A BOGEYMAN TEMPLAR PARENTS TOLD THEIR CHILDREN TO MAKE THEM TURN THEIR LIGHTS OUT AND GO TO SLEEP...
I AM ACTUALLY RATHER PLEASED TO LEARN THE MYTHS ARE REAL. IN THE COLD LIGHT OF REALITY LEGENDS SO OFTEN ... DISAPPOINT.
BALDERDASH! I, FOR ONE, REFUSE TO BE INTIMIDATED, FESSENDEN! WE ALL KNOW WHAT HAPPENED TO THAT BOUNDER THADDEUS GIFT!
I RESPECT YOUR POSITION AS GRAND MASTER OF THIS RITE, BUT I DEMAND TO SEE THE FACE OF THIS MAN, WHO WOULD BE MY JUDGE, JURY AND EXECUTIONER!
CIVILIZED MEN GET TO MEET THEIR ACCUSERS, TO LOOK THEM IN THE EYE!

YES. WELL. HENCE THE NEED FOR *THIS* MEETING.

YOU WILL NOT KNOW THE TRUE NAME OR FACE OF THE BLACK CROSS. I DO NOT.

FOR ALL I KNOW HE IS MORE THAN ONE MAN.

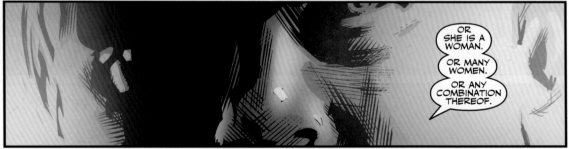

OR SHE IS A WOMAN.

OR MANY WOMEN.

OR ANY COMBINATION THEREOF.

THE INSTRUCTIONS FROM THE INNER SANCTUM ARE QUITE CLEAR:

NONE OF YOUR RESPECTIVE CONCESSIONS IS TO INTERFERE WITH BLACK CROSS IN HIS DUTIES. IF HE REQUESTS YOUR AID, YOU MUST GIVE HIM WHATEVER HE ASKS.

BUT YOU MUST NOT INFORM ANYONE THAT HE HAS CONTACTED YOU. INCLUDING ME.

OR BETRAY *ANYTHING* ABOUT HIS IDENTITY.

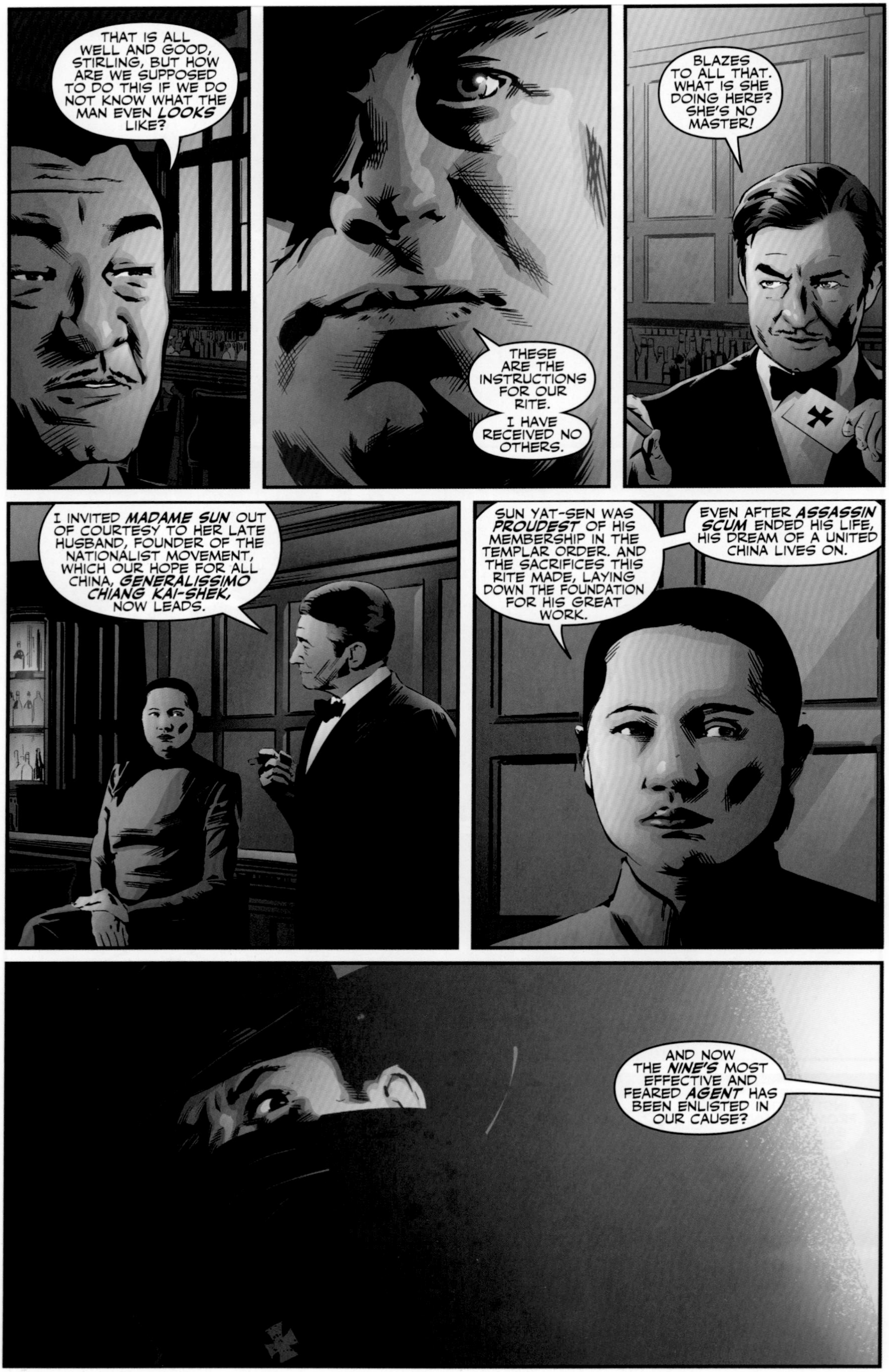
THAT IS ALL WELL AND GOOD, STIRLING, BUT HOW ARE WE SUPPOSED TO DO THIS IF WE DO NOT KNOW WHAT THE MAN EVEN *LOOKS* LIKE?
THESE ARE THE INSTRUCTIONS FOR OUR RITE.
I HAVE RECEIVED NO OTHERS.
BLAZES TO ALL THAT. WHAT IS SHE DOING HERE? SHE'S NO MASTER!
I INVITED *MADAME SUN* OUT OF COURTESY TO HER LATE HUSBAND, FOUNDER OF THE NATIONALIST MOVEMENT, WHICH OUR HOPE FOR ALL CHINA, *GENERALISSIMO CHIANG KAI-SHEK,* NOW LEADS.
SUN YAT-SEN WAS *PROUDEST* OF HIS MEMBERSHIP IN THE TEMPLAR ORDER. AND THE SACRIFICES THIS RITE MADE, LAYING DOWN THE FOUNDATION FOR HIS GREAT WORK.
EVEN AFTER *ASSASSIN SCUM* ENDED HIS LIFE, HIS DREAM OF A UNITED CHINA LIVES ON.
AND NOW THE *NINE'S* MOST EFFECTIVE AND FEARED *AGENT* HAS BEEN ENLISTED IN OUR CAUSE?

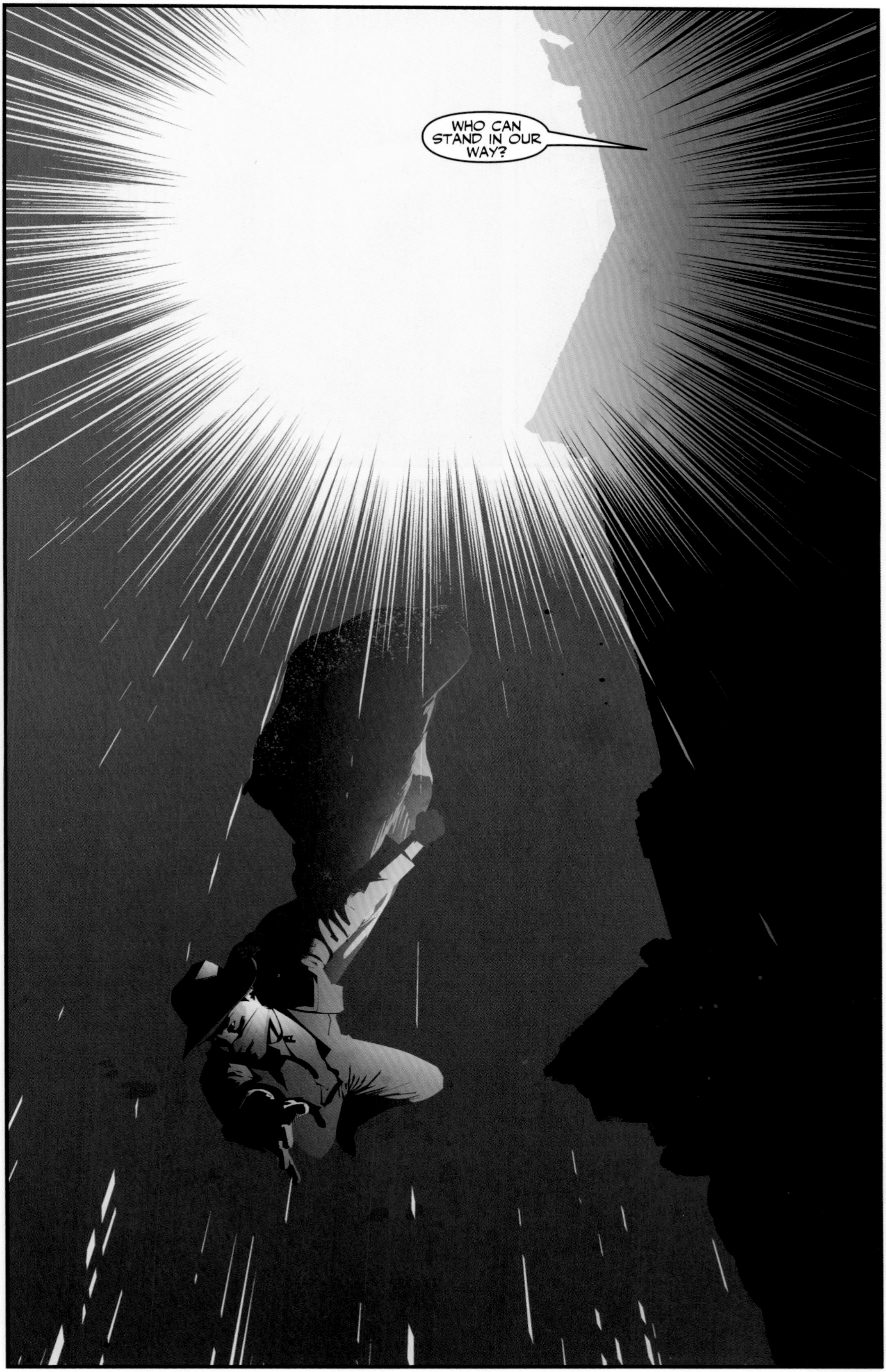
WHO CAN STAND IN OUR WAY?

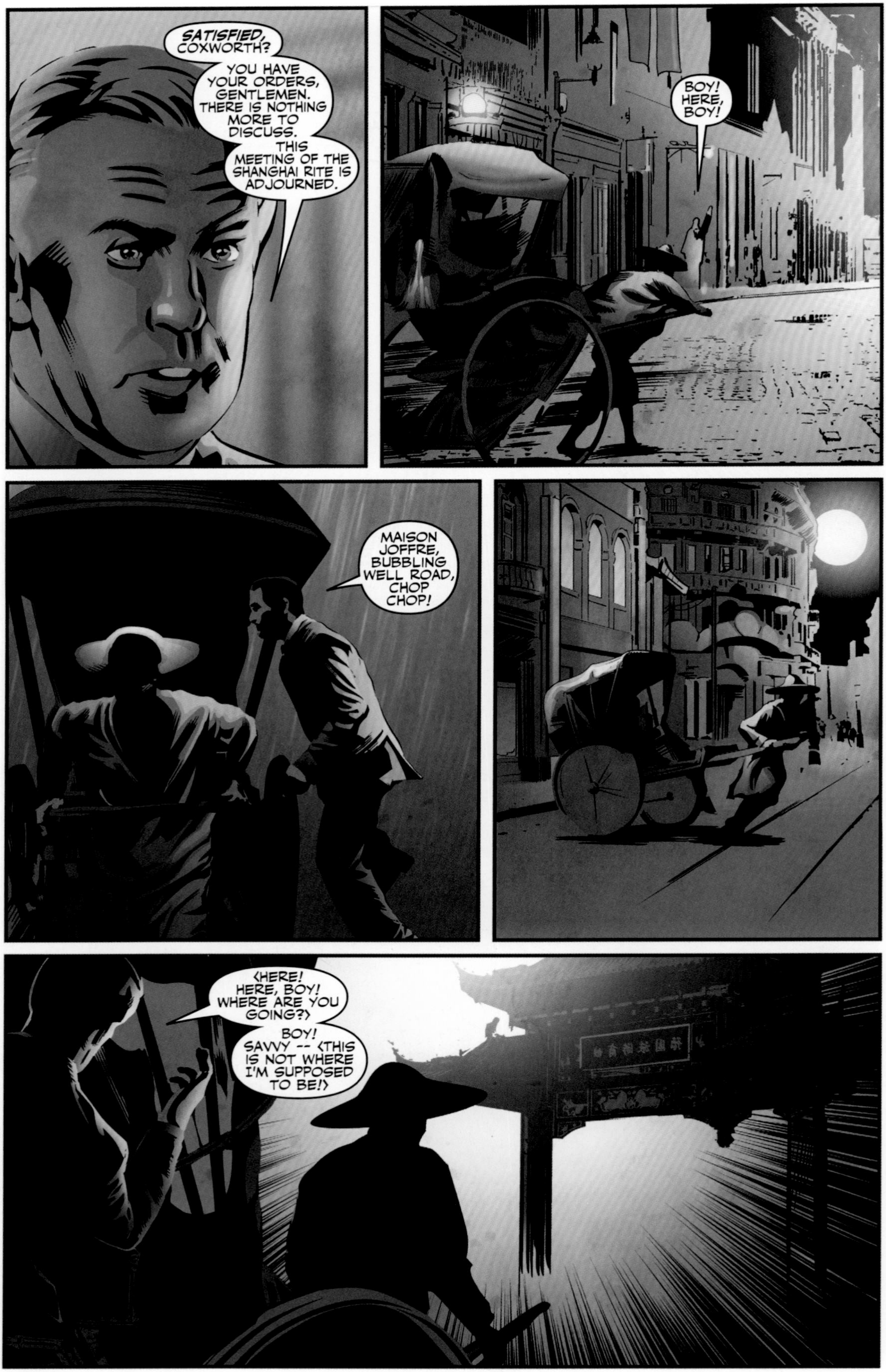
SATISFIED, COXWORTH?
YOU HAVE YOUR ORDERS, GENTLEMEN. THERE IS NOTHING MORE TO DISCUSS.
THIS MEETING OF THE SHANGHAI RITE IS ADJOURNED.
BOY! HERE, BOY!
MAISON JOFFRE, BUBBLING WELL ROAD, CHOP CHOP!
<HERE! HERE, BOY! WHERE ARE YOU GOING?>
BOY!
SAVVY -- <THIS IS NOT WHERE I'M SUPPOSED TO BE!>

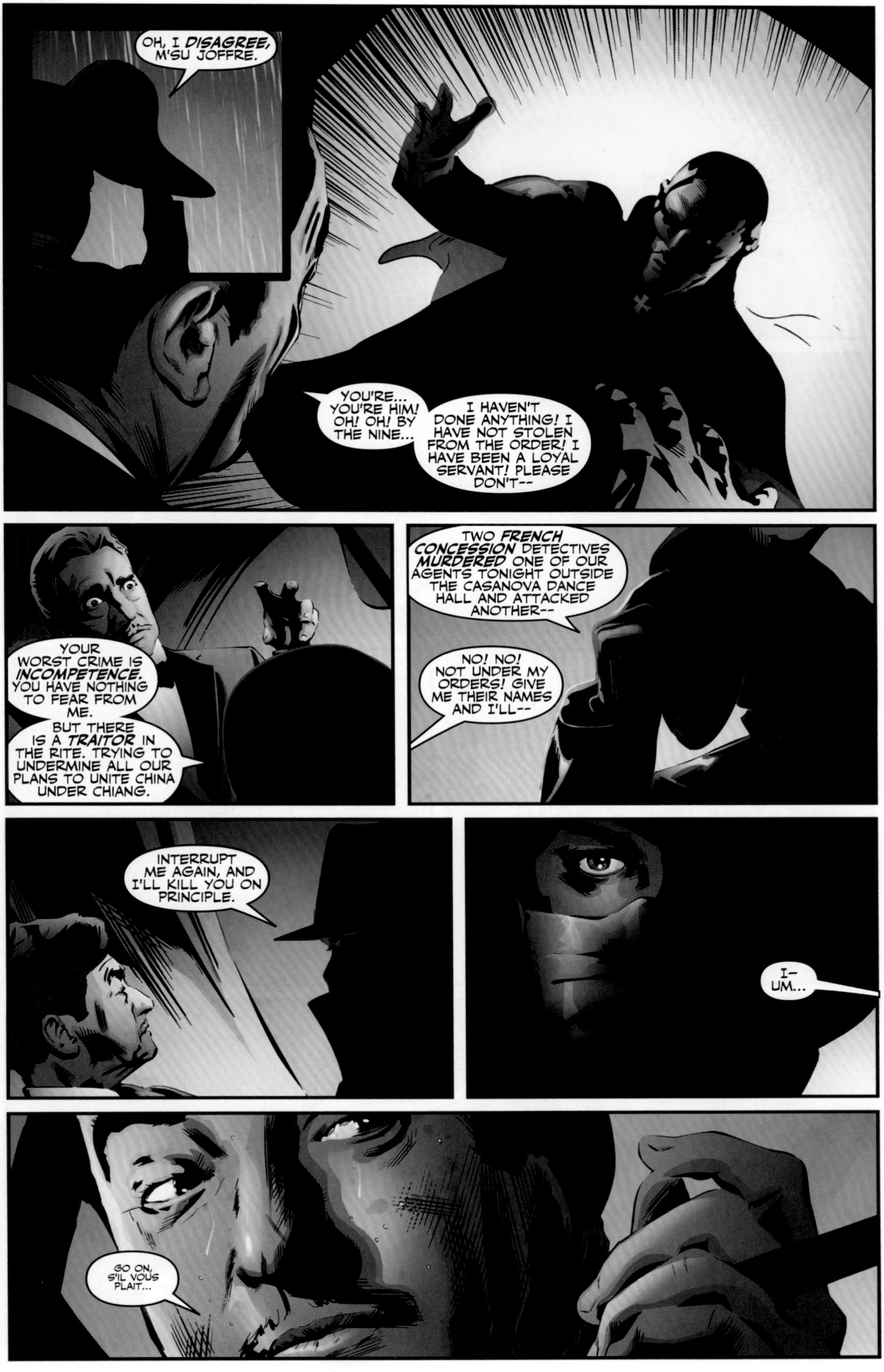
OH, I DISAGREE, M'SU JOFFRE.
YOU'RE... YOU'RE HIM! OH! OH! BY THE NINE...
I HAVEN'T DONE ANYTHING! I HAVE NOT STOLEN FROM THE ORDER! I HAVE BEEN A LOYAL SERVANT! PLEASE DON'T--
YOUR WORST CRIME IS INCOMPETENCE. YOU HAVE NOTHING TO FEAR FROM ME.
BUT THERE IS A TRAITOR IN THE RITE. TRYING TO UNDERMINE ALL OUR PLANS TO UNITE CHINA UNDER CHIANG.
TWO FRENCH CONCESSION DETECTIVES MURDERED ONE OF OUR AGENTS TONIGHT OUTSIDE THE CASANOVA DANCE HALL AND ATTACKED ANOTHER--
NO! NO! NOT UNDER MY ORDERS! GIVE ME THEIR NAMES AND I'LL--
INTERRUPT ME AGAIN, AND I'LL KILL YOU ON PRINCIPLE.
I-- UM...
GO ON, S'IL VOUS PLAIT...

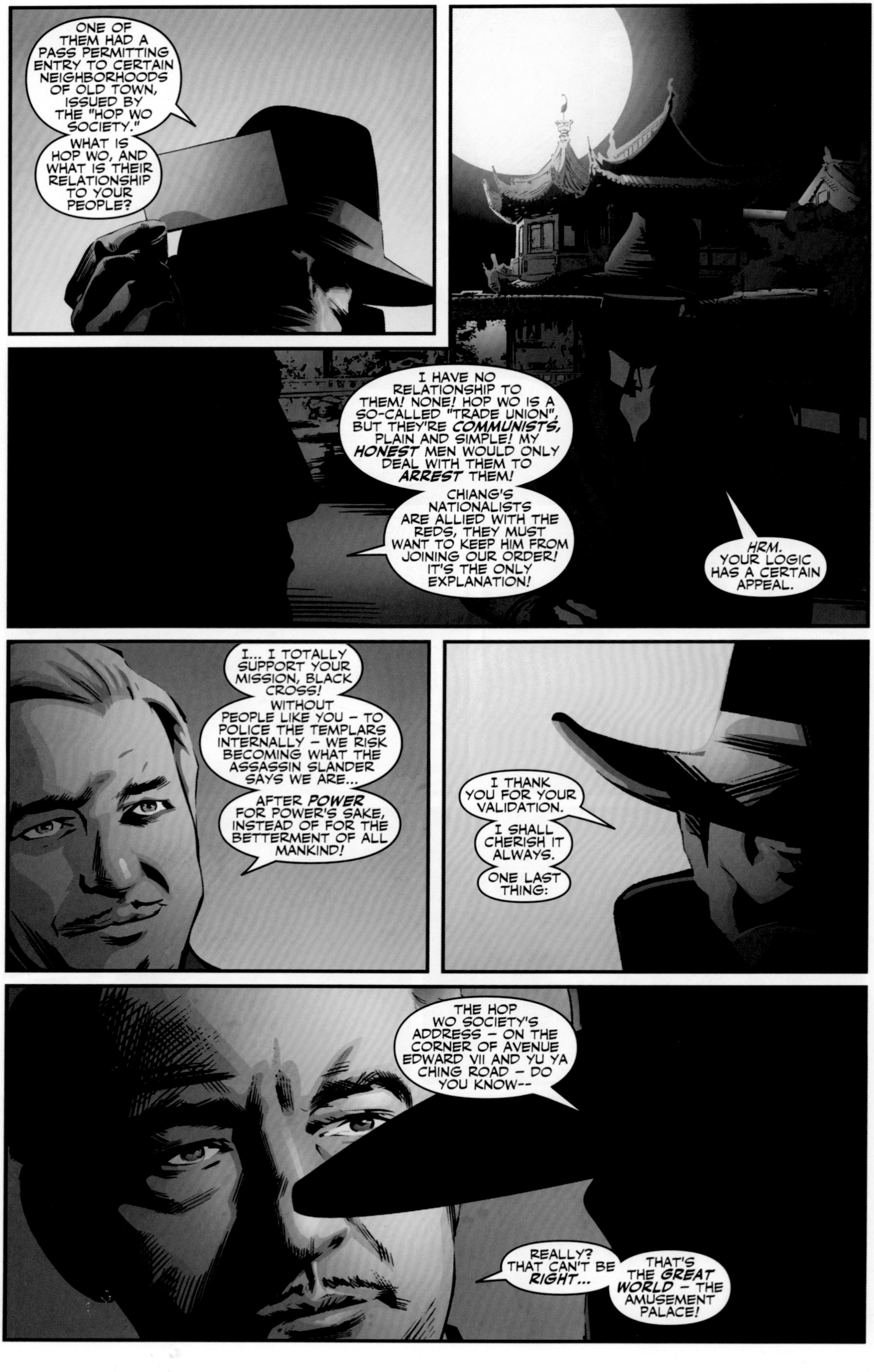
ONE OF THEM HAD A PASS PERMITTING ENTRY TO CERTAIN NEIGHBORHOODS OF OLD TOWN, ISSUED BY THE "HOP WO SOCIETY."
WHAT IS HOP WO, AND WHAT IS THEIR RELATIONSHIP TO YOUR PEOPLE?
I HAVE NO RELATIONSHIP TO THEM! NONE! HOP WO IS A SO-CALLED "TRADE UNION", BUT THEY'RE *COMMUNISTS,* PLAIN AND SIMPLE! MY *HONEST* MEN WOULD ONLY DEAL WITH THEM TO *ARREST* THEM!
CHIANG'S NATIONALISTS ARE ALLIED WITH THE REDS, THEY MUST WANT TO KEEP HIM FROM JOINING OUR ORDER! IT'S THE ONLY EXPLANATION!
HRM. YOUR LOGIC HAS A CERTAIN APPEAL.
I... I TOTALLY SUPPORT YOUR MISSION, BLACK CROSS!
WITHOUT PEOPLE LIKE YOU – TO POLICE THE TEMPLARS INTERNALLY – WE RISK BECOMING WHAT THE ASSASSIN SLANDER SAYS WE ARE...
AFTER *POWER* FOR POWER'S SAKE, INSTEAD OF FOR THE BETTERMENT OF ALL MANKIND!
I THANK YOU FOR YOUR VALIDATION.
I SHALL CHERISH IT ALWAYS.
ONE LAST THING:
THE HOP WO SOCIETY'S ADDRESS – ON THE CORNER OF AVENUE EDWARD VII AND YU YA CHING ROAD – DO YOU KNOW--
REALLY? THAT CAN'T BE *RIGHT...*
THAT'S THE *GREAT WORLD* – THE AMUSEMENT PALACE!

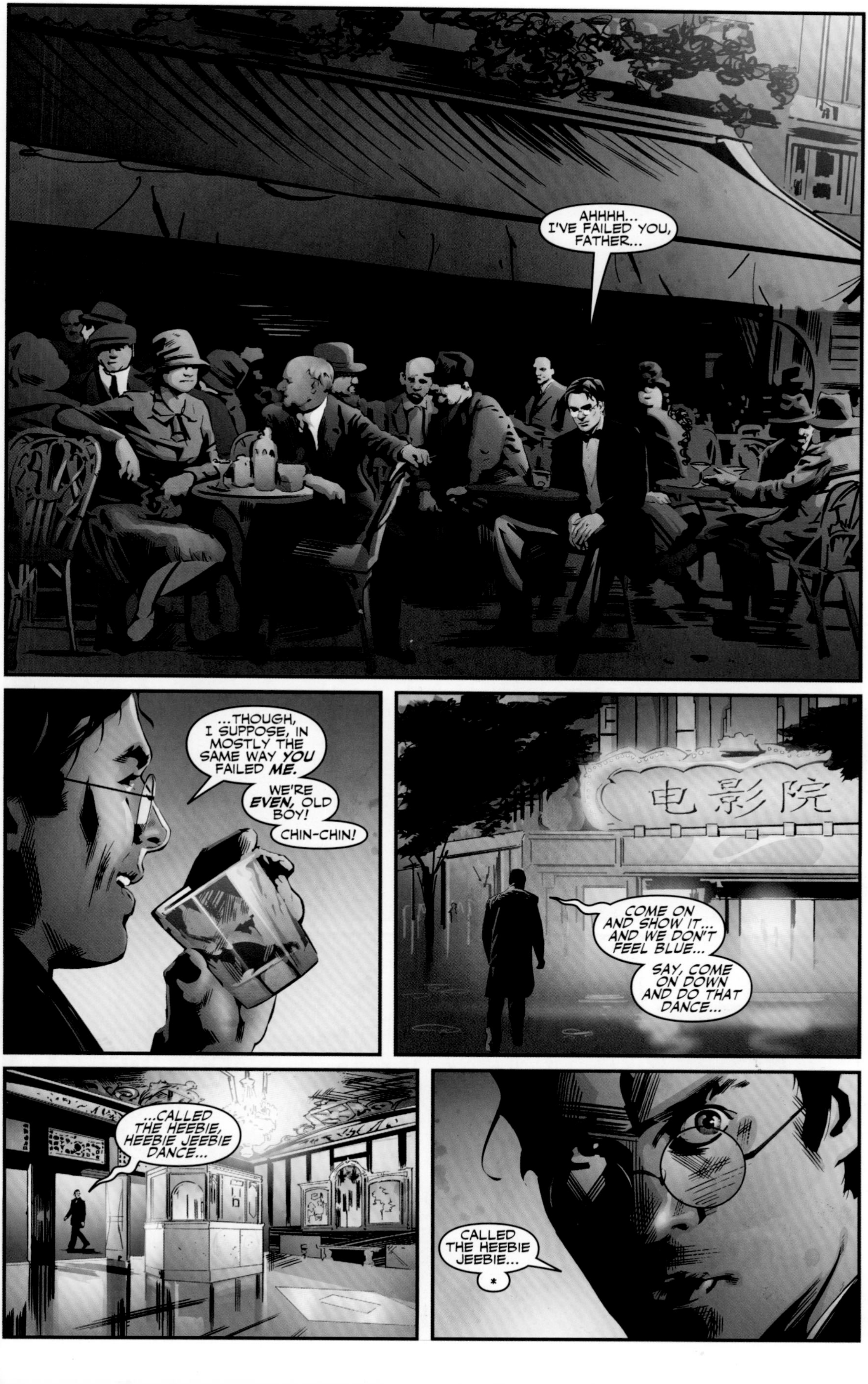
AHHHH...
I'VE FAILED YOU,
FATHER...
...THOUGH, I SUPPOSE, IN MOSTLY THE SAME WAY *YOU* FAILED *ME.*
WE'RE *EVEN*, OLD BOY!
CHIN-CHIN!
电影院
COME ON AND SHOW IT... AND WE DON'T FEEL BLUE...
SAY, COME ON DOWN AND DO THAT DANCE...
...CALLED THE HEEBIE, HEEBIE JEEBIE DANCE...
CALLED THE HEEBIE JEEBIE...
*

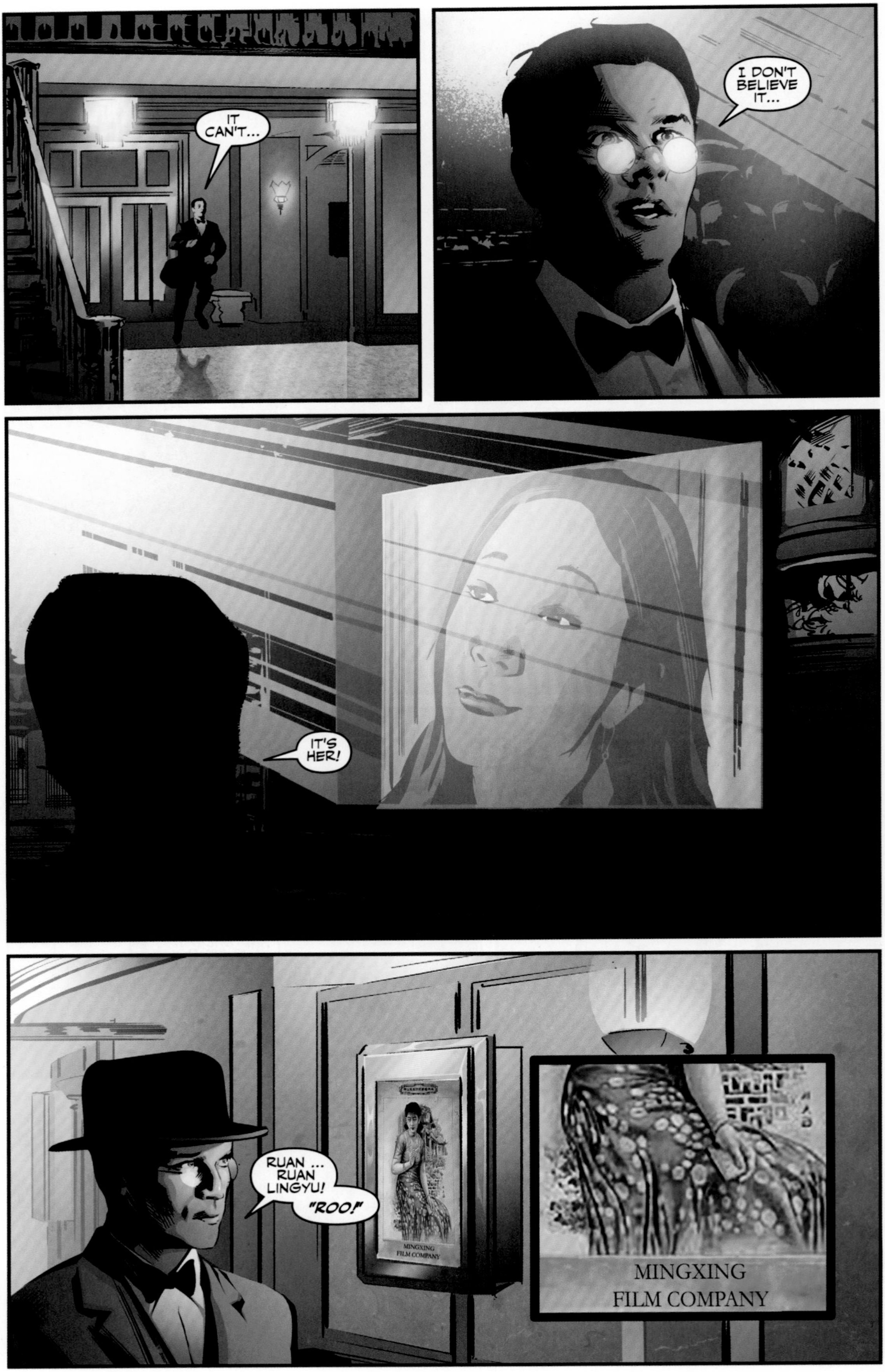
IT CAN'T...
I DON'T BELIEVE IT...
IT'S HER!
RUAN ... RUAN LINGYU!
"ROO!"
MINGXING FILM COMPANY
MINGXING FILM COMPANY

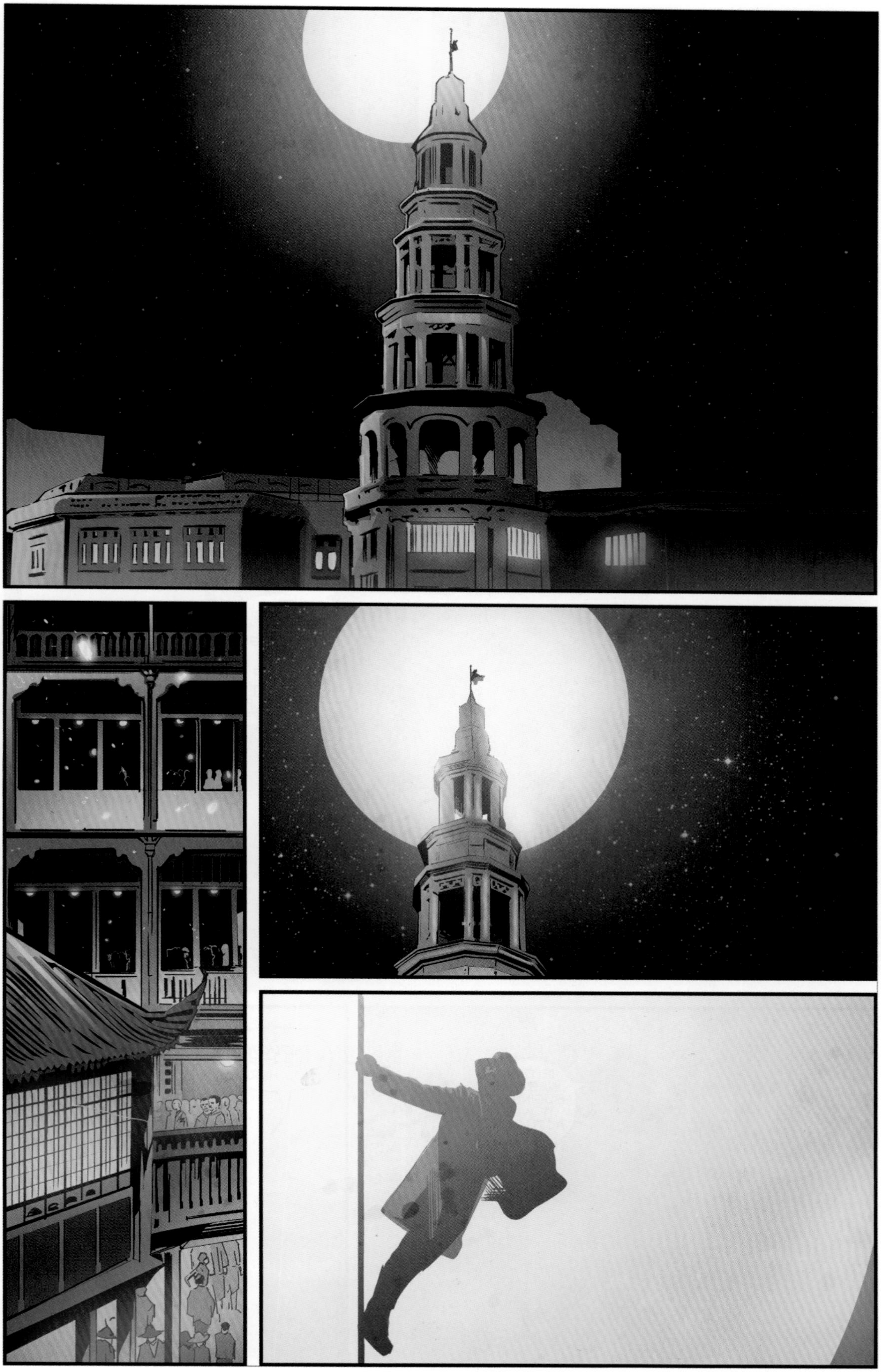

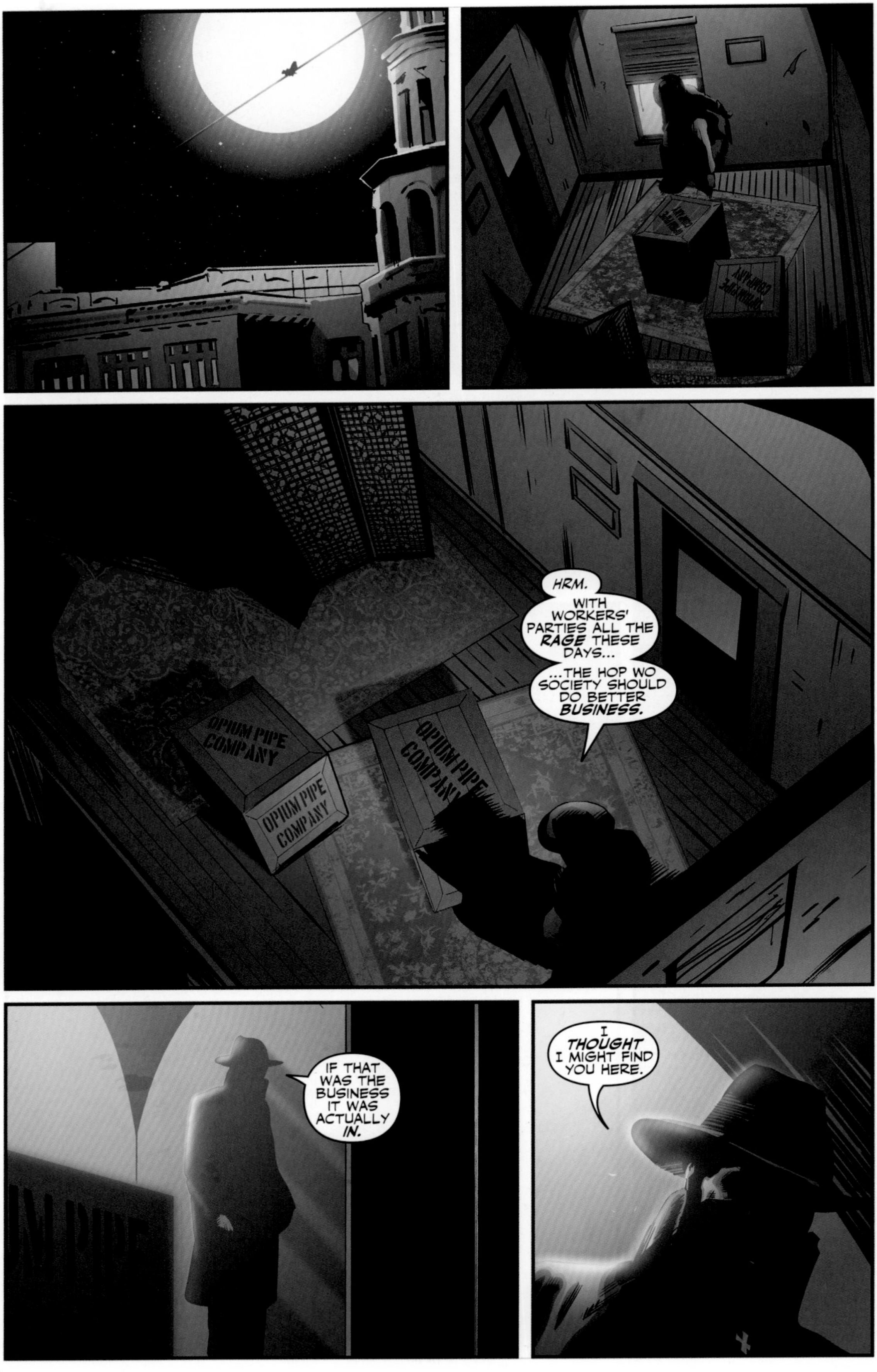
HRM.
WITH WORKERS' PARTIES ALL THE RAGE THESE DAYS...
...THE HOP WO SOCIETY SHOULD DO BETTER BUSINESS.
OPIUM PIPE COMPANY
OPIUM PIPE COMPANY
OPIUM PIPE COMPANY
IF THAT WAS THE BUSINESS IT WAS ACTUALLY IN.
I THOUGHT I MIGHT FIND YOU HERE.

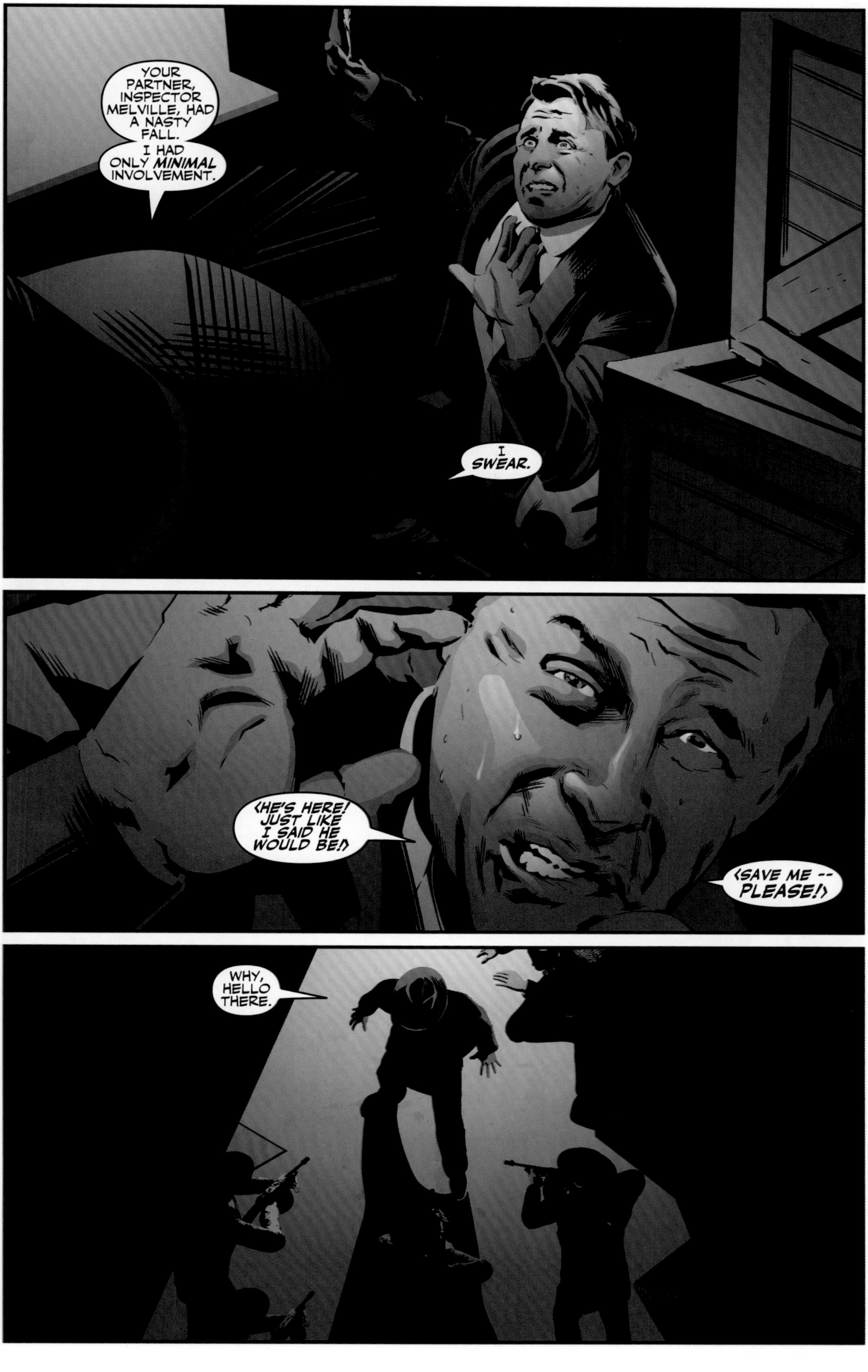
YOUR PARTNER, INSPECTOR MELVILLE, HAD A NASTY FALL.
I HAD ONLY MINIMAL INVOLVEMENT.
I SWEAR.
‹HE'S HERE! JUST LIKE I SAID HE WOULD BE!›
‹SAVE ME -- PLEASE!›
WHY, HELLO THERE.

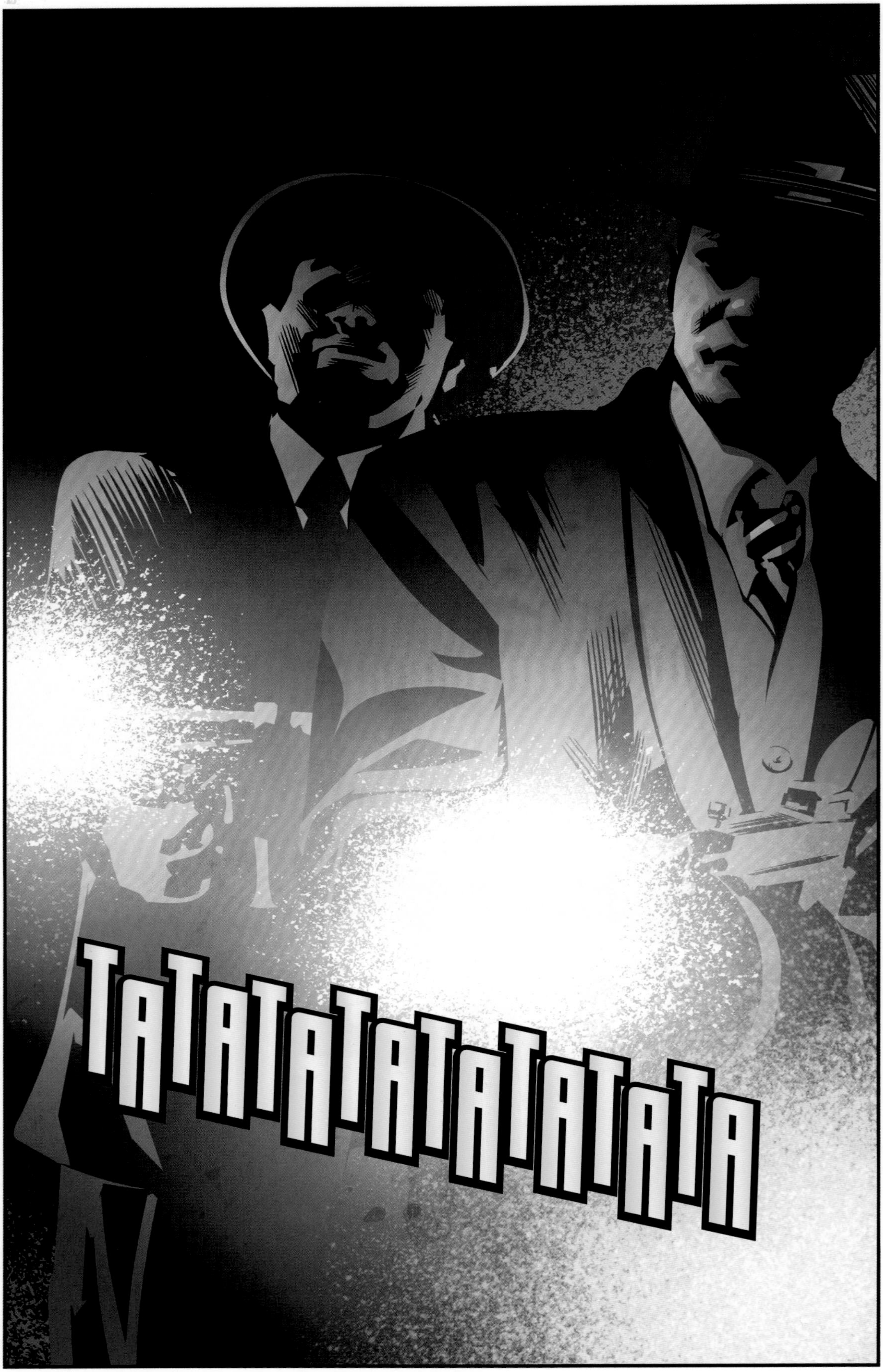
TATATATATATATATA

CHAPTER THREE

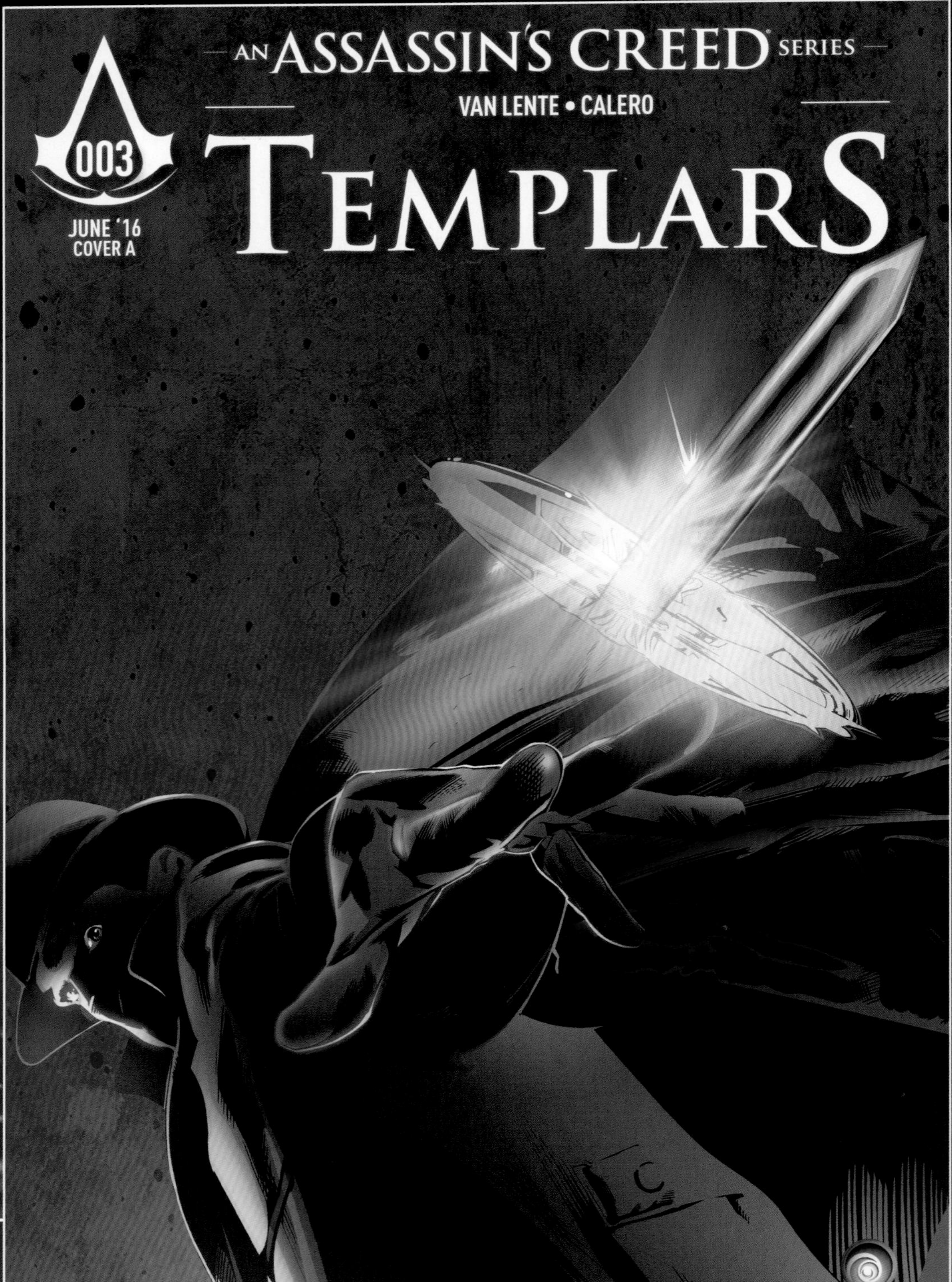
AN ASSASSIN'S CREED SERIES
VAN LENTE • CALERO
003
TEMPLARS
JUNE '16
COVER A
UBISOFT
TITAN COMICS

ISSUE 3 - COVER A
DENNIS CALERO

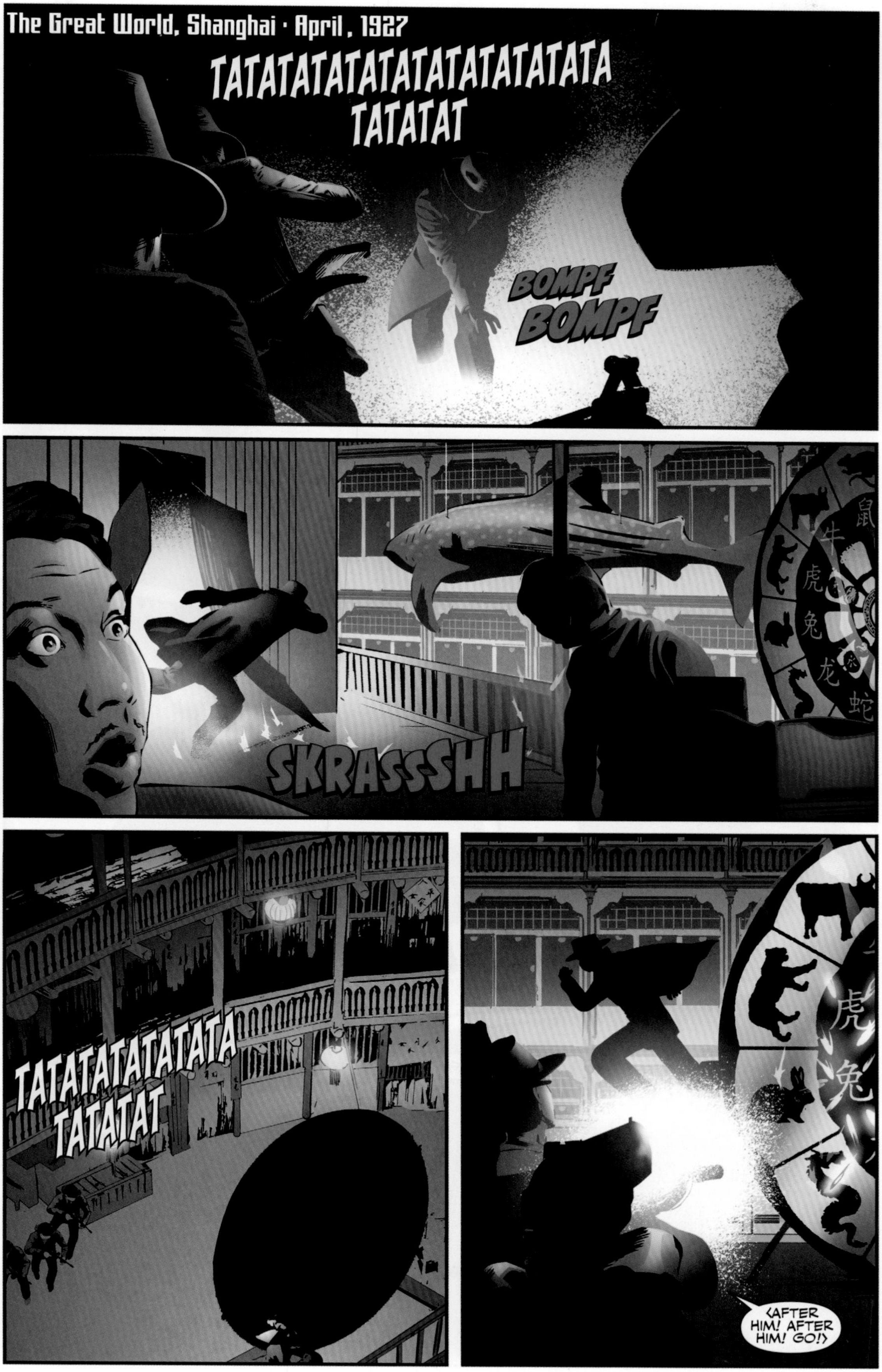
The Great World, Shanghai · April, 1927
TATATATATATATATATATATATA
TATATAT
BOMPF
BOMPF
SKRASSSHH
鼠
牛
虎
兔
龙
蛇
TATATATATATATA
TATATAT
虎
兔
<AFTER HIM! AFTER HIM! GO!>

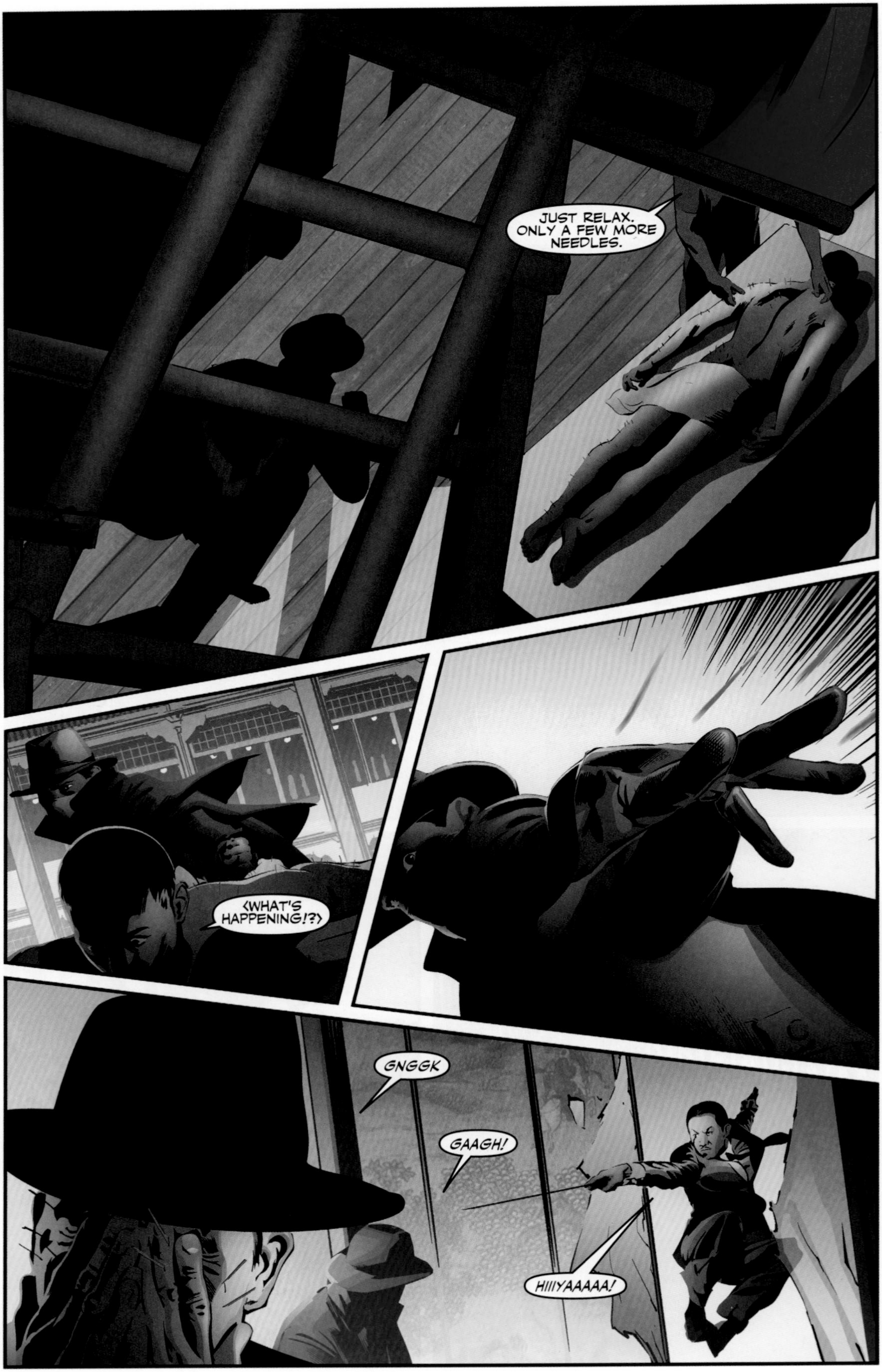
JUST RELAX. ONLY A FEW MORE NEEDLES.
‹WHAT'S HAPPENING!?›
GNGGK
GAAGH!
HIIIYAAAAA!

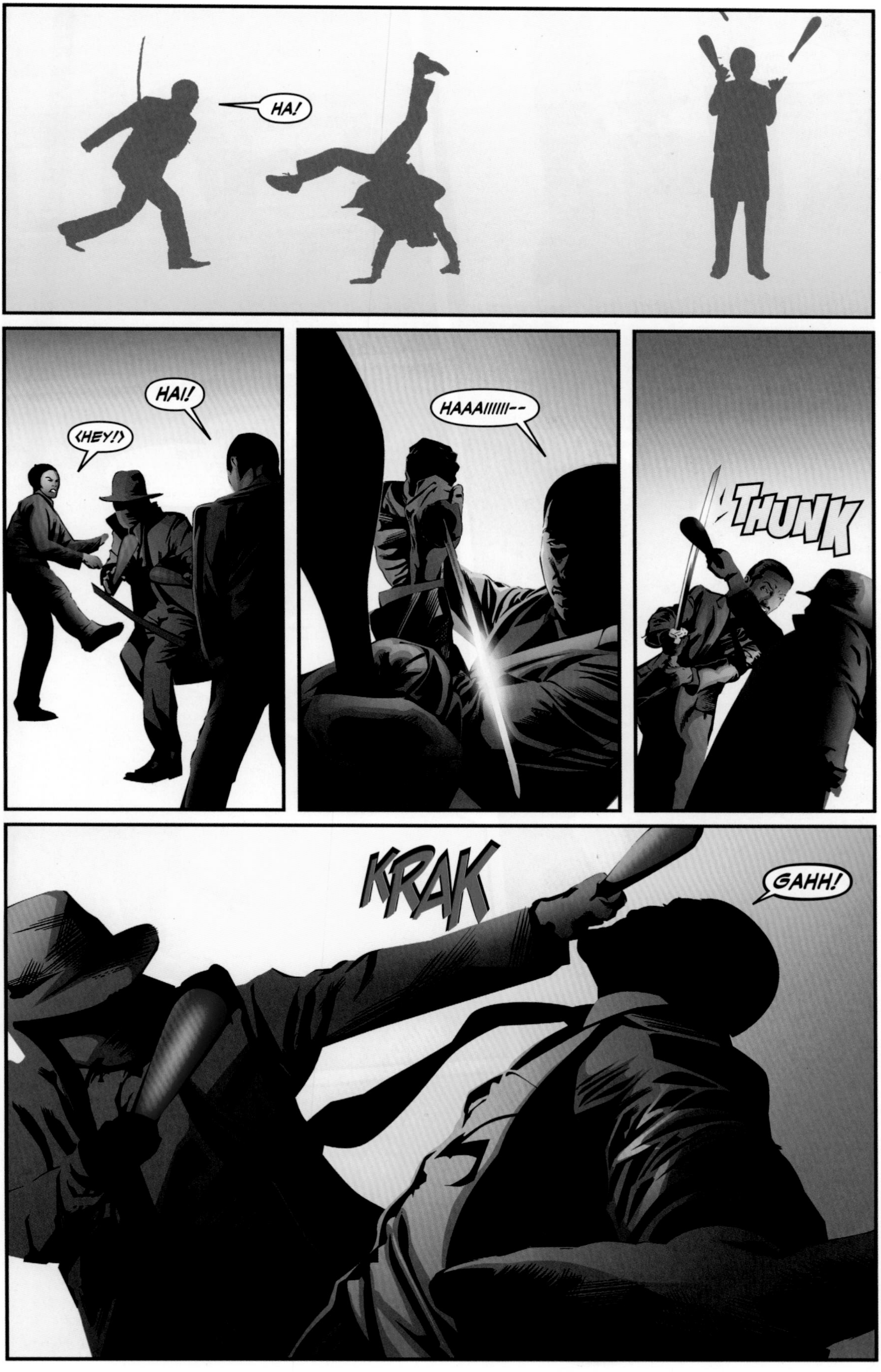
HA!
HAI!
‹HEY!›
HAAAIIIIII--
THUNK
KRAK
GAHH!

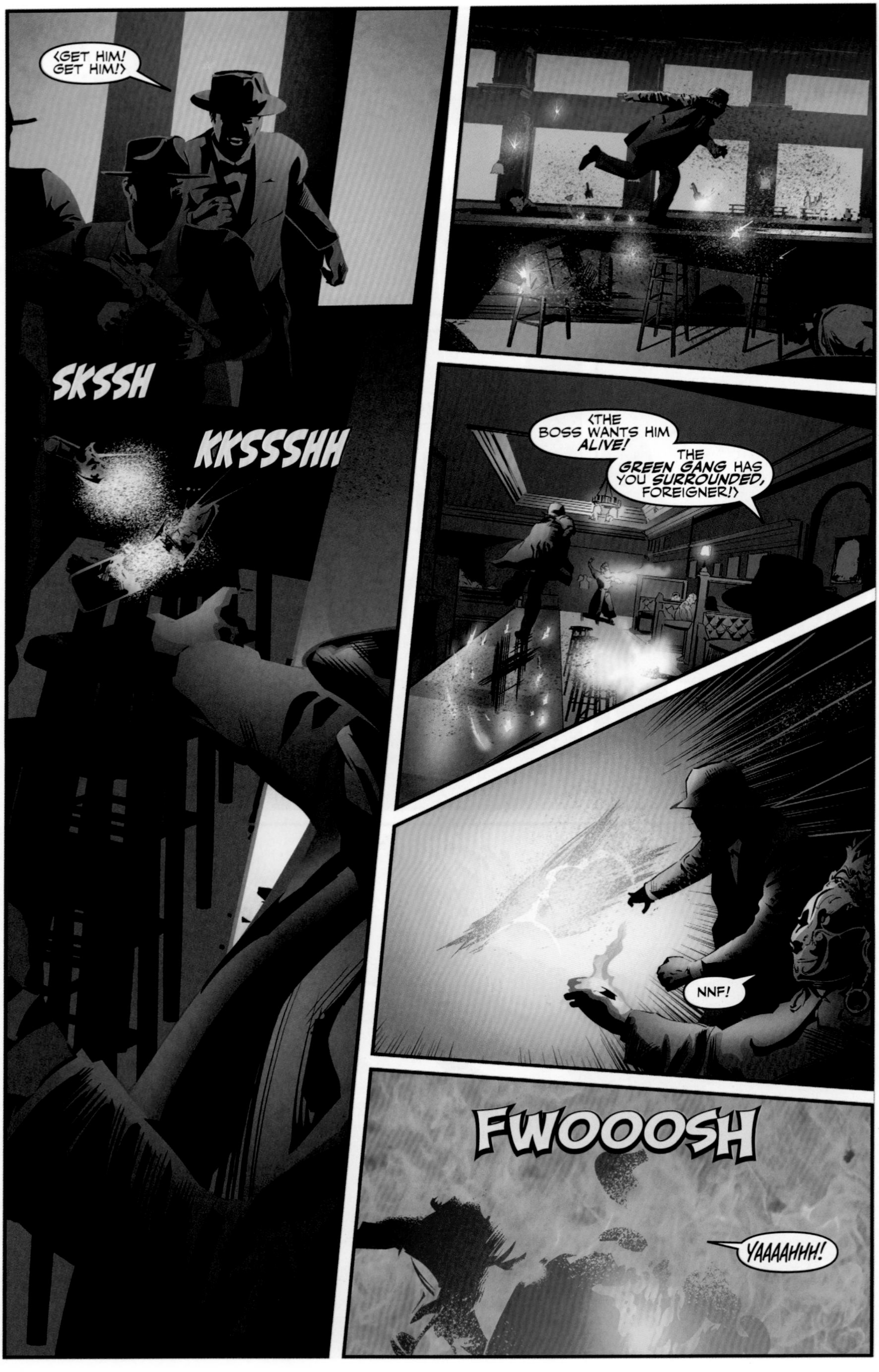
‹GET HIM! GET HIM!›
SKSSH
KKSSSHH
‹THE BOSS WANTS HIM *ALIVE!*
THE *GREEN GANG* HAS YOU *SURROUNDED,* FOREIGNER!›
NNF!
FWOOOSH
YAAAAHHH!

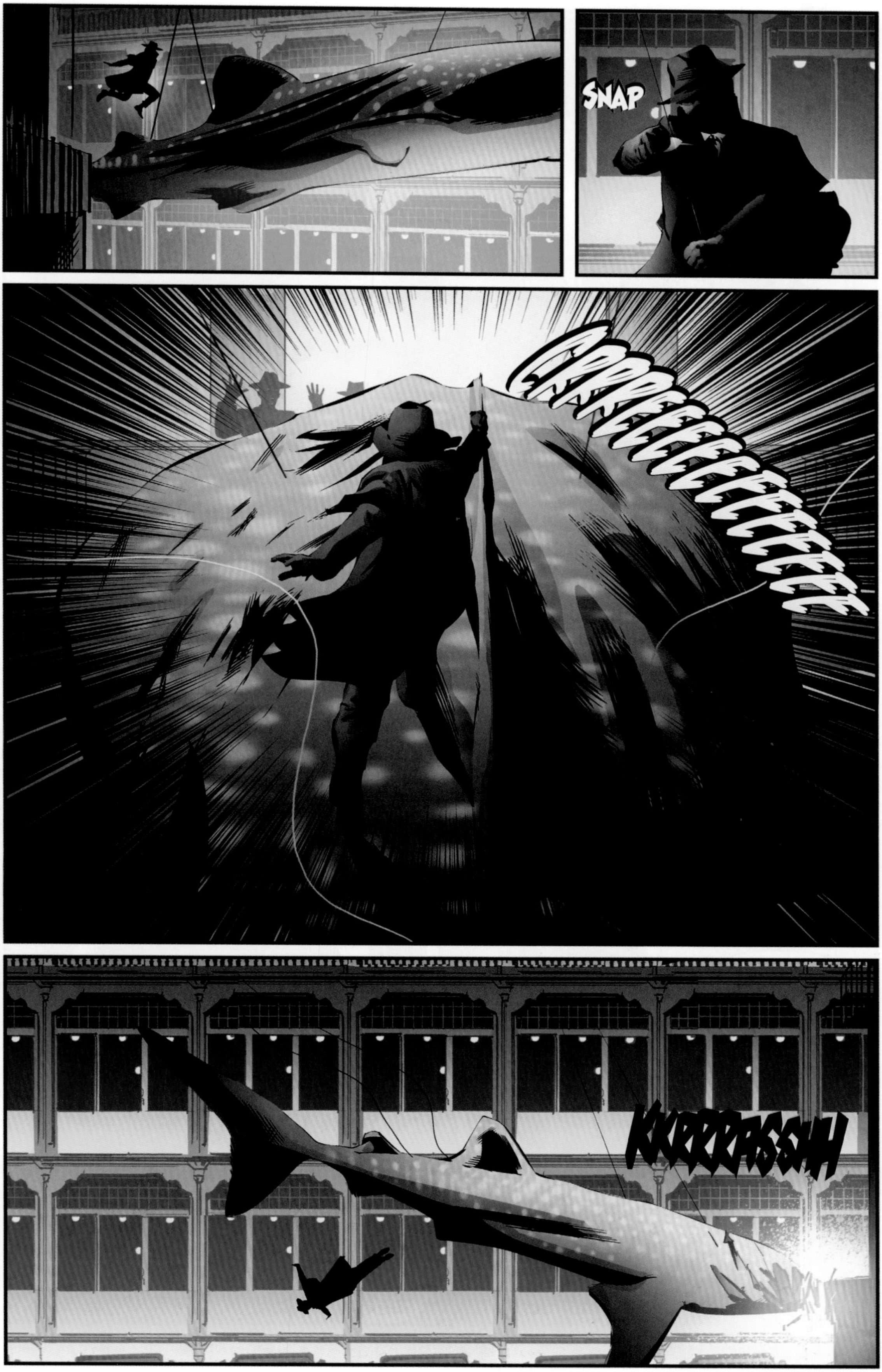
SNAP
CRRREEEEEEEEEEE
KKRRRASSHH

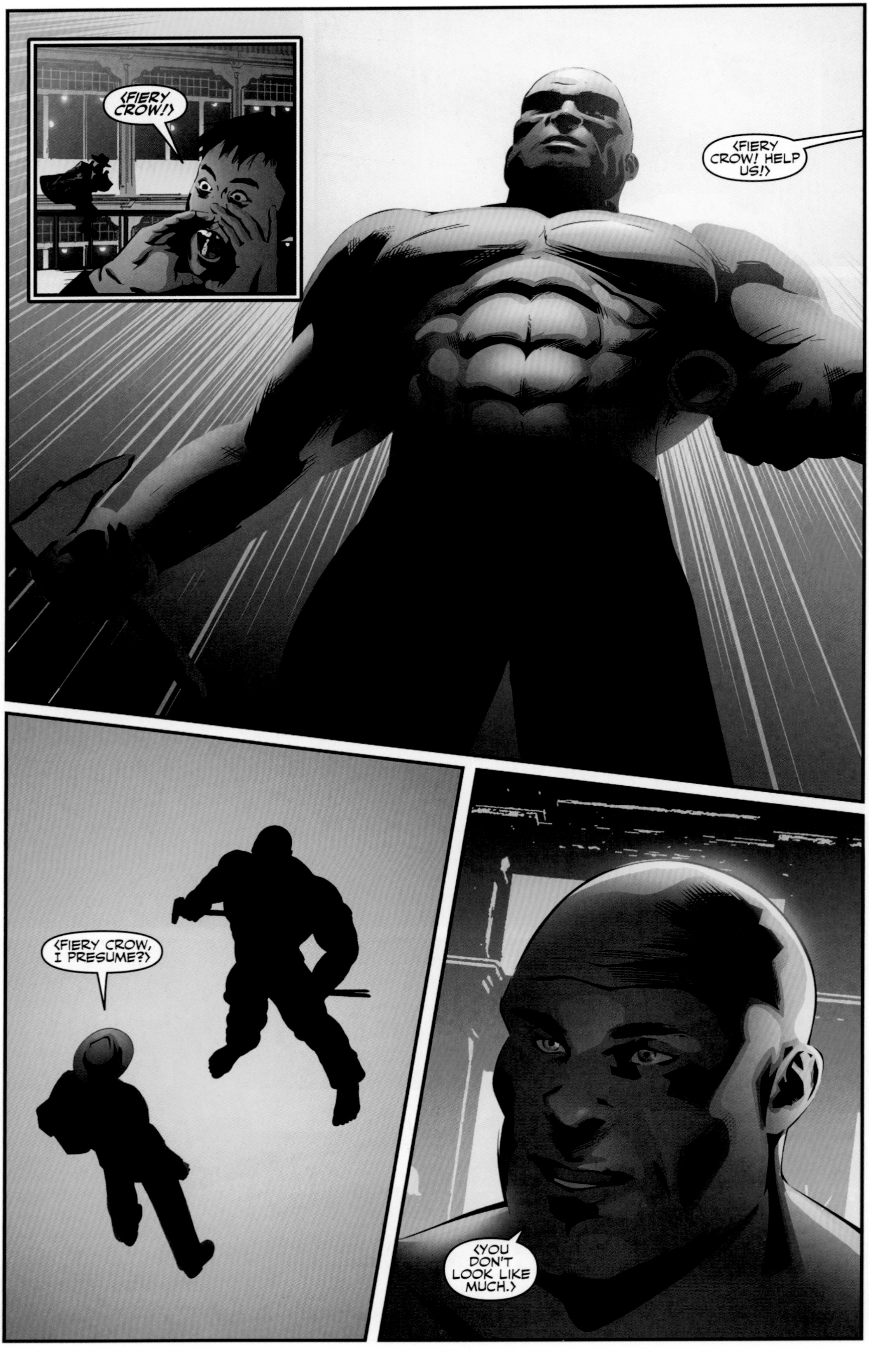
<FIERY CROW!>
<FIERY CROW! HELP US!>
<FIERY CROW, I PRESUME?>
<YOU DON'T LOOK LIKE MUCH.>

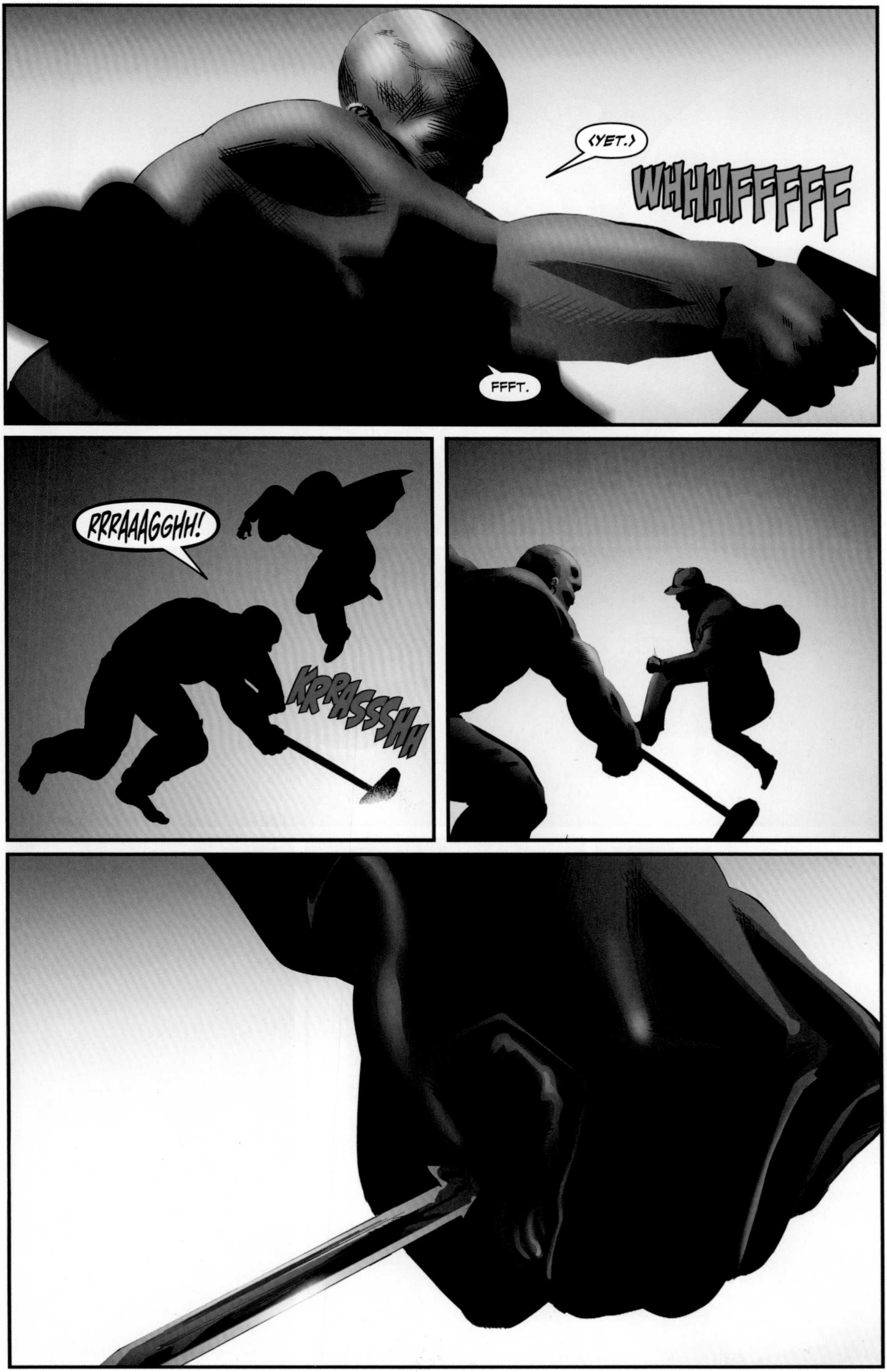
<YET.>
WHHHFFFFF
FFFT.
RRRAAAGGHH!
KRRASSSHH

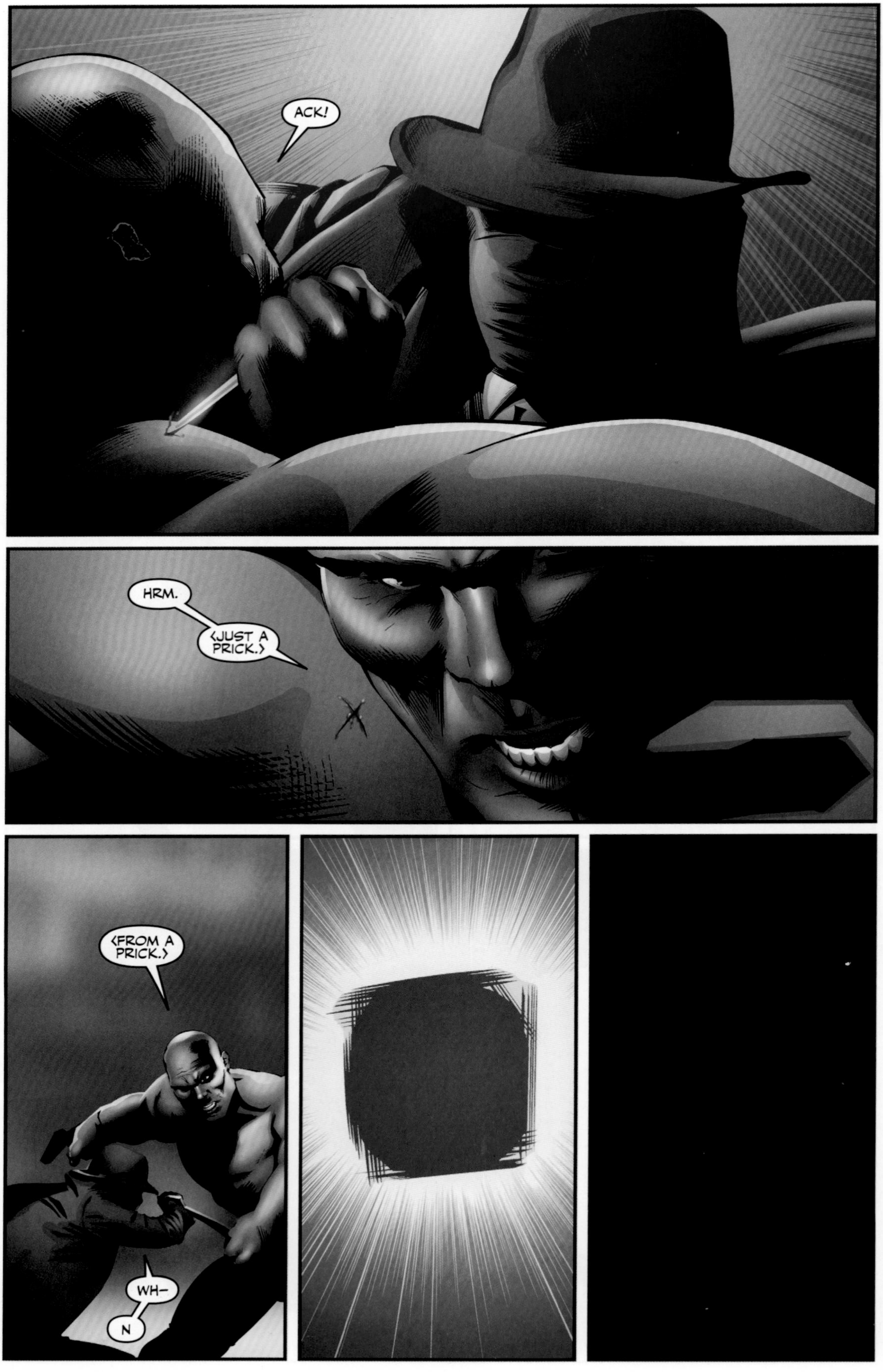
ACK!
HRM.
<JUST A PRICK.>
<FROM A PRICK.>
WH-
N

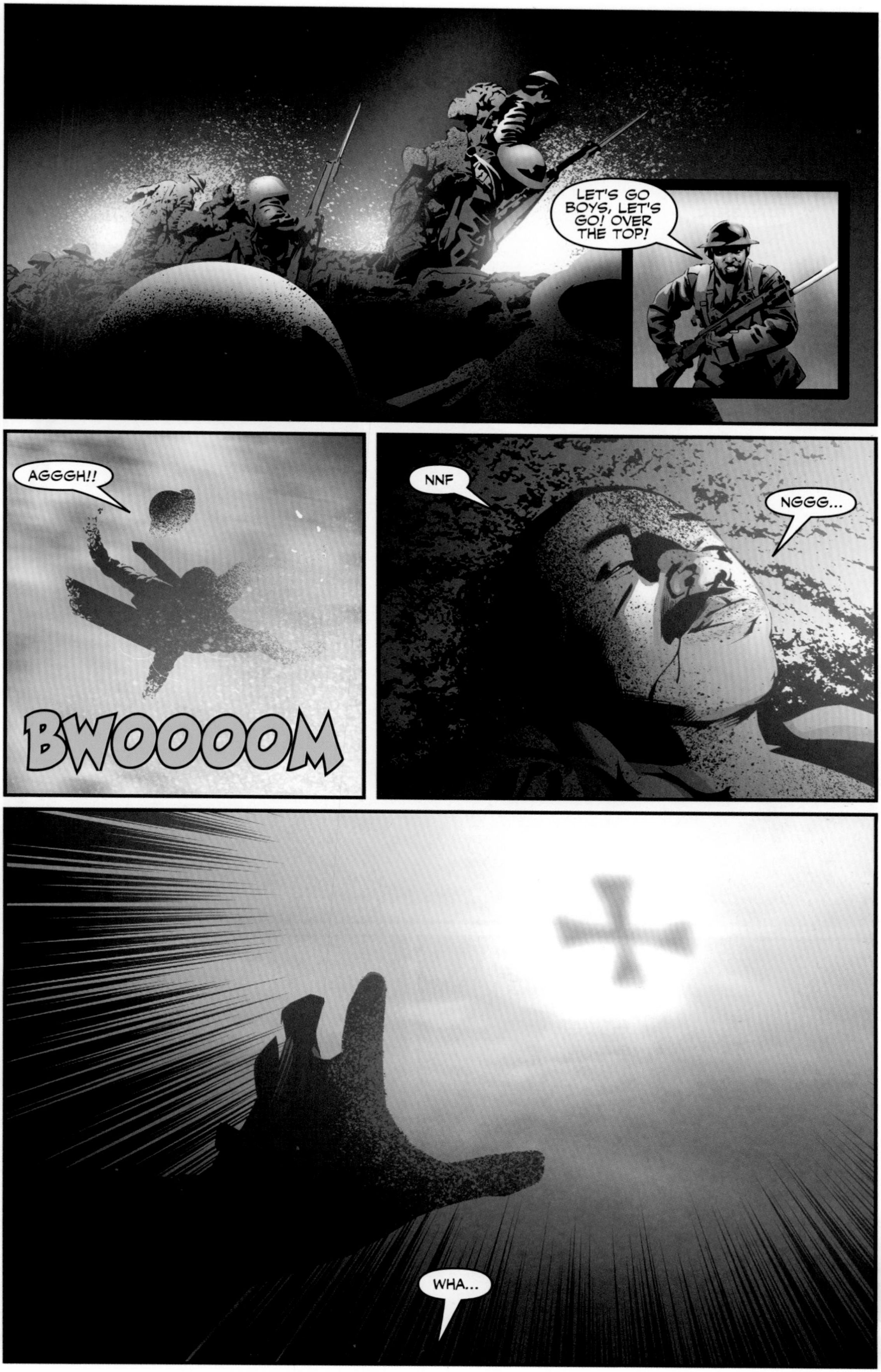
LET'S GO BOYS, LET'S GO! OVER THE TOP!
AGGGH!!
BWOOOOM
NNF
NGGG...
WHA...

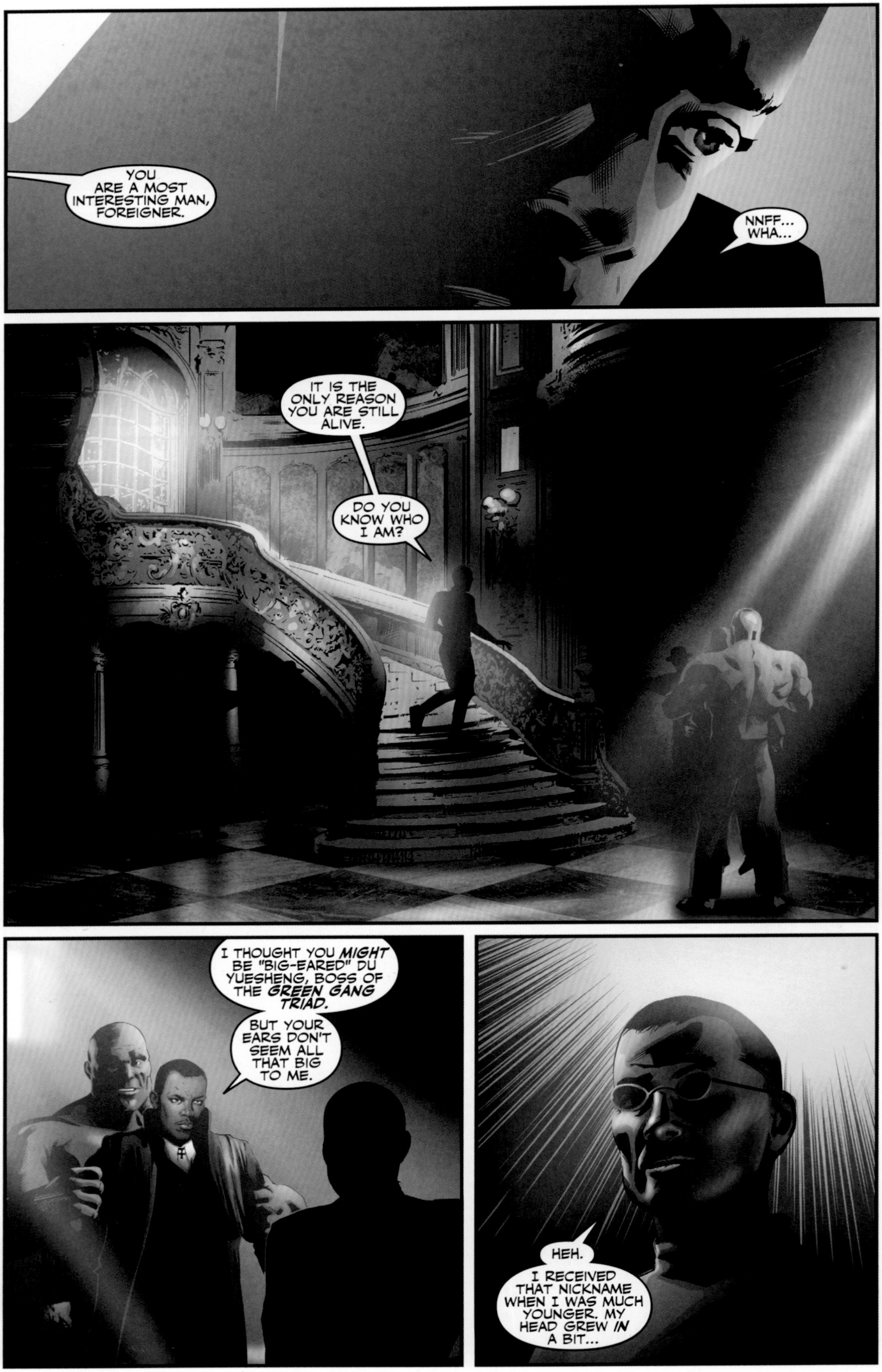
YOU ARE A MOST INTERESTING MAN, FOREIGNER.
NNFF... WHA...
IT IS THE ONLY REASON YOU ARE STILL ALIVE.
DO YOU KNOW WHO I AM?
I THOUGHT YOU *MIGHT* BE "BIG-EARED" DU YUESHENG, BOSS OF THE *GREEN GANG TRIAD.*
BUT YOUR EARS DON'T SEEM ALL THAT BIG TO ME.
HEH.
I RECEIVED THAT NICKNAME WHEN I WAS MUCH YOUNGER. MY HEAD GREW *IN* A BIT...

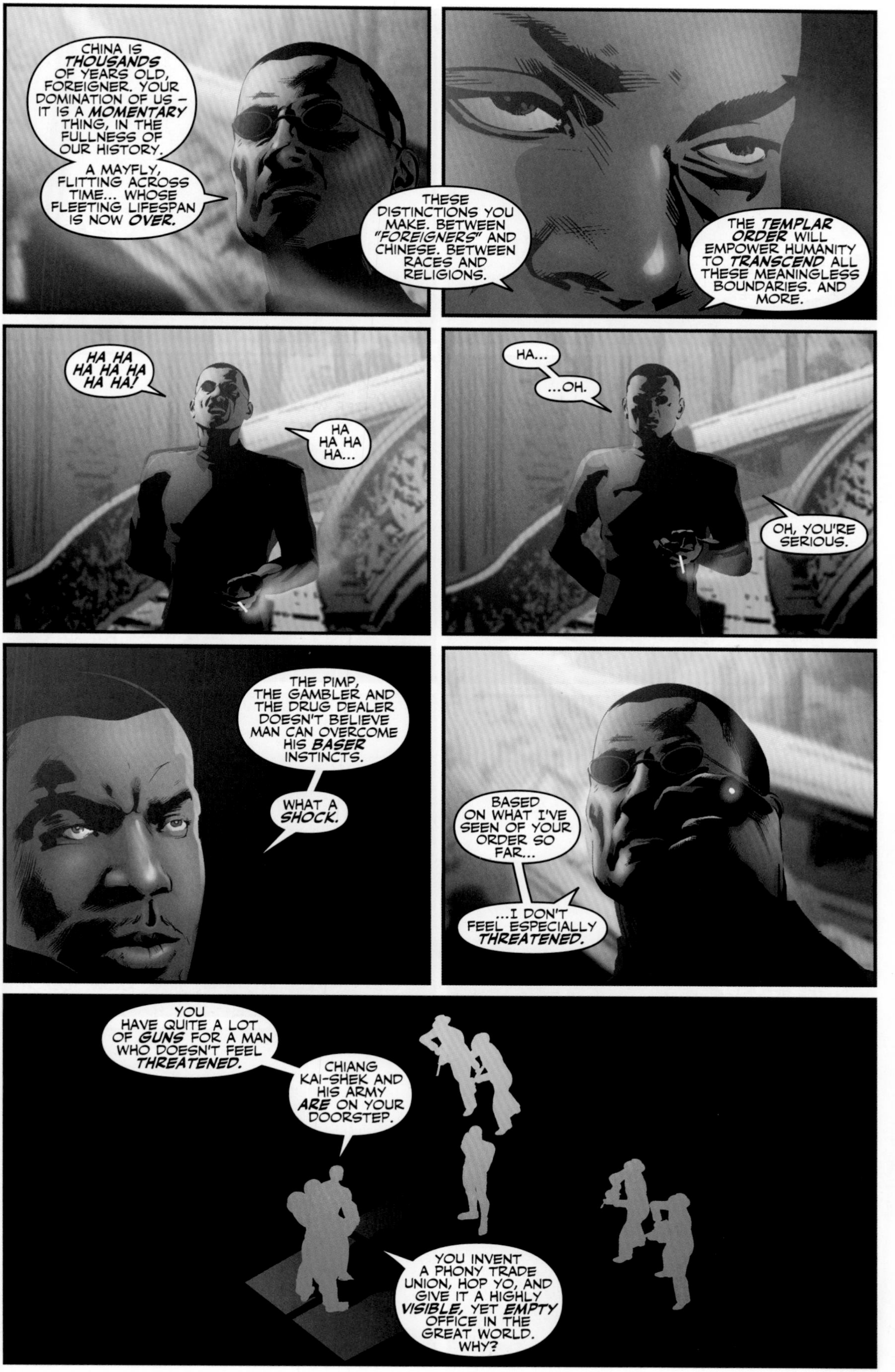
CHINA IS THOUSANDS OF YEARS OLD, FOREIGNER. YOUR DOMINATION OF US – IT IS A MOMENTARY THING, IN THE FULLNESS OF OUR HISTORY.
A MAYFLY, FLITTING ACROSS TIME... WHOSE FLEETING LIFESPAN IS NOW OVER.
THESE DISTINCTIONS YOU MAKE. BETWEEN "FOREIGNERS" AND CHINESE. BETWEEN RACES AND RELIGIONS.
THE TEMPLAR ORDER WILL EMPOWER HUMANITY TO TRANSCEND ALL THESE MEANINGLESS BOUNDARIES. AND MORE.
HA HA HA HA HA HA HA!
HA HA HA HA...
HA...
...OH.
OH, YOU'RE SERIOUS.
THE PIMP, THE GAMBLER AND THE DRUG DEALER DOESN'T BELIEVE MAN CAN OVERCOME HIS BASER INSTINCTS.
WHAT A SHOCK.
BASED ON WHAT I'VE SEEN OF YOUR ORDER SO FAR...
...I DON'T FEEL ESPECIALLY THREATENED.
YOU HAVE QUITE A LOT OF GUNS FOR A MAN WHO DOESN'T FEEL THREATENED.
CHIANG KAI-SHEK AND HIS ARMY ARE ON YOUR DOORSTEP.
YOU INVENT A PHONY TRADE UNION, HOP YO, AND GIVE IT A HIGHLY VISIBLE, YET EMPTY OFFICE IN THE GREAT WORLD. WHY?

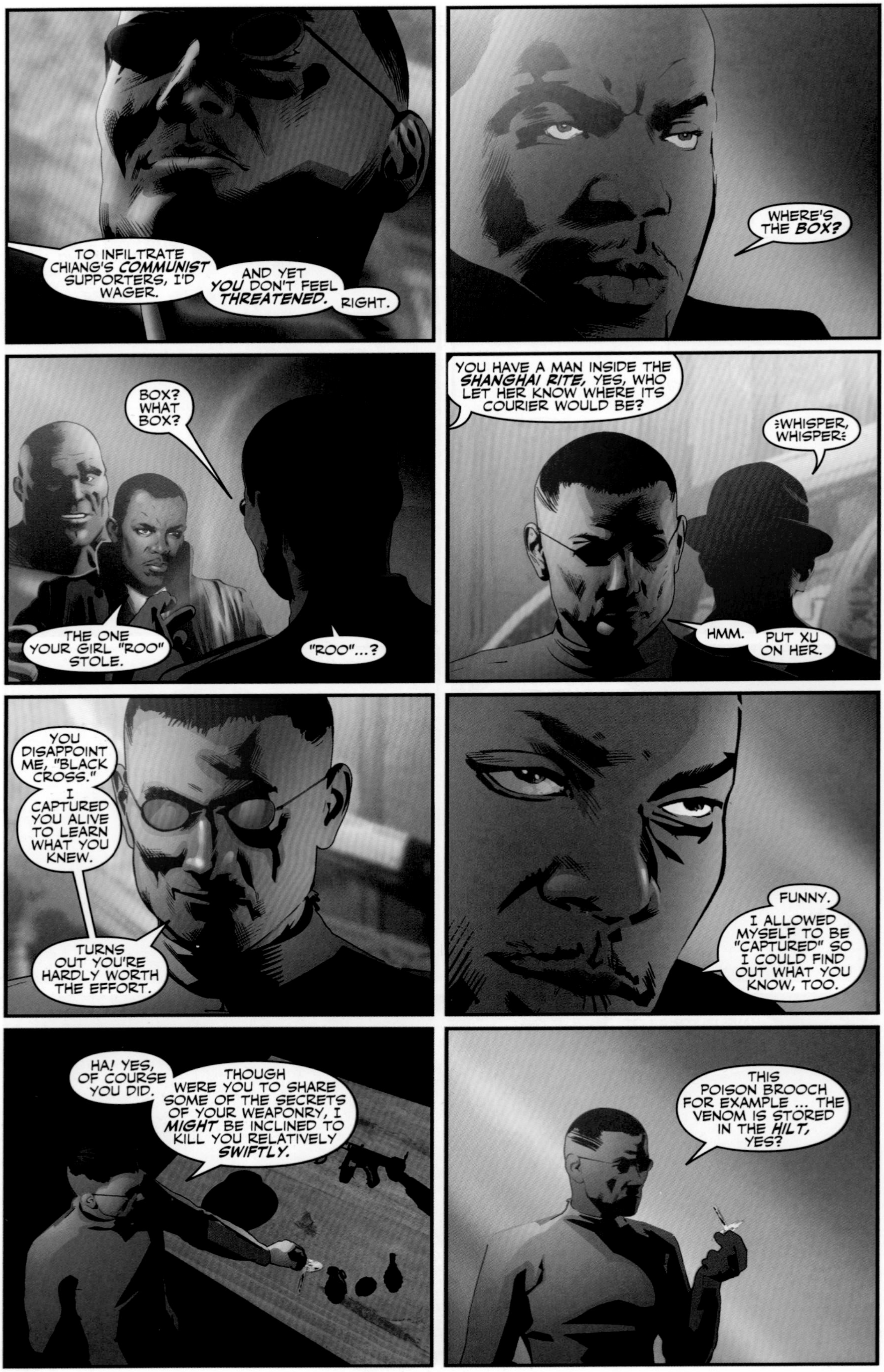
TO INFILTRATE CHIANG'S COMMUNIST SUPPORTERS, I'D WAGER.
AND YET YOU DON'T FEEL THREATENED. RIGHT.
WHERE'S THE BOX?
BOX? WHAT BOX?
THE ONE YOUR GIRL "ROO" STOLE.
"ROO"...?
YOU HAVE A MAN INSIDE THE SHANGHAI RITE, YES, WHO LET HER KNOW WHERE ITS COURIER WOULD BE?
WHISPER, WHISPER
HMM.
PUT XU ON HER.
YOU DISAPPOINT ME, "BLACK CROSS." I CAPTURED YOU ALIVE TO LEARN WHAT YOU KNEW.
TURNS OUT YOU'RE HARDLY WORTH THE EFFORT.
FUNNY. I ALLOWED MYSELF TO BE "CAPTURED" SO I COULD FIND OUT WHAT YOU KNOW, TOO.
HA! YES, OF COURSE YOU DID.
THOUGH WERE YOU TO SHARE SOME OF THE SECRETS OF YOUR WEAPONRY, I MIGHT BE INCLINED TO KILL YOU RELATIVELY SWIFTLY.
THIS POISON BROOCH FOR EXAMPLE ... THE VENOM IS STORED IN THE HILT, YES?

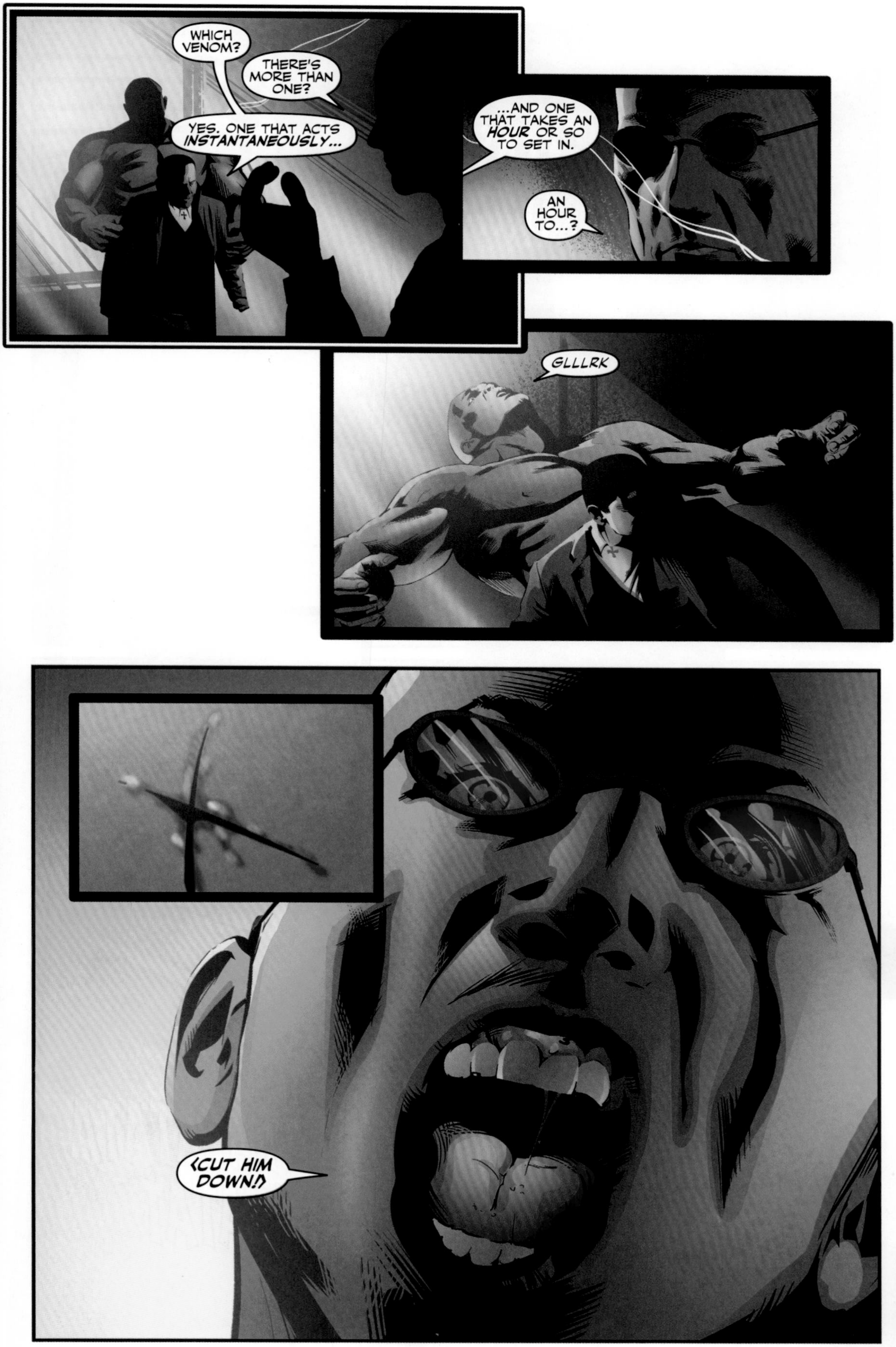
WHICH VENOM?
THERE'S MORE THAN ONE?
YES. ONE THAT ACTS *INSTANTANEOUSLY*...
...AND ONE THAT TAKES AN *HOUR* OR SO TO SET IN.
AN HOUR TO...?
GLLLRK
‹CUT HIM DOWN!›

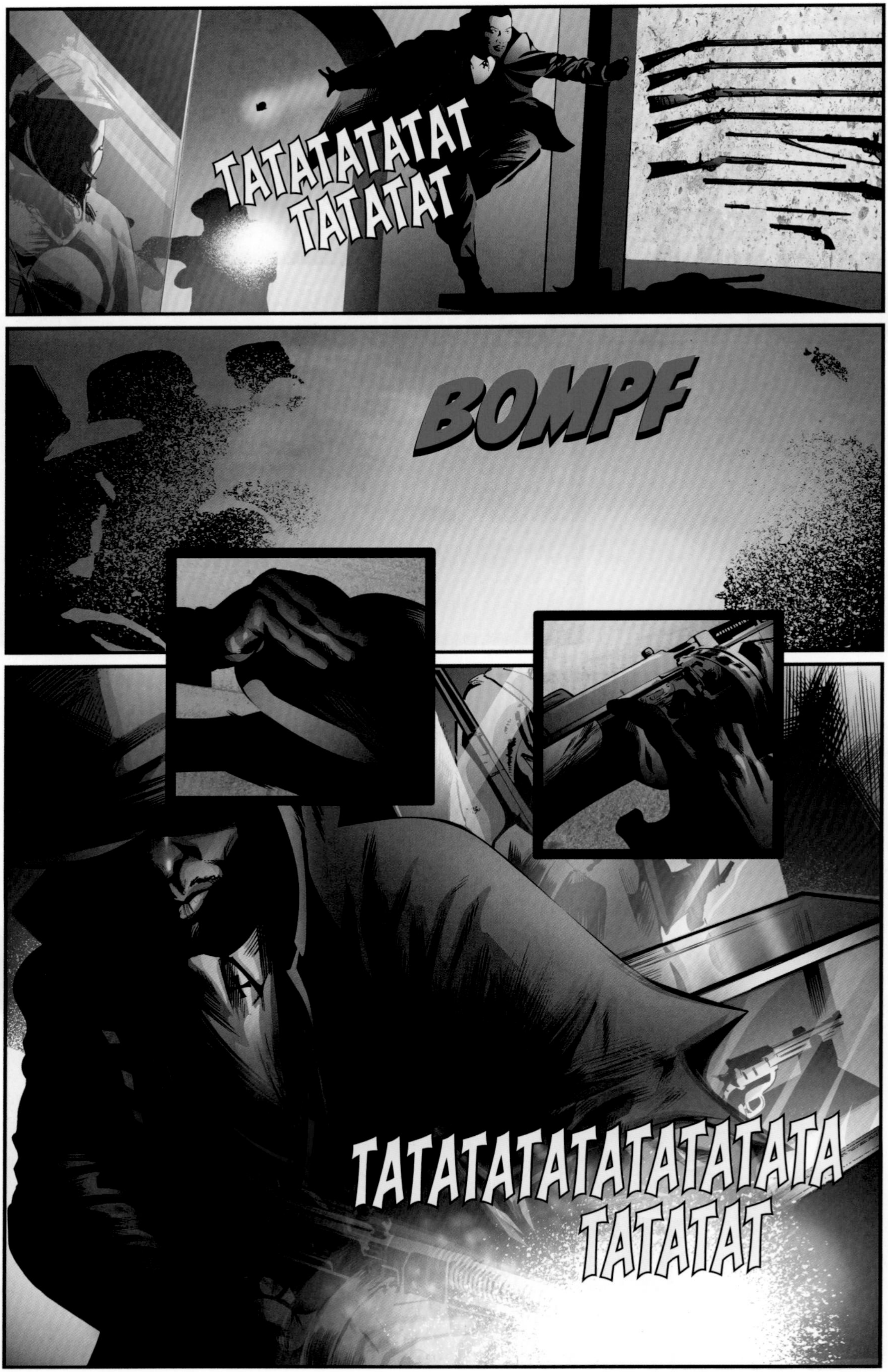
TATATATATAT
TATATAT
BOMPF
TATATATATATATATATA
TATATAT

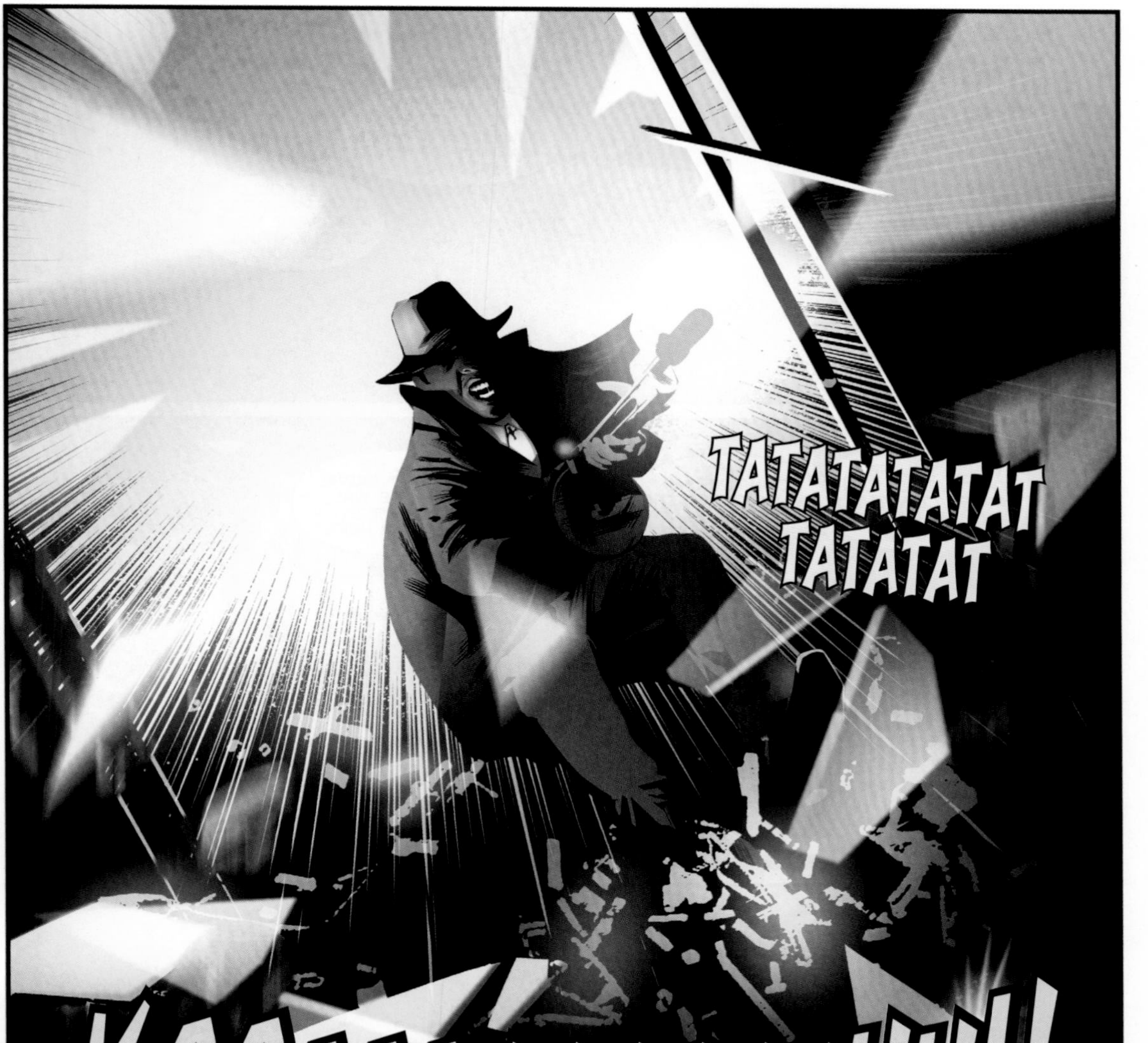
TATATATATAT
TATATAT
KSSSSSHHHHHHHHH

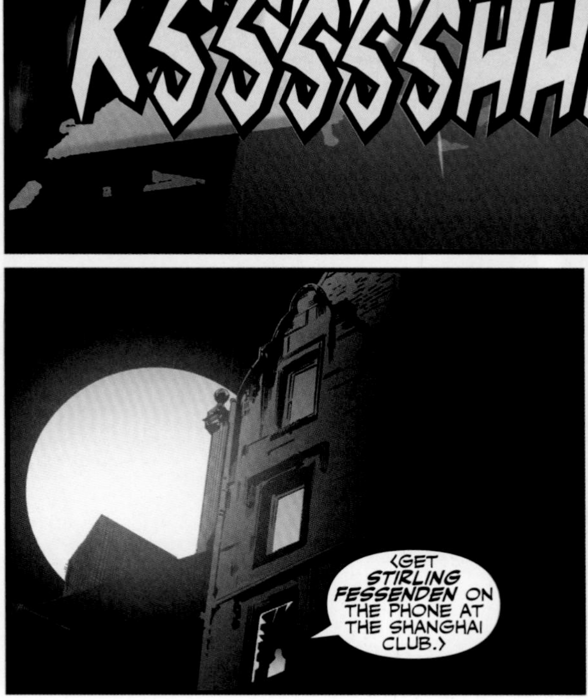
<GET STIRLING FESSENDEN ON THE PHONE AT THE SHANGHAI CLUB.>

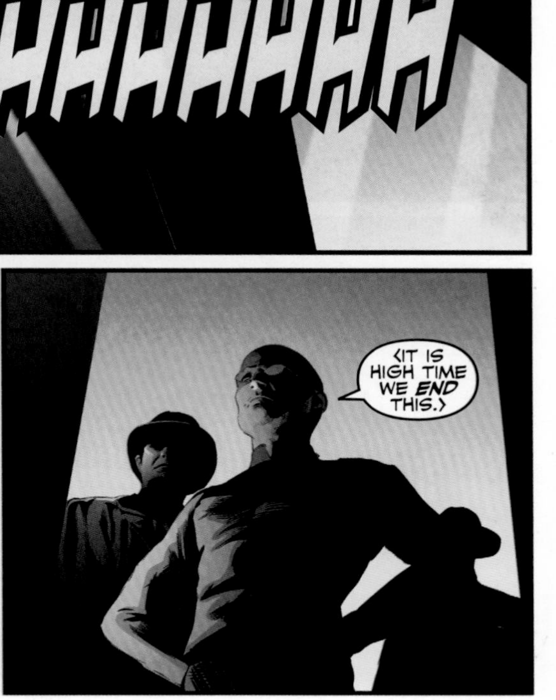
<IT IS HIGH TIME WE END THIS.>

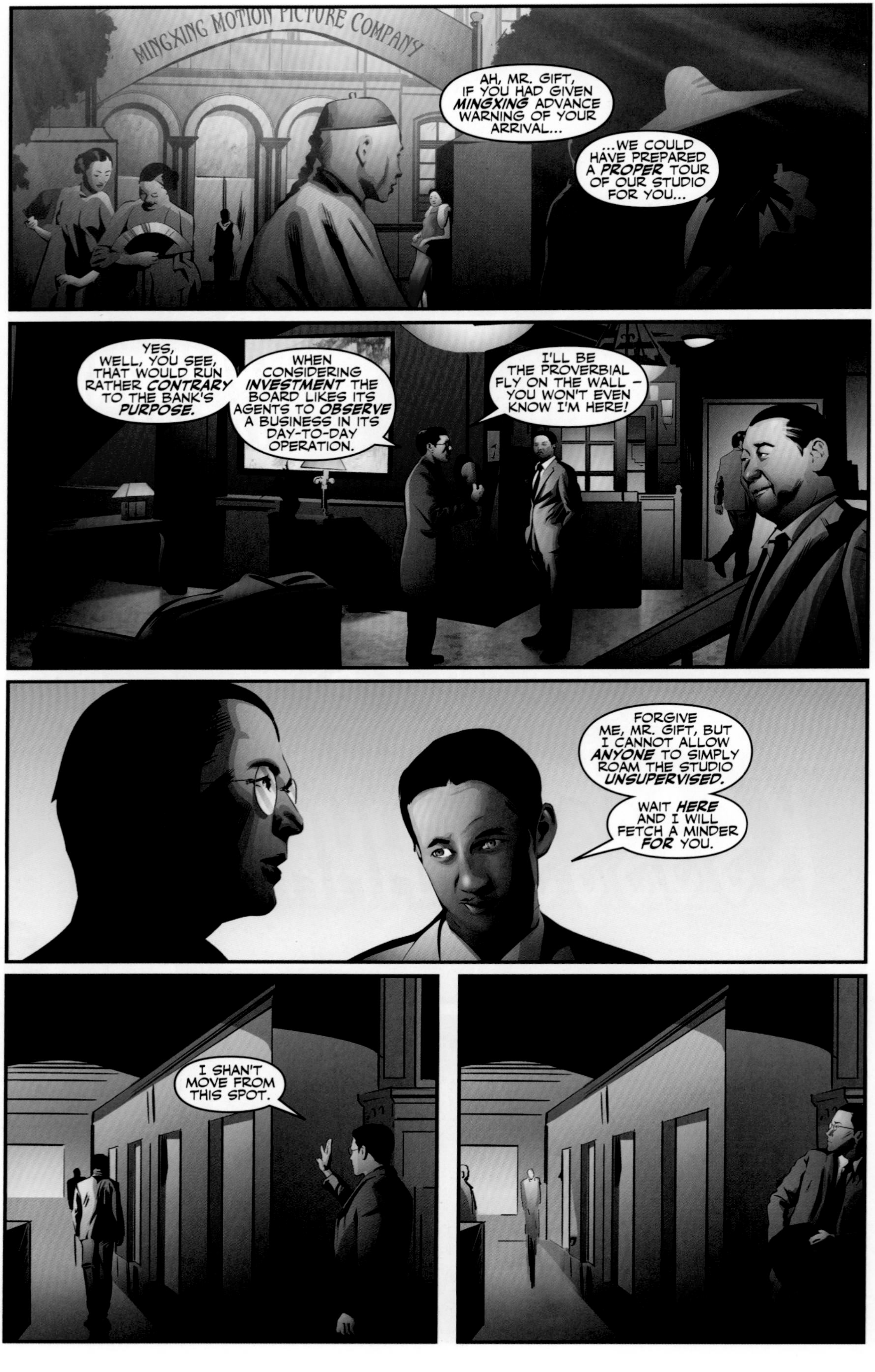
MINGXING MOTION PICTURE COMPANY
AH, MR. GIFT, IF YOU HAD GIVEN MINGXING ADVANCE WARNING OF YOUR ARRIVAL...
...WE COULD HAVE PREPARED A PROPER TOUR OF OUR STUDIO FOR YOU...
YES, WELL, YOU SEE, THAT WOULD RUN RATHER CONTRARY TO THE BANK'S PURPOSE.
WHEN CONSIDERING INVESTMENT THE BOARD LIKES ITS AGENTS TO OBSERVE A BUSINESS IN ITS DAY-TO-DAY OPERATION.
I'LL BE THE PROVERBIAL FLY ON THE WALL – YOU WON'T EVEN KNOW I'M HERE!
FORGIVE ME, MR. GIFT, BUT I CANNOT ALLOW ANYONE TO SIMPLY ROAM THE STUDIO UNSUPERVISED.
WAIT HERE AND I WILL FETCH A MINDER FOR YOU.
I SHAN'T MOVE FROM THIS SPOT.

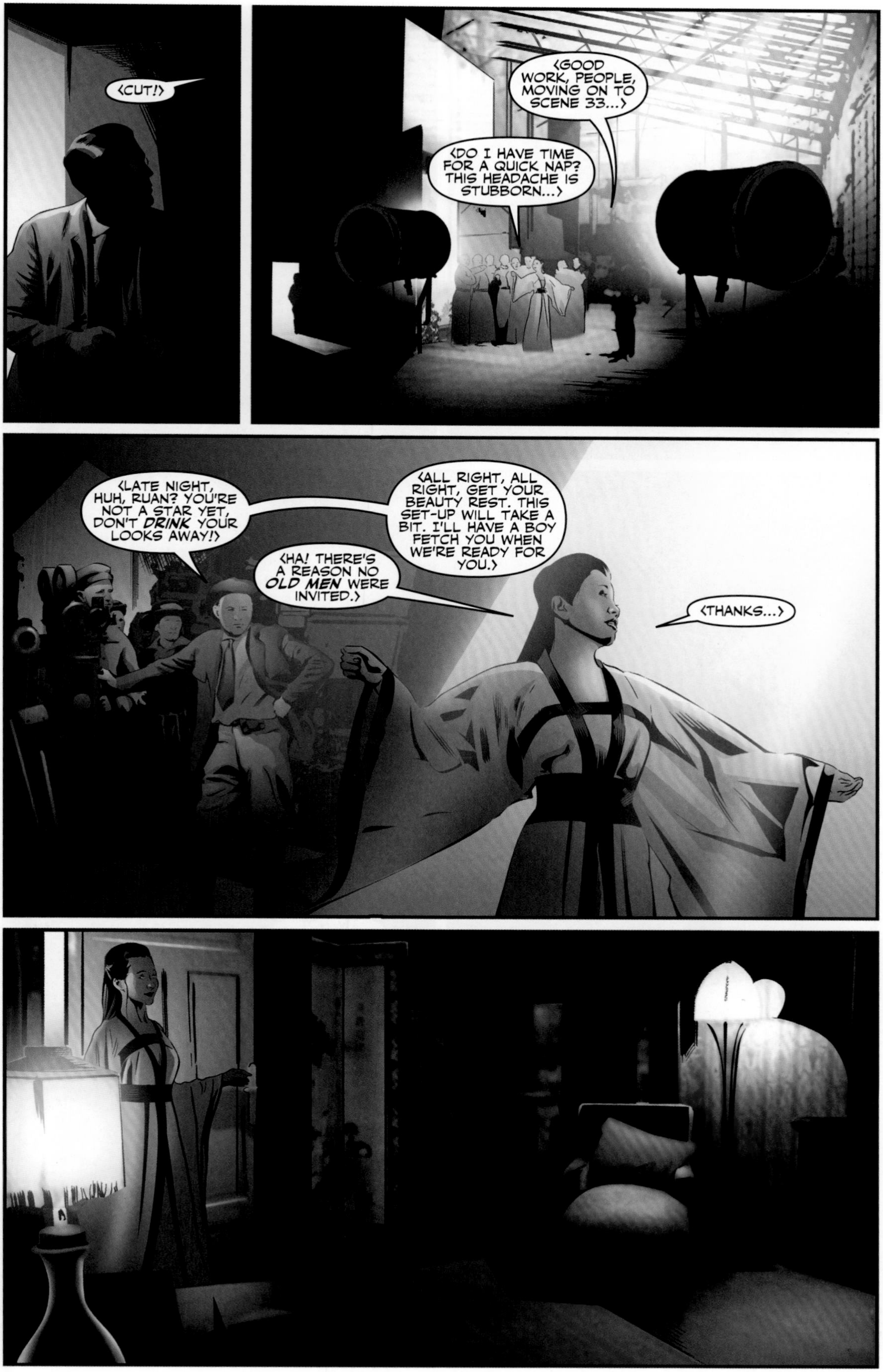
<CUT!>
<GOOD WORK, PEOPLE, MOVING ON TO SCENE 33...>
<DO I HAVE TIME FOR A QUICK NAP? THIS HEADACHE IS STUBBORN...>
<LATE NIGHT, HUH, RUAN? YOU'RE NOT A STAR YET, DON'T DRINK YOUR LOOKS AWAY!>
<HA! THERE'S A REASON NO OLD MEN WERE INVITED.>
<ALL RIGHT, ALL RIGHT, GET YOUR BEAUTY REST. THIS SET-UP WILL TAKE A BIT. I'LL HAVE A BOY FETCH YOU WHEN WE'RE READY FOR YOU.>
<THANKS...>

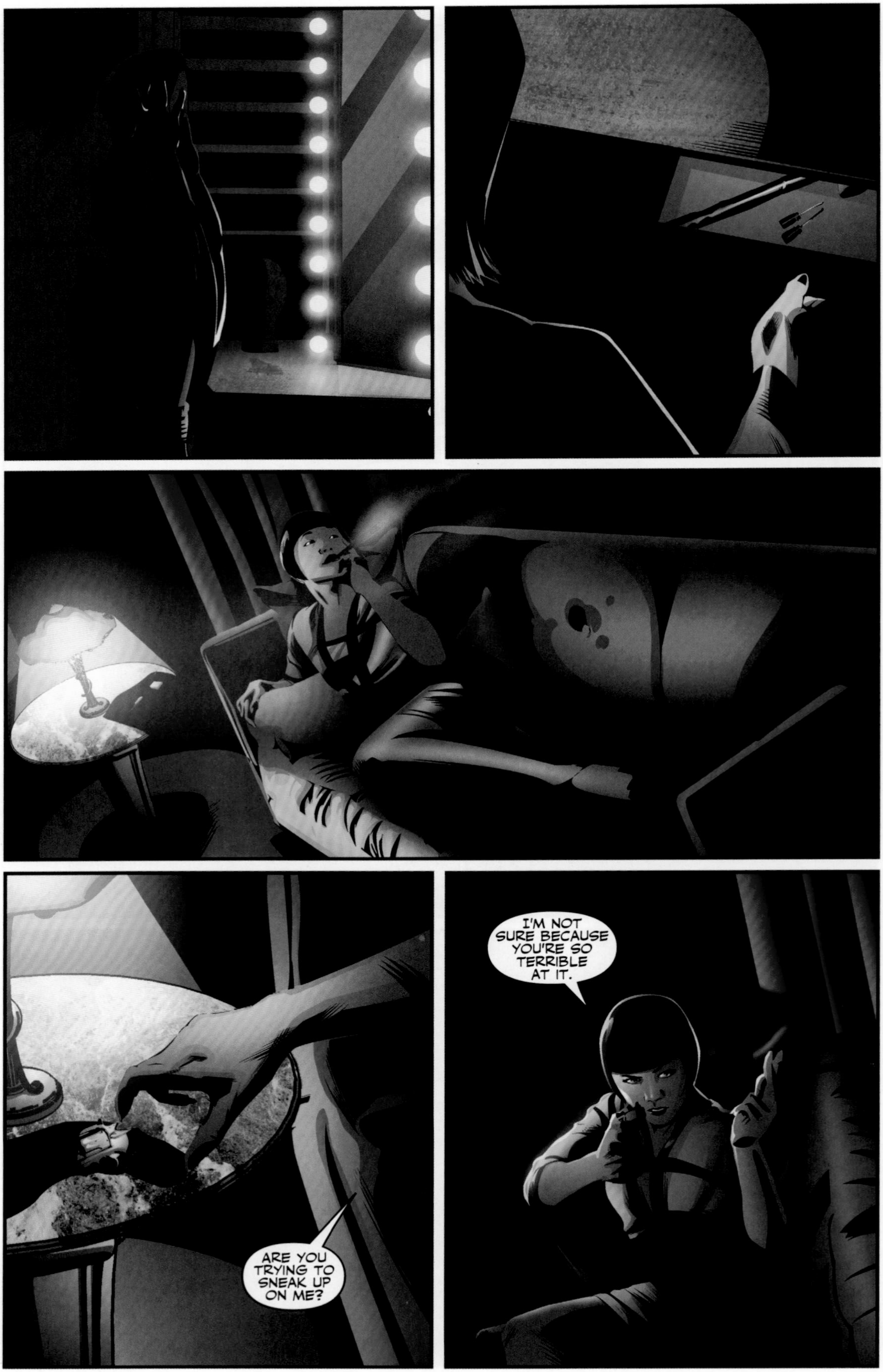

ARE YOU TRYING TO SNEAK UP ON ME?
I'M NOT SURE BECAUSE YOU'RE SO TERRIBLE AT IT.

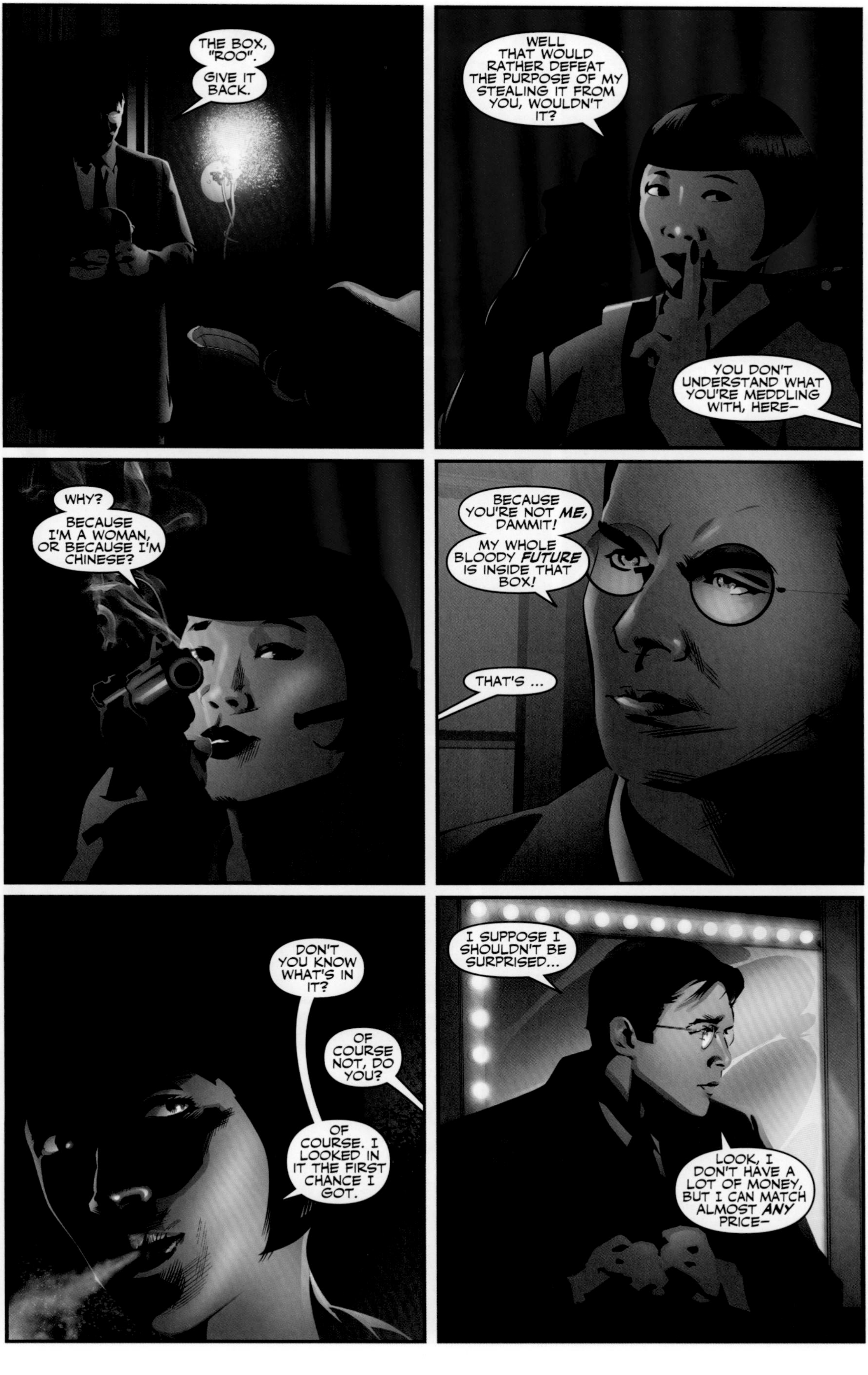
THE BOX, "ROO".
GIVE IT BACK.
WELL THAT WOULD RATHER DEFEAT THE PURPOSE OF MY STEALING IT FROM YOU, WOULDN'T IT?
YOU DON'T UNDERSTAND WHAT YOU'RE MEDDLING WITH, HERE–
WHY?
BECAUSE I'M A WOMAN, OR BECAUSE I'M CHINESE?
BECAUSE YOU'RE NOT *ME*, DAMMIT!
MY WHOLE BLOODY *FUTURE* IS INSIDE THAT BOX!
THAT'S ...
DON'T YOU KNOW WHAT'S IN IT?
OF COURSE NOT, DO YOU?
OF COURSE. I LOOKED IN IT THE FIRST CHANCE I GOT.
I SUPPOSE I SHOULDN'T BE SURPRISED...
LOOK, I DON'T HAVE A LOT OF MONEY, BUT I CAN MATCH ALMOST *ANY* PRICE–

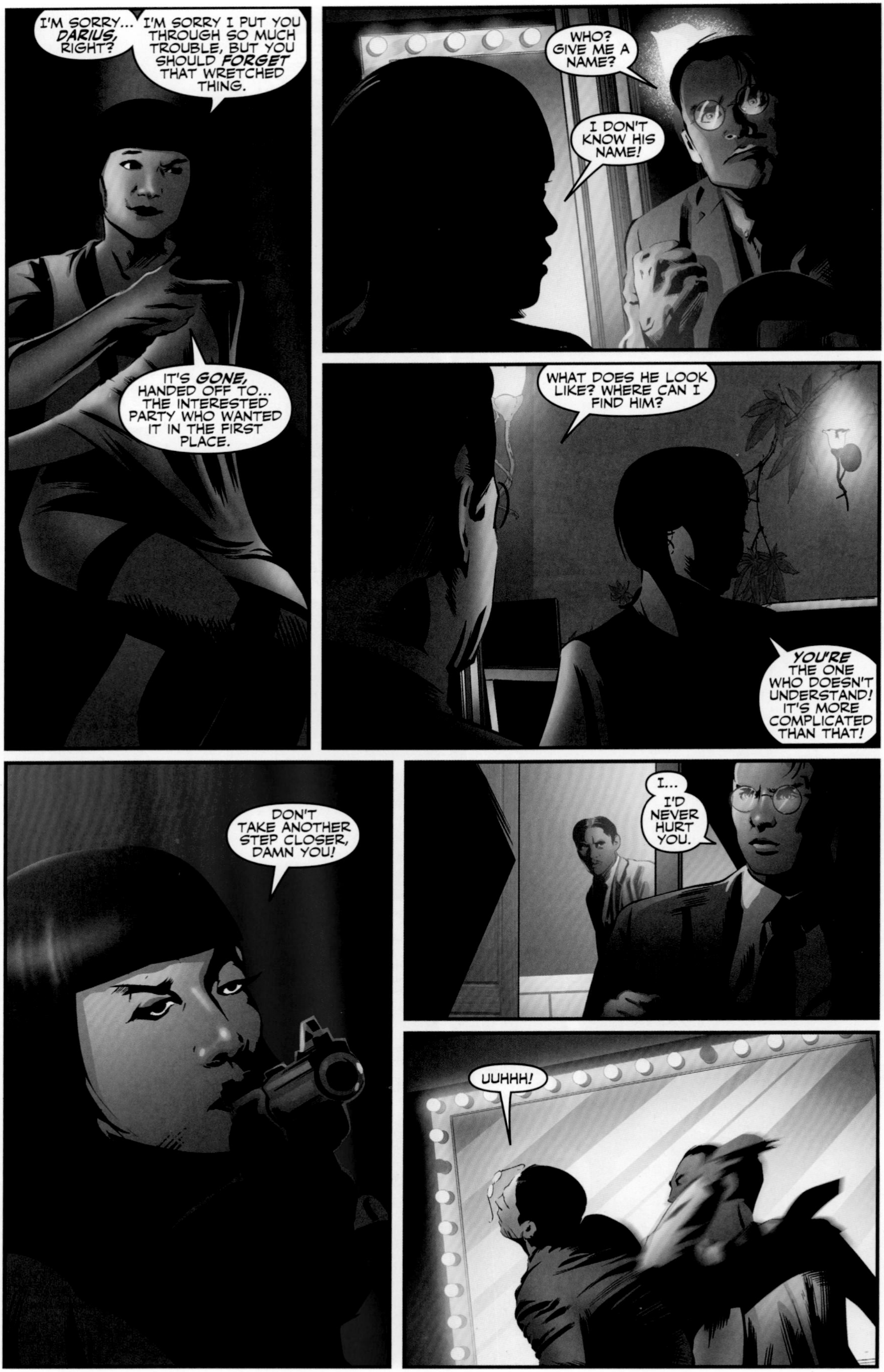
I'M SORRY... DARIUS, RIGHT?
I'M SORRY I PUT YOU THROUGH SO MUCH TROUBLE, BUT YOU SHOULD FORGET THAT WRETCHED THING.
IT'S GONE, HANDED OFF TO... THE INTERESTED PARTY WHO WANTED IT IN THE FIRST PLACE.
WHO? GIVE ME A NAME?
I DON'T KNOW HIS NAME!
WHAT DOES HE LOOK LIKE? WHERE CAN I FIND HIM?
YOU'RE THE ONE WHO DOESN'T UNDERSTAND! IT'S MORE COMPLICATED THAN THAT!
DON'T TAKE ANOTHER STEP CLOSER, DAMN YOU!
I... I'D NEVER HURT YOU.
UUHHH!

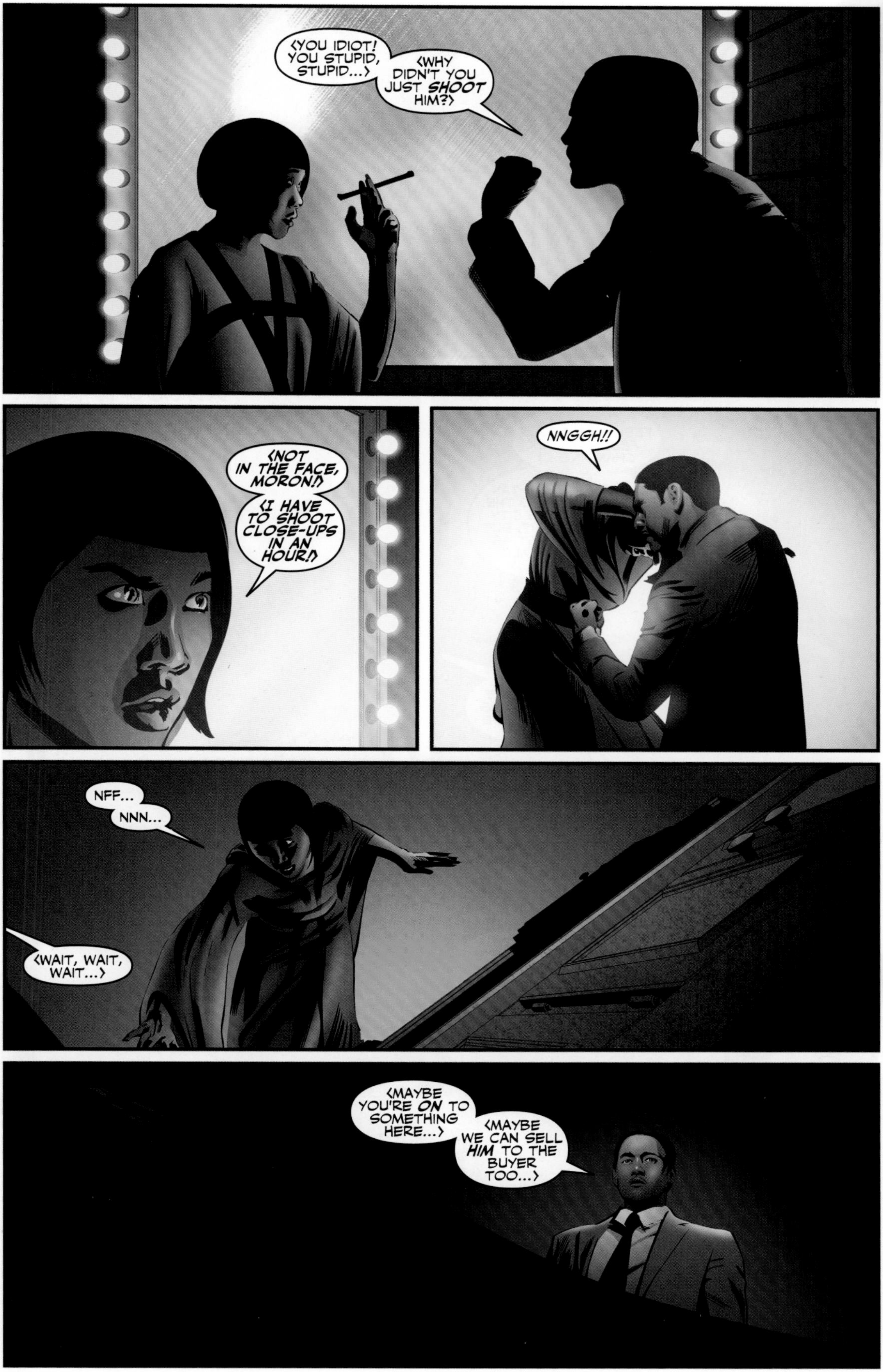
‹YOU IDIOT! YOU STUPID, STUPID...›
‹WHY DIDN'T YOU JUST SHOOT HIM?›
‹NOT IN THE FACE, MORON!›
‹I HAVE TO SHOOT CLOSE-UPS IN AN HOUR!›
NNGGH!!
NFF...
NNN...
‹WAIT, WAIT, WAIT...›
‹MAYBE YOU'RE ON TO SOMETHING HERE...›
‹MAYBE WE CAN SELL HIM TO THE BUYER TOO...›

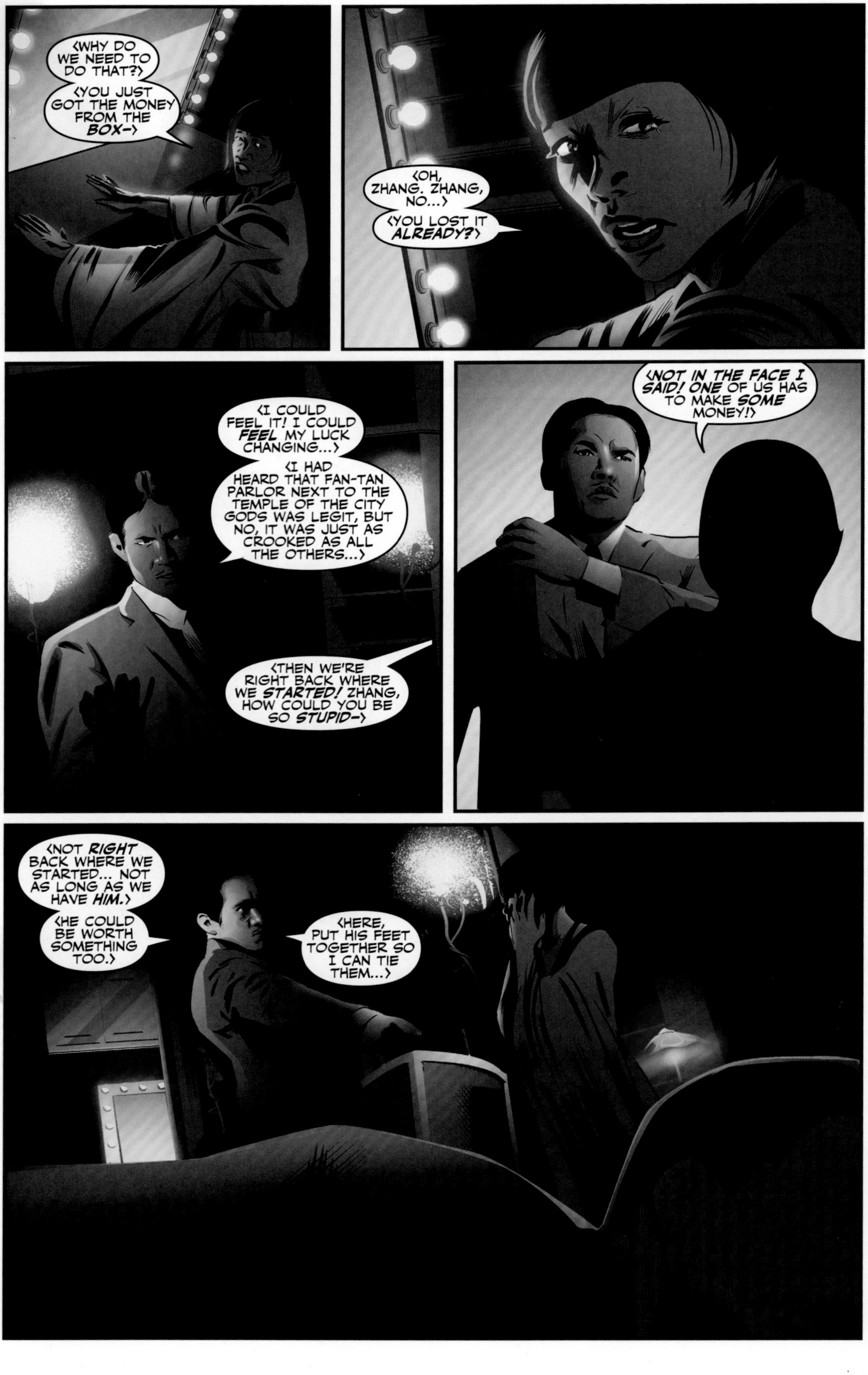
<WHY DO WE NEED TO DO THAT?>
<YOU JUST GOT THE MONEY FROM THE BOX–>
<OH, ZHANG. ZHANG, NO...>
<YOU LOST IT ALREADY?>
<I COULD FEEL IT! I COULD FEEL MY LUCK CHANGING...>
<I HAD HEARD THAT FAN-TAN PARLOR NEXT TO THE TEMPLE OF THE CITY GODS WAS LEGIT, BUT NO, IT WAS JUST AS CROOKED AS ALL THE OTHERS...>
<THEN WE'RE RIGHT BACK WHERE WE STARTED! ZHANG, HOW COULD YOU BE SO STUPID–>
<NOT IN THE FACE I SAID! ONE OF US HAS TO MAKE SOME MONEY!>
<NOT RIGHT BACK WHERE WE STARTED... NOT AS LONG AS WE HAVE HIM.>
<HE COULD BE WORTH SOMETHING TOO.>
<HERE, PUT HIS FEET TOGETHER SO I CAN TIE THEM...>

CHAPTER FOUR

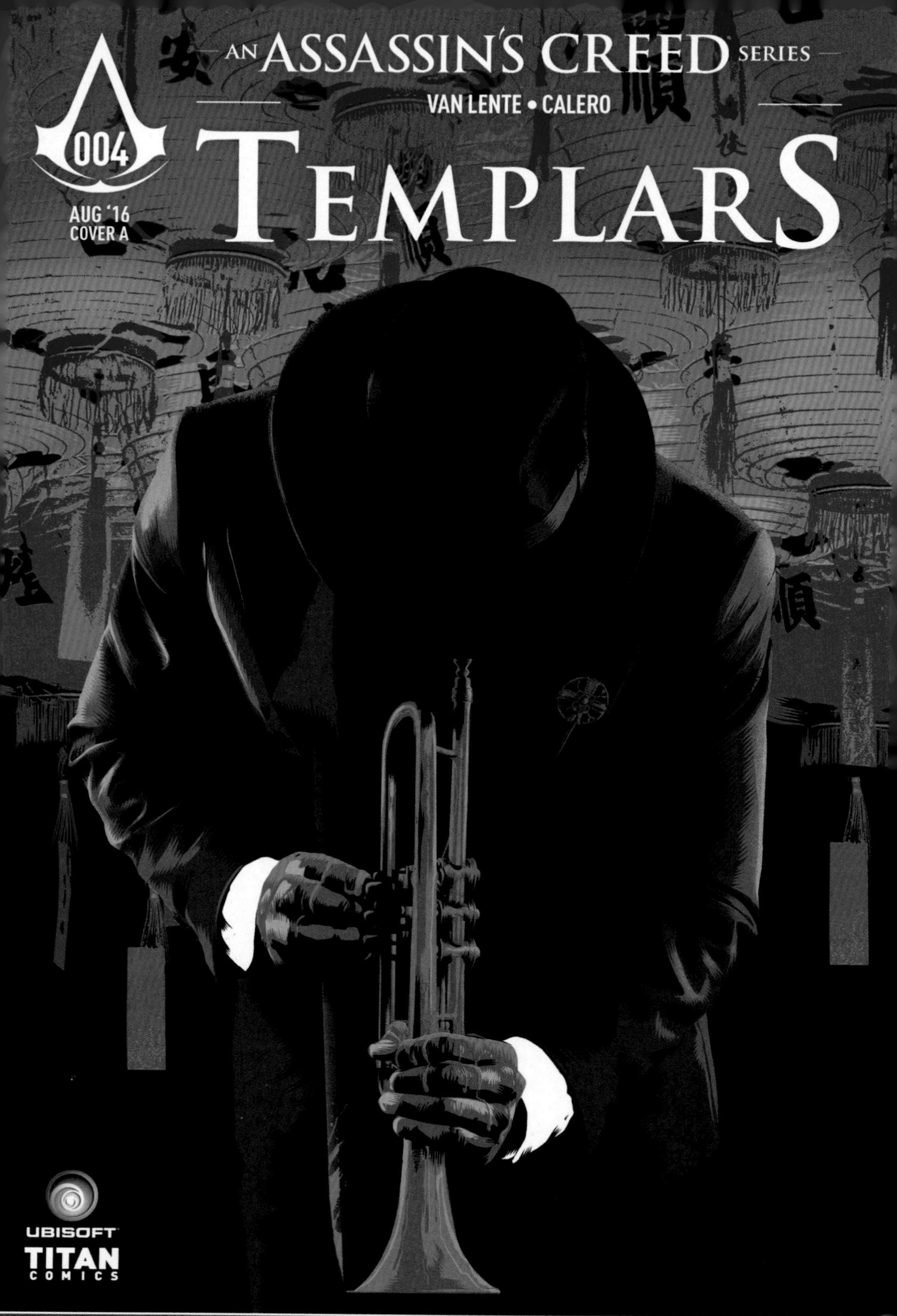
AN ASSASSIN'S CREED SERIES
VAN LENTE • CALERO
004
TEMPLARS
AUG '16
COVER A
UBISOFT
TITAN
COMICS

SSUE 4 - COVER A
MATT TAYLOR

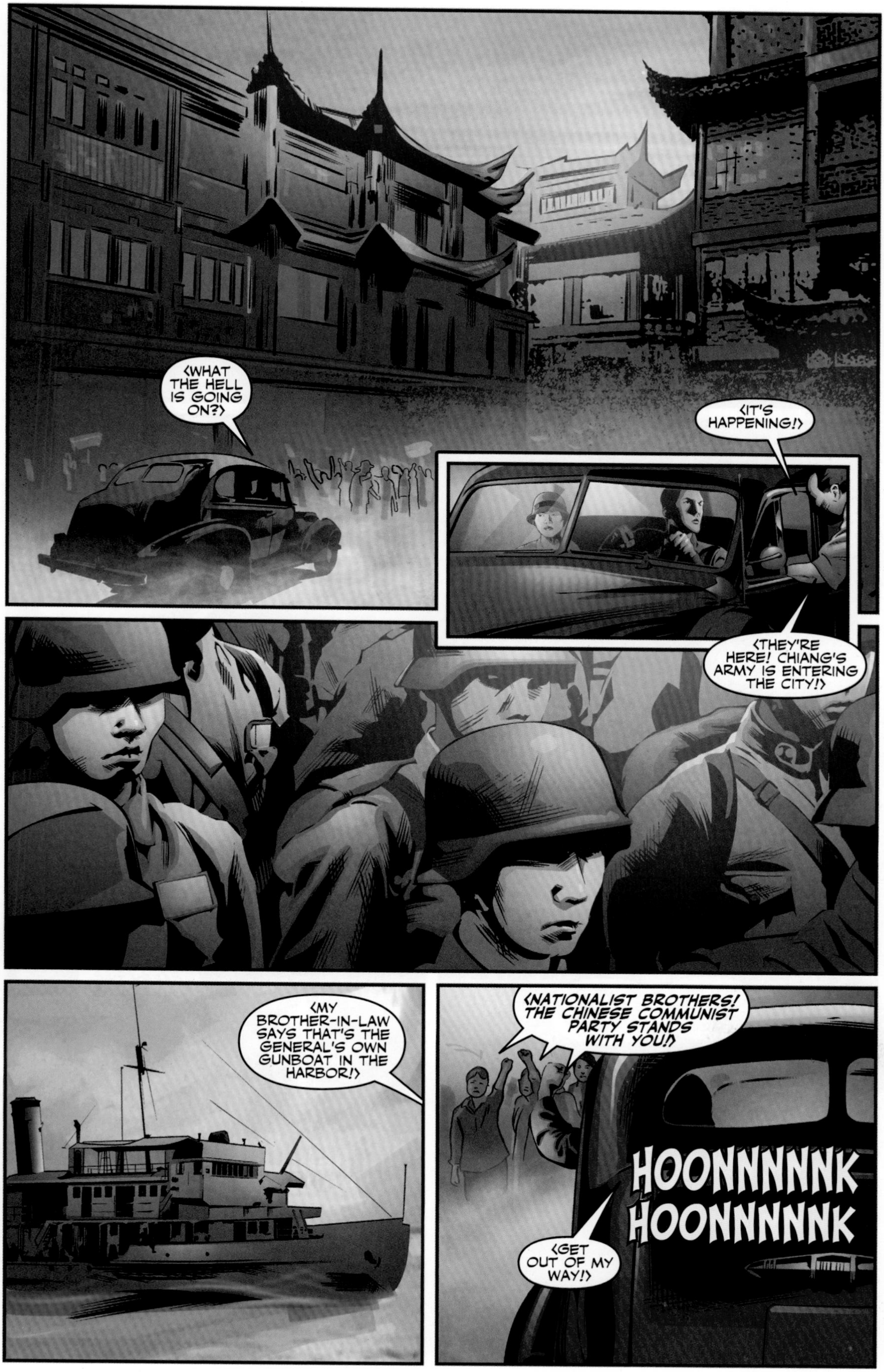

<WHAT THE HELL IS GOING ON?>
<IT'S HAPPENING!>
<THEY'RE HERE! CHIANG'S ARMY IS ENTERING THE CITY!>
<MY BROTHER-IN-LAW SAYS THAT'S THE GENERAL'S OWN GUNBOAT IN THE HARBOR!>
<NATIONALIST BROTHERS! THE CHINESE COMMUNIST PARTY STANDS WITH YOU!>
HOONNNNNK
HOONNNNNK
<GET OUT OF MY WAY!>

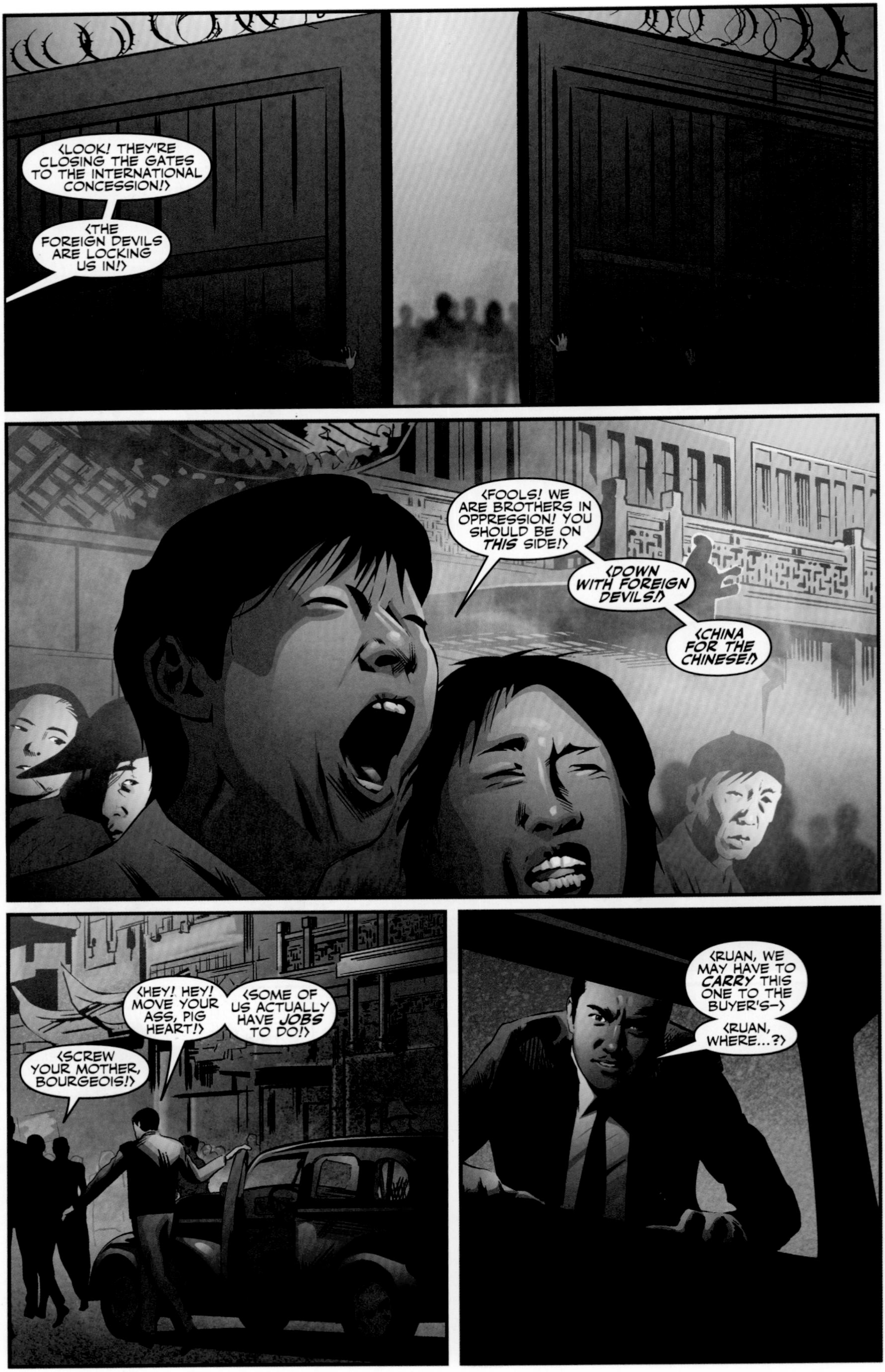
‹LOOK! THEY'RE CLOSING THE GATES TO THE INTERNATIONAL CONCESSION!›
‹THE FOREIGN DEVILS ARE LOCKING US IN!›
‹FOOLS! WE ARE BROTHERS IN OPPRESSION! YOU SHOULD BE ON *THIS* SIDE!›
‹*DOWN WITH FOREIGN DEVILS!*›
‹*CHINA FOR THE CHINESE!*›
‹HEY! HEY! MOVE YOUR ASS, PIG HEART!›
‹SOME OF US ACTUALLY HAVE *JOBS* TO DO!›
‹SCREW YOUR MOTHER, BOURGEOIS!›
‹RUAN, WE MAY HAVE TO *CARRY* THIS ONE TO THE BUYER'S–›
‹RUAN, WHERE...?›

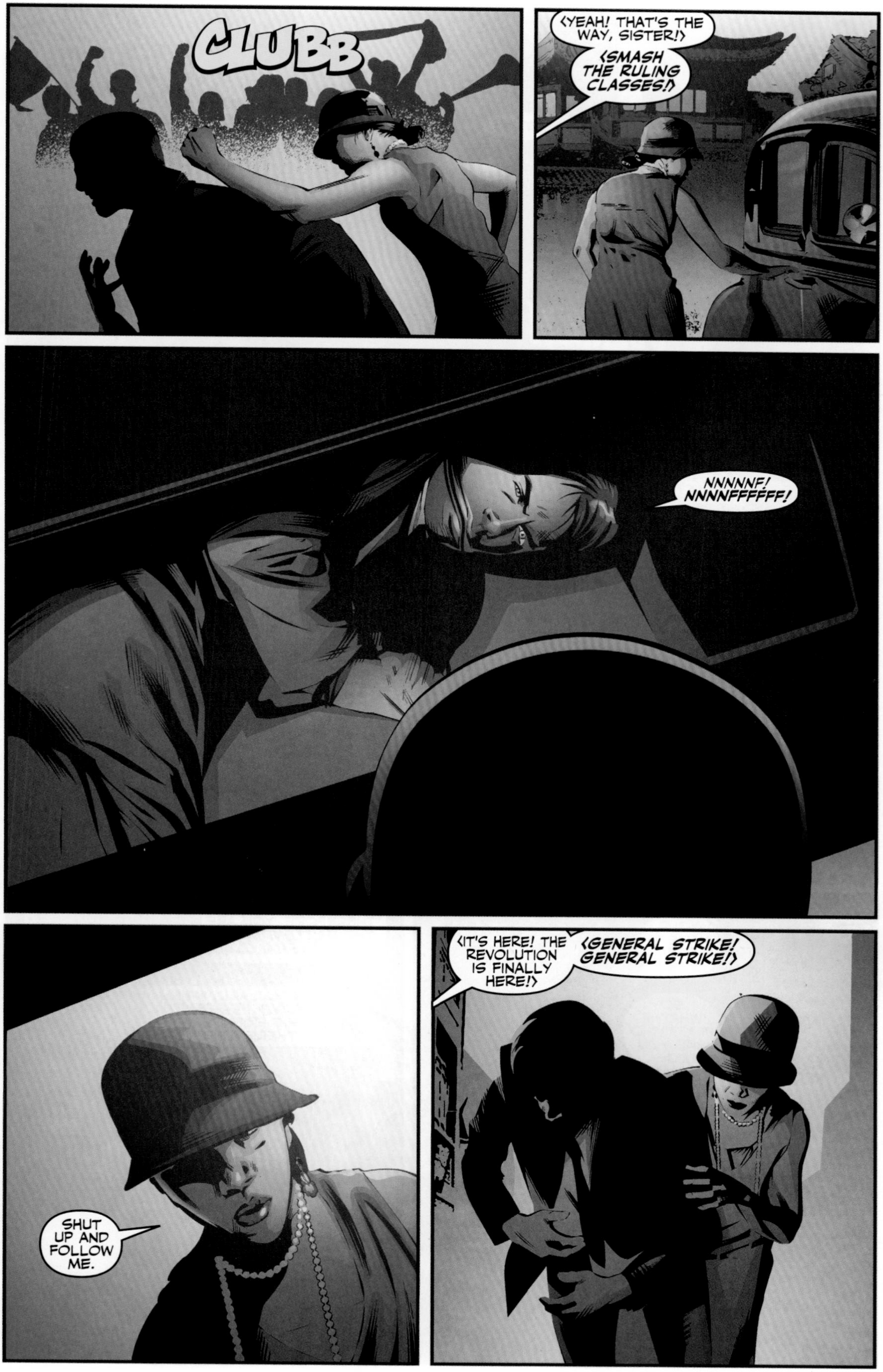
CLUBB
<YEAH! THAT'S THE WAY, SISTER!>
<SMASH THE RULING CLASSES!>
NNNNNF! NNNNFFFFFF!
SHUT UP AND FOLLOW ME.
<IT'S HERE! THE REVOLUTION IS FINALLY HERE!>
<GENERAL STRIKE! GENERAL STRIKE!>

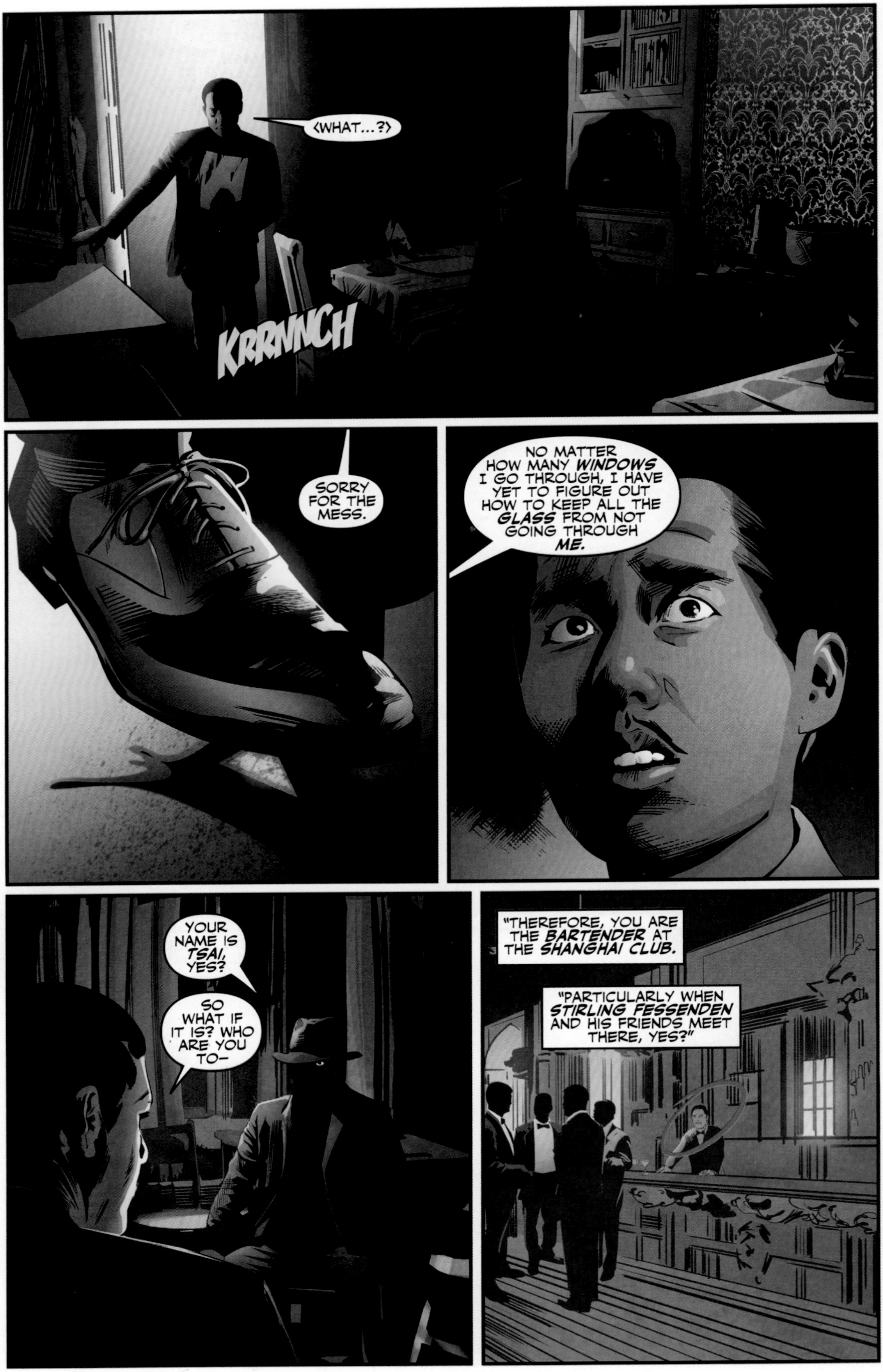

‹WHAT...?›
KRRNNCH
SORRY FOR THE MESS.
NO MATTER HOW MANY WINDOWS I GO THROUGH, I HAVE YET TO FIGURE OUT HOW TO KEEP ALL THE GLASS FROM NOT GOING THROUGH ME.
YOUR NAME IS TSAI, YES?
SO WHAT IF IT IS? WHO ARE YOU TO–
"THEREFORE, YOU ARE THE BARTENDER AT THE SHANGHAI CLUB.
"PARTICULARLY WHEN STIRLING FESSENDEN AND HIS FRIENDS MEET THERE, YES?"

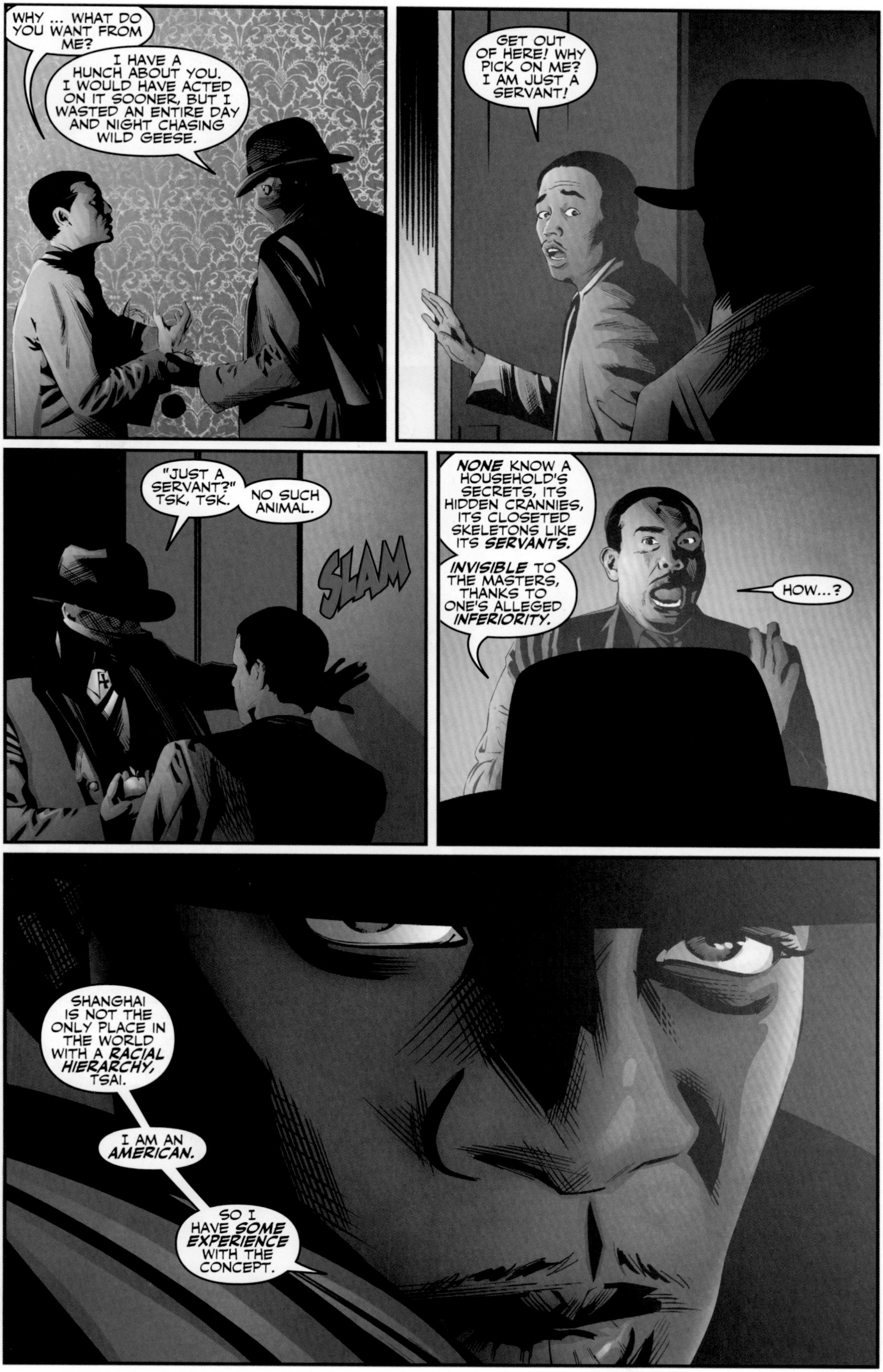
WHY ... WHAT DO YOU WANT FROM ME?
I HAVE A HUNCH ABOUT YOU. I WOULD HAVE ACTED ON IT SOONER, BUT I WASTED AN ENTIRE DAY AND NIGHT CHASING WILD GEESE.
GET OUT OF HERE! WHY PICK ON ME? I AM JUST A SERVANT!
"JUST A SERVANT?" TSK, TSK.
NO SUCH ANIMAL.
SLAM
NONE KNOW A HOUSEHOLD'S SECRETS, ITS HIDDEN CRANNIES, ITS CLOSETED SKELETONS LIKE ITS SERVANTS.
INVISIBLE TO THE MASTERS, THANKS TO ONE'S ALLEGED INFERIORITY.
HOW...?
SHANGHAI IS NOT THE ONLY PLACE IN THE WORLD WITH A RACIAL HIERARCHY, TSAI.
I AM AN AMERICAN.
SO I HAVE SOME EXPERIENCE WITH THE CONCEPT.

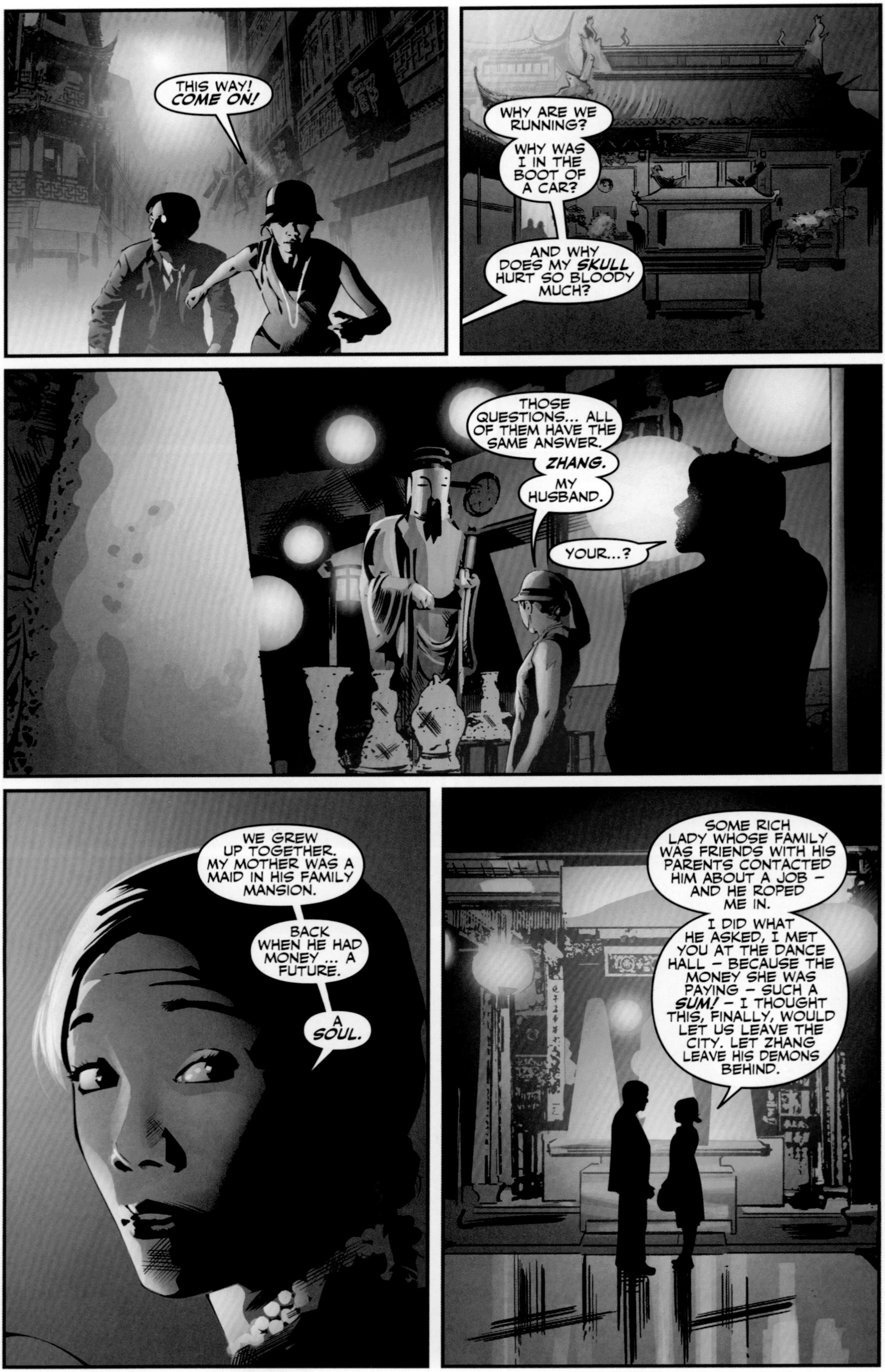
THIS WAY! COME ON!
WHY ARE WE RUNNING?
WHY WAS I IN THE BOOT OF A CAR?
AND WHY DOES MY SKULL HURT SO BLOODY MUCH?
THOSE QUESTIONS... ALL OF THEM HAVE THE SAME ANSWER.
ZHANG.
MY HUSBAND.
YOUR...?
WE GREW UP TOGETHER. MY MOTHER WAS A MAID IN HIS FAMILY MANSION.
BACK WHEN HE HAD MONEY ... A FUTURE.
A SOUL.
SOME RICH LADY WHOSE FAMILY WAS FRIENDS WITH HIS PARENTS CONTACTED HIM ABOUT A JOB – AND HE ROPED ME IN.
I DID WHAT HE ASKED, I MET YOU AT THE DANCE HALL – BECAUSE THE MONEY SHE WAS PAYING – SUCH A SUM! – I THOUGHT THIS, FINALLY, WOULD LET US LEAVE THE CITY. LET ZHANG LEAVE HIS DEMONS BEHIND.

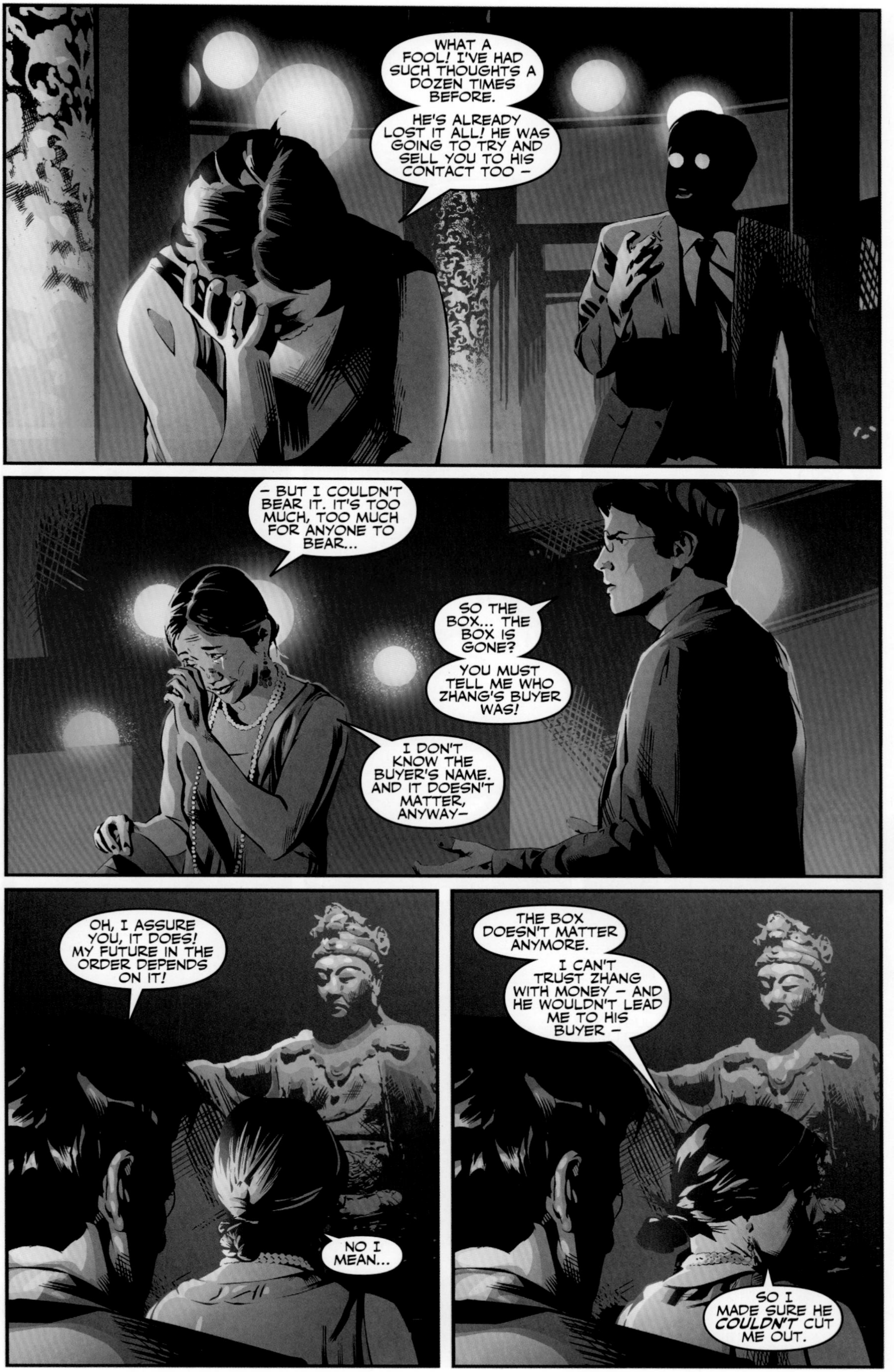
WHAT A FOOL! I'VE HAD SUCH THOUGHTS A DOZEN TIMES BEFORE.
HE'S ALREADY LOST IT ALL! HE WAS GOING TO TRY AND SELL YOU TO HIS CONTACT TOO –
– BUT I COULDN'T BEAR IT. IT'S TOO MUCH, TOO MUCH FOR ANYONE TO BEAR...
SO THE BOX... THE BOX IS GONE?
YOU MUST TELL ME WHO ZHANG'S BUYER WAS!
I DON'T KNOW THE BUYER'S NAME. AND IT DOESN'T MATTER, ANYWAY–
OH, I ASSURE YOU, IT DOES! MY FUTURE IN THE ORDER DEPENDS ON IT!
NO I MEAN...
THE BOX DOESN'T MATTER ANYMORE.
I CAN'T TRUST ZHANG WITH MONEY – AND HE WOULDN'T LEAD ME TO HIS BUYER –
SO I MADE SURE HE *COULDN'T* CUT ME OUT.

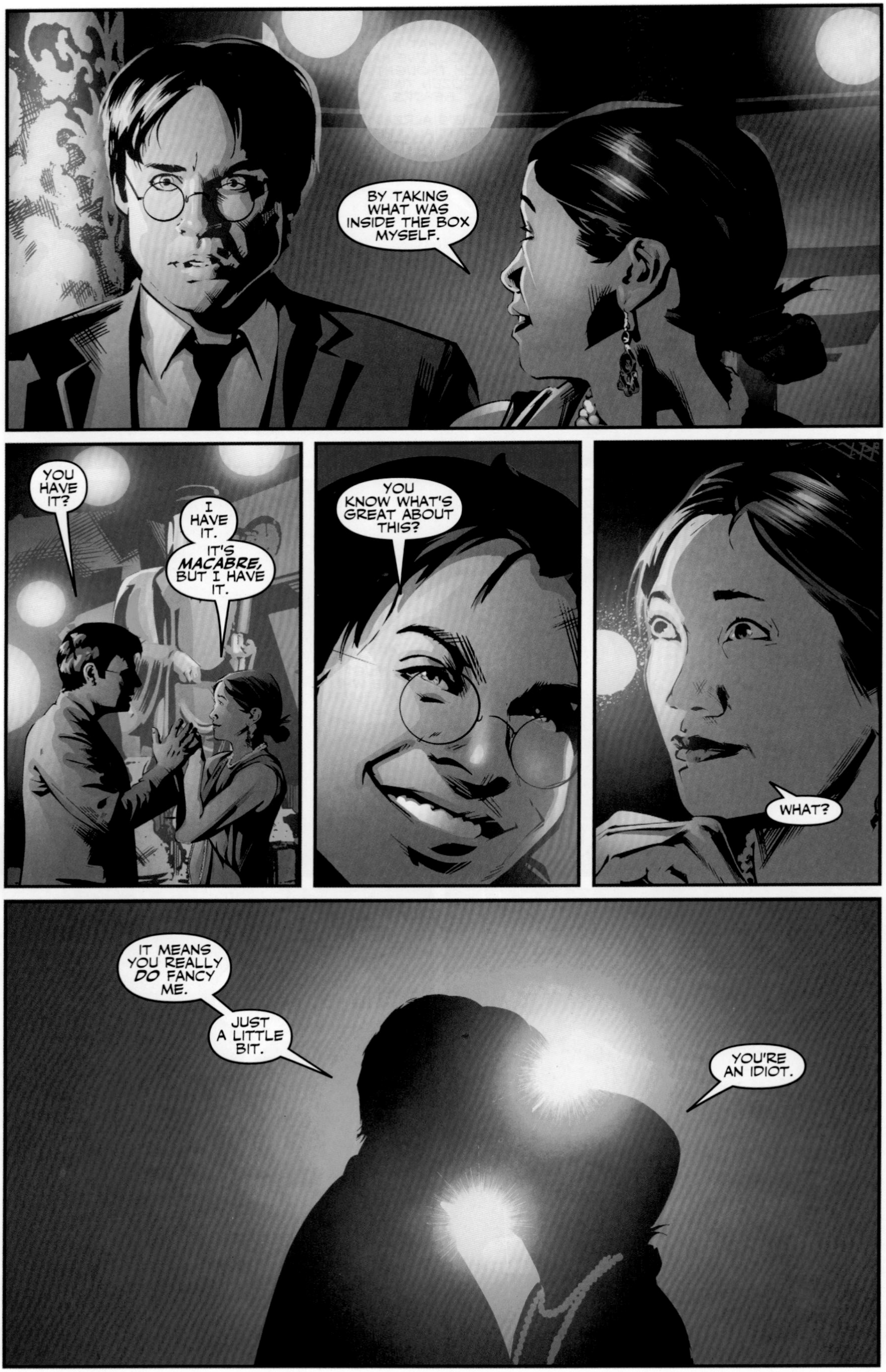
BY TAKING WHAT WAS INSIDE THE BOX MYSELF.
YOU HAVE IT?
I HAVE IT.
IT'S *MACABRE,* BUT I HAVE IT.
YOU KNOW WHAT'S GREAT ABOUT THIS?
WHAT?
IT MEANS YOU REALLY *DO* FANCY ME.
JUST A LITTLE BIT.
YOU'RE AN IDIOT.

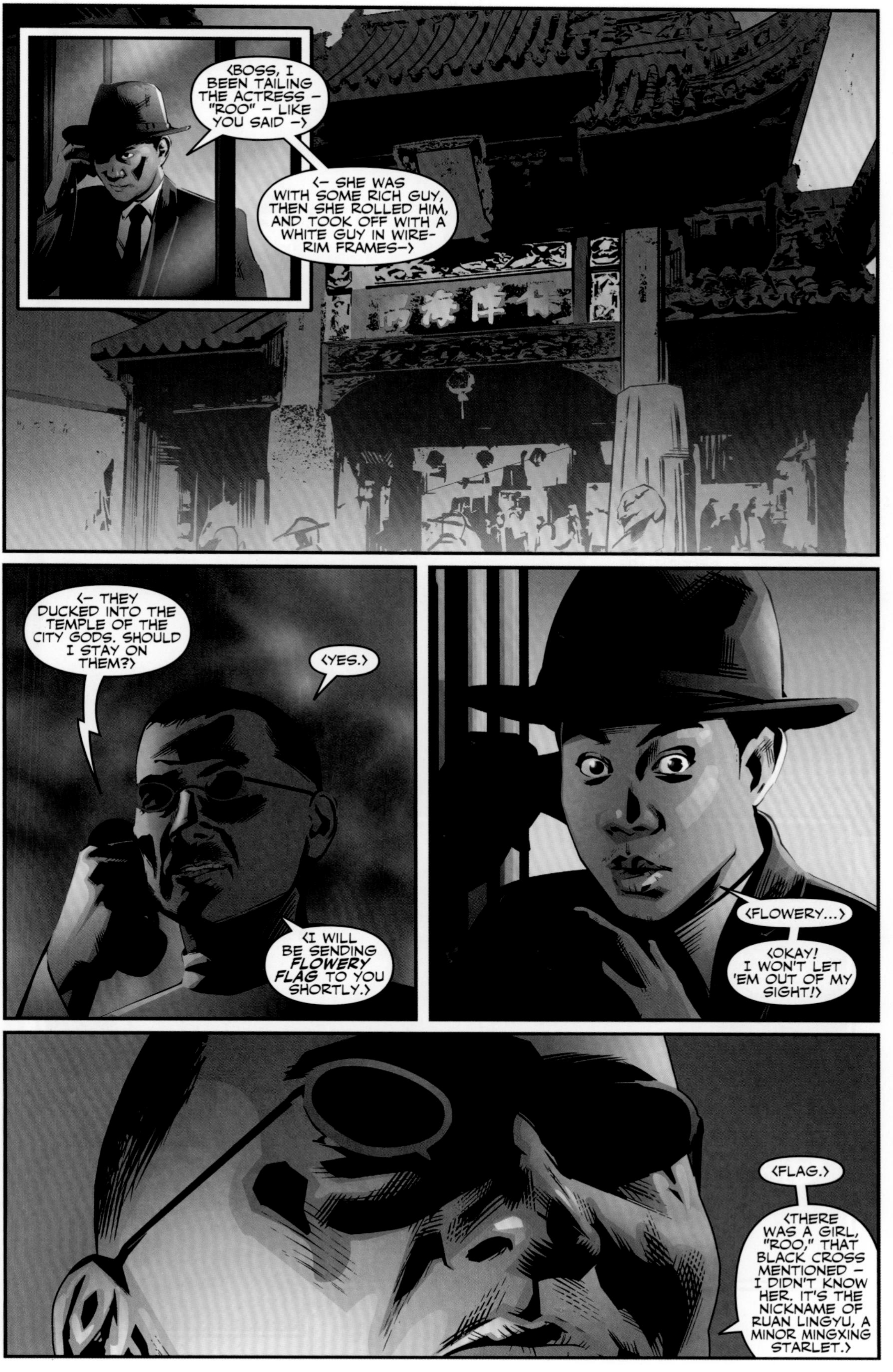

‹BOSS, I BEEN TAILING THE ACTRESS – "ROO" – LIKE YOU SAID –›
‹– SHE WAS WITH SOME RICH GUY, THEN SHE ROLLED HIM, AND TOOK OFF WITH A WHITE GUY IN WIRE-RIM FRAMES–›
‹– THEY DUCKED INTO THE TEMPLE OF THE CITY GODS. SHOULD I STAY ON THEM?›
‹YES.›
‹I WILL BE SENDING FLOWERY FLAG TO YOU SHORTLY.›
‹FLOWERY...›
‹OKAY! I WON'T LET 'EM OUT OF MY SIGHT!›
‹FLAG.›
‹THERE WAS A GIRL, "ROO," THAT BLACK CROSS MENTIONED – I DIDN'T KNOW HER. IT'S THE NICKNAME OF RUAN LINGYU, A MINOR MINGXING STARLET.›

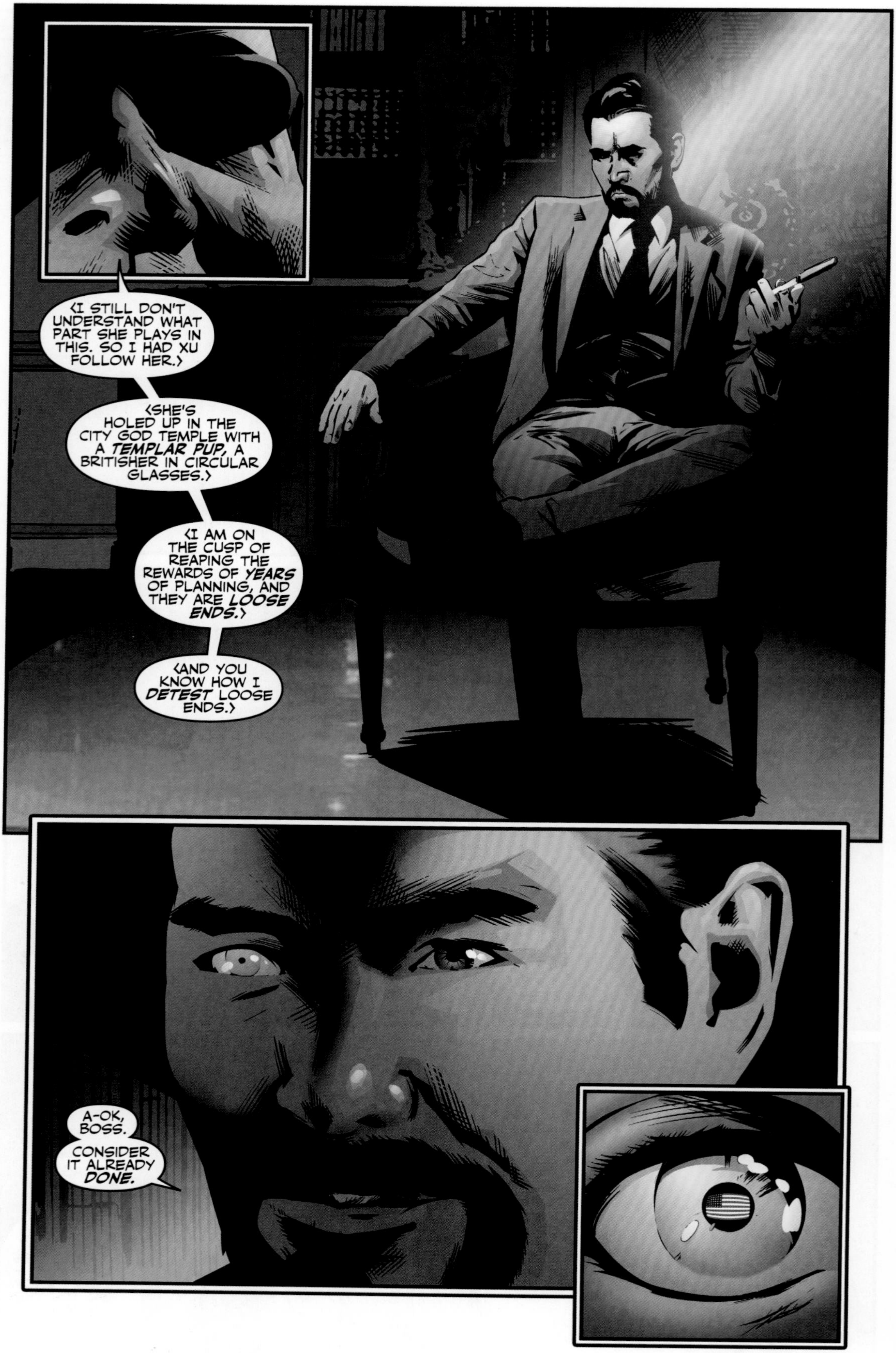
<I STILL DON'T UNDERSTAND WHAT PART SHE PLAYS IN THIS. SO I HAD XU FOLLOW HER.>
<SHE'S HOLED UP IN THE CITY GOD TEMPLE WITH A *TEMPLAR PUP*, A BRITISHER IN CIRCULAR GLASSES.>
<I AM ON THE CUSP OF REAPING THE REWARDS OF *YEARS* OF PLANNING, AND THEY ARE *LOOSE ENDS*.>
<AND YOU KNOW HOW I *DETEST* LOOSE ENDS.>
A-OK, BOSS.
CONSIDER IT ALREADY *DONE*.

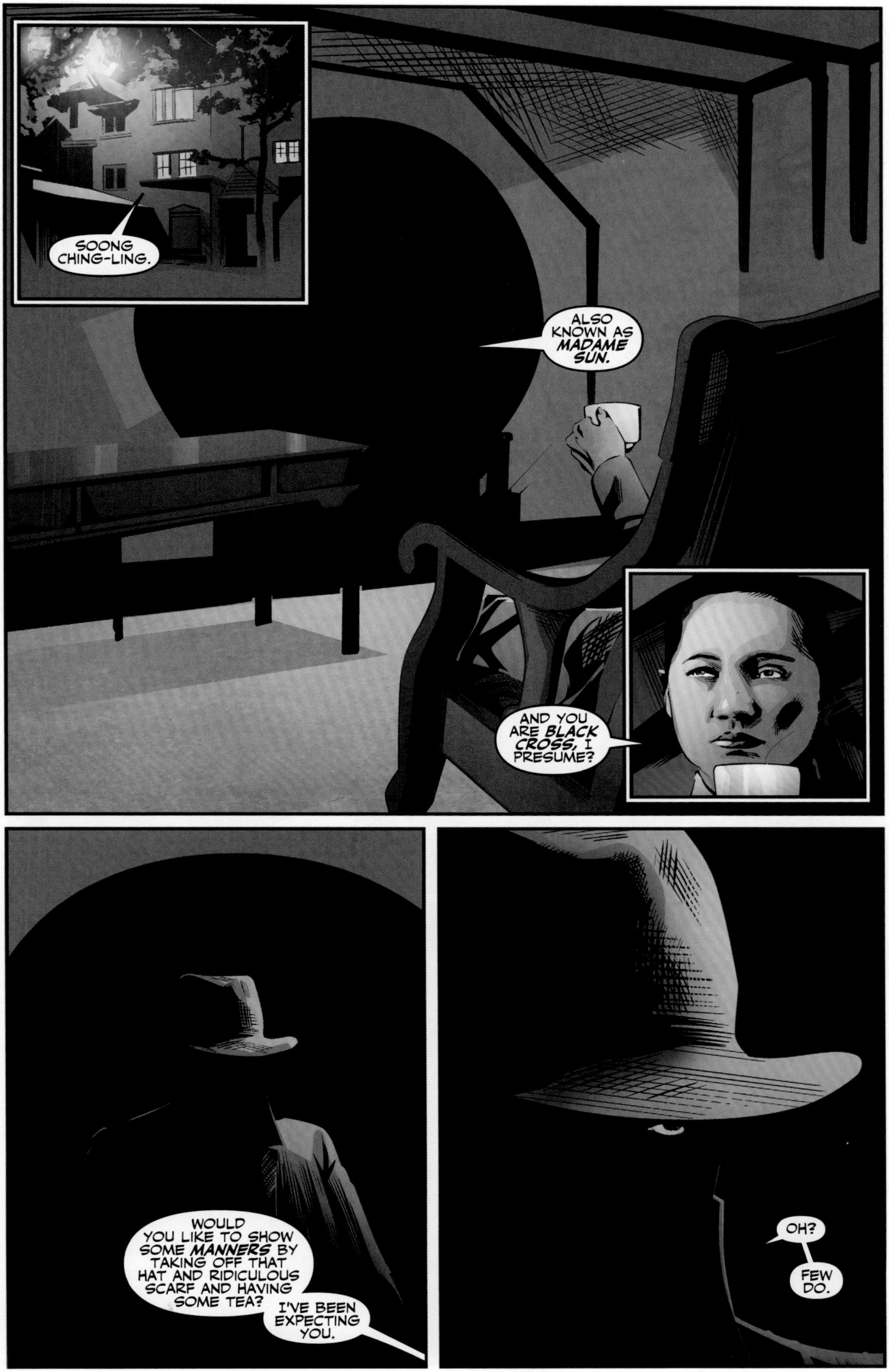
SOONG CHING-LING.
ALSO KNOWN AS MADAME SUN.
AND YOU ARE BLACK CROSS, I PRESUME?
WOULD YOU LIKE TO SHOW SOME MANNERS BY TAKING OFF THAT HAT AND RIDICULOUS SCARF AND HAVING SOME TEA?
I'VE BEEN EXPECTING YOU.
OH?
FEW DO.

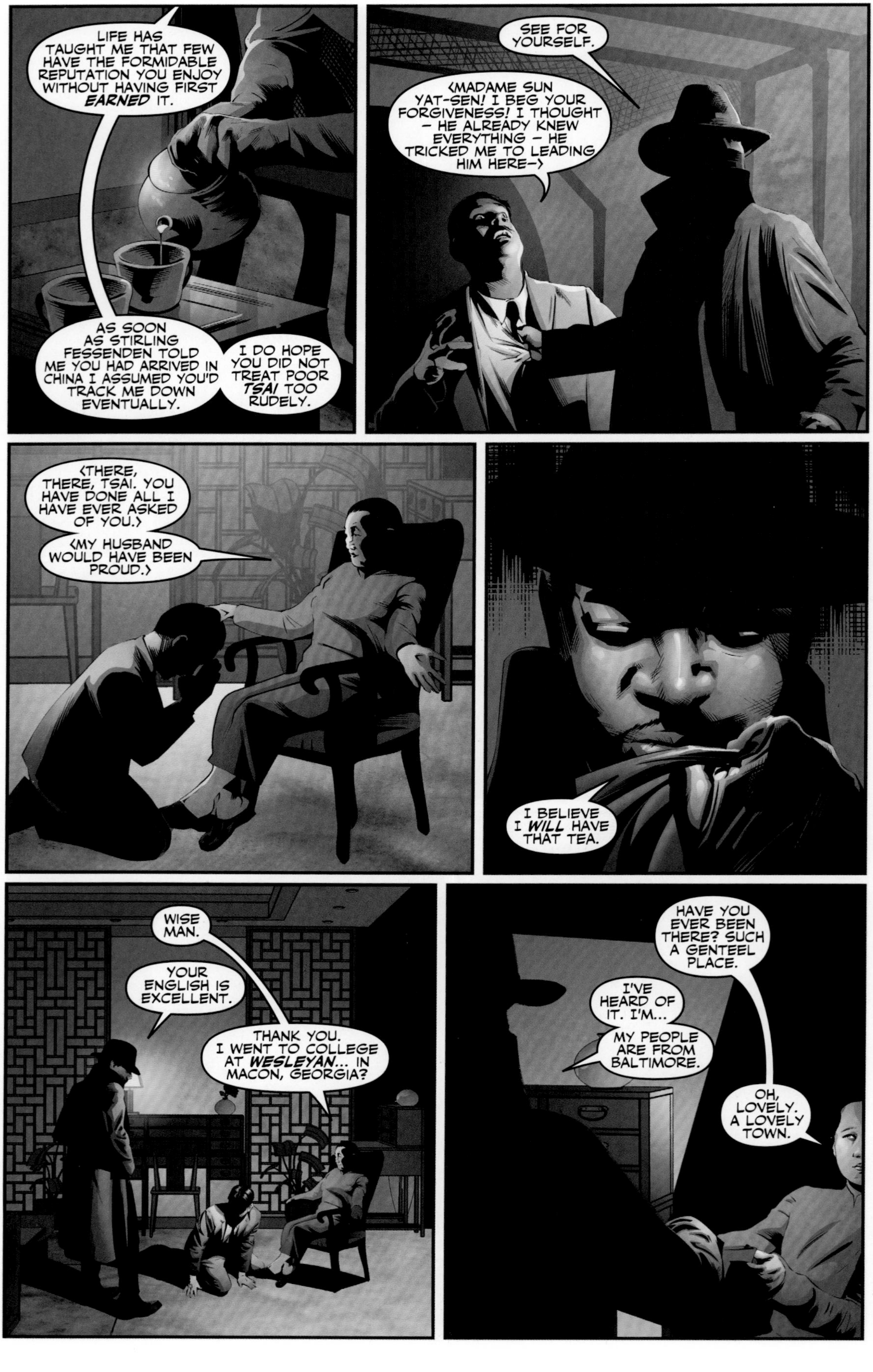
LIFE HAS TAUGHT ME THAT FEW HAVE THE FORMIDABLE REPUTATION YOU ENJOY WITHOUT HAVING FIRST *EARNED* IT.
AS SOON AS STIRLING FESSENDEN TOLD ME YOU HAD ARRIVED IN CHINA I ASSUMED YOU'D TRACK ME DOWN EVENTUALLY.
I DO HOPE YOU DID NOT TREAT POOR *TSAI* TOO RUDELY.
SEE FOR YOURSELF.
<MADAME SUN YAT-SEN! I BEG YOUR FORGIVENESS! I THOUGHT – HE ALREADY KNEW EVERYTHING – HE TRICKED ME TO LEADING HIM HERE–>
<THERE, THERE, TSAI. YOU HAVE DONE ALL I HAVE EVER ASKED OF YOU.>
<MY HUSBAND WOULD HAVE BEEN PROUD.>
I BELIEVE I *WILL* HAVE THAT TEA.
WISE MAN.
YOUR ENGLISH IS EXCELLENT.
THANK YOU. I WENT TO COLLEGE AT *WESLEYAN*... IN MACON, GEORGIA?
HAVE YOU EVER BEEN THERE? SUCH A GENTEEL PLACE.
I'VE HEARD OF IT. I'M...
MY PEOPLE ARE FROM BALTIMORE.
OH, LOVELY. A LOVELY TOWN.

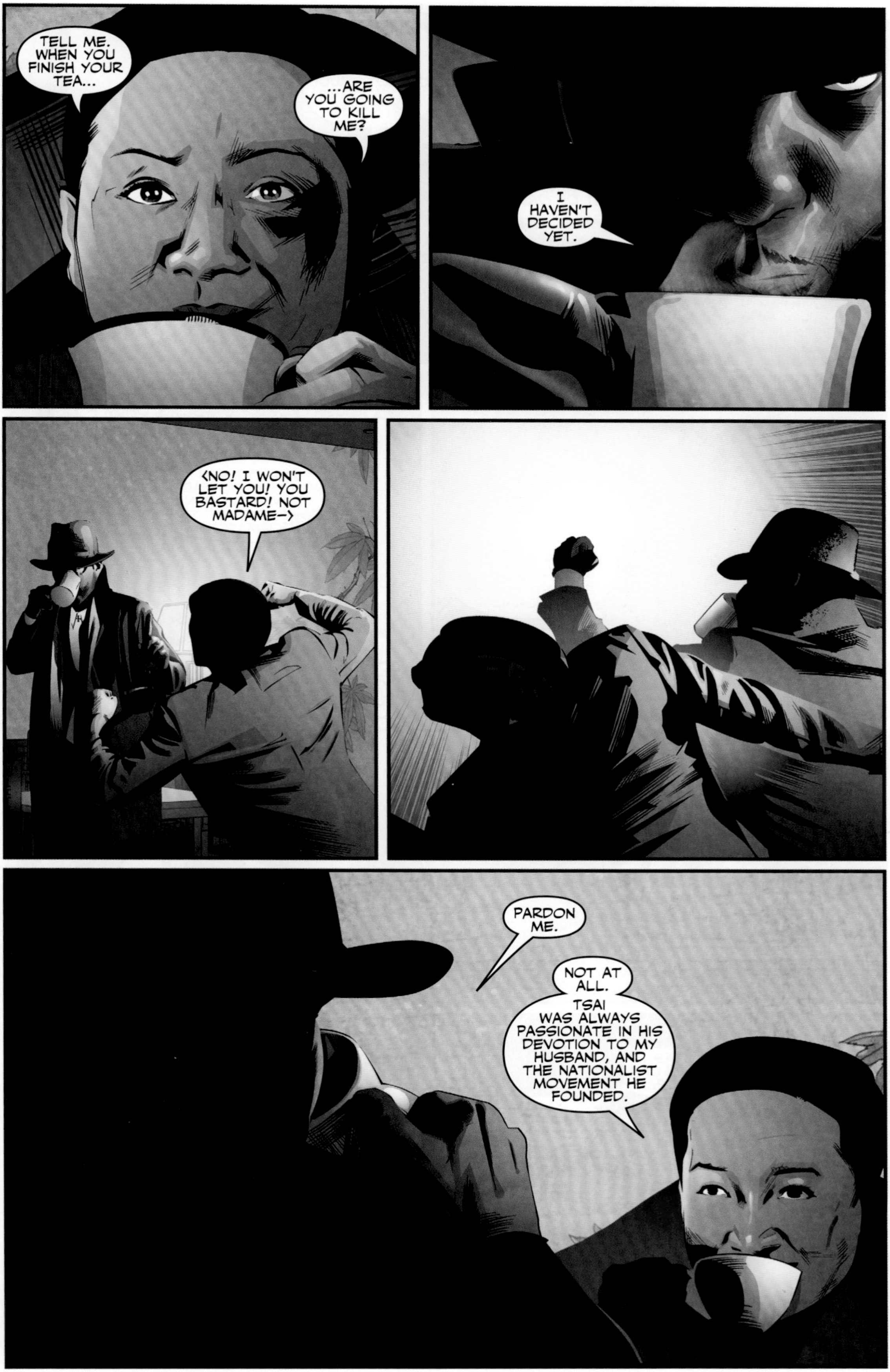
TELL ME. WHEN YOU FINISH YOUR TEA...
...ARE YOU GOING TO KILL ME?
I HAVEN'T DECIDED YET.
<NO! I WON'T LET YOU! YOU BASTARD! NOT MADAME—>
PARDON ME.
NOT AT ALL.
TSAI WAS ALWAYS PASSIONATE IN HIS DEVOTION TO MY HUSBAND, AND THE NATIONALIST MOVEMENT HE FOUNDED.

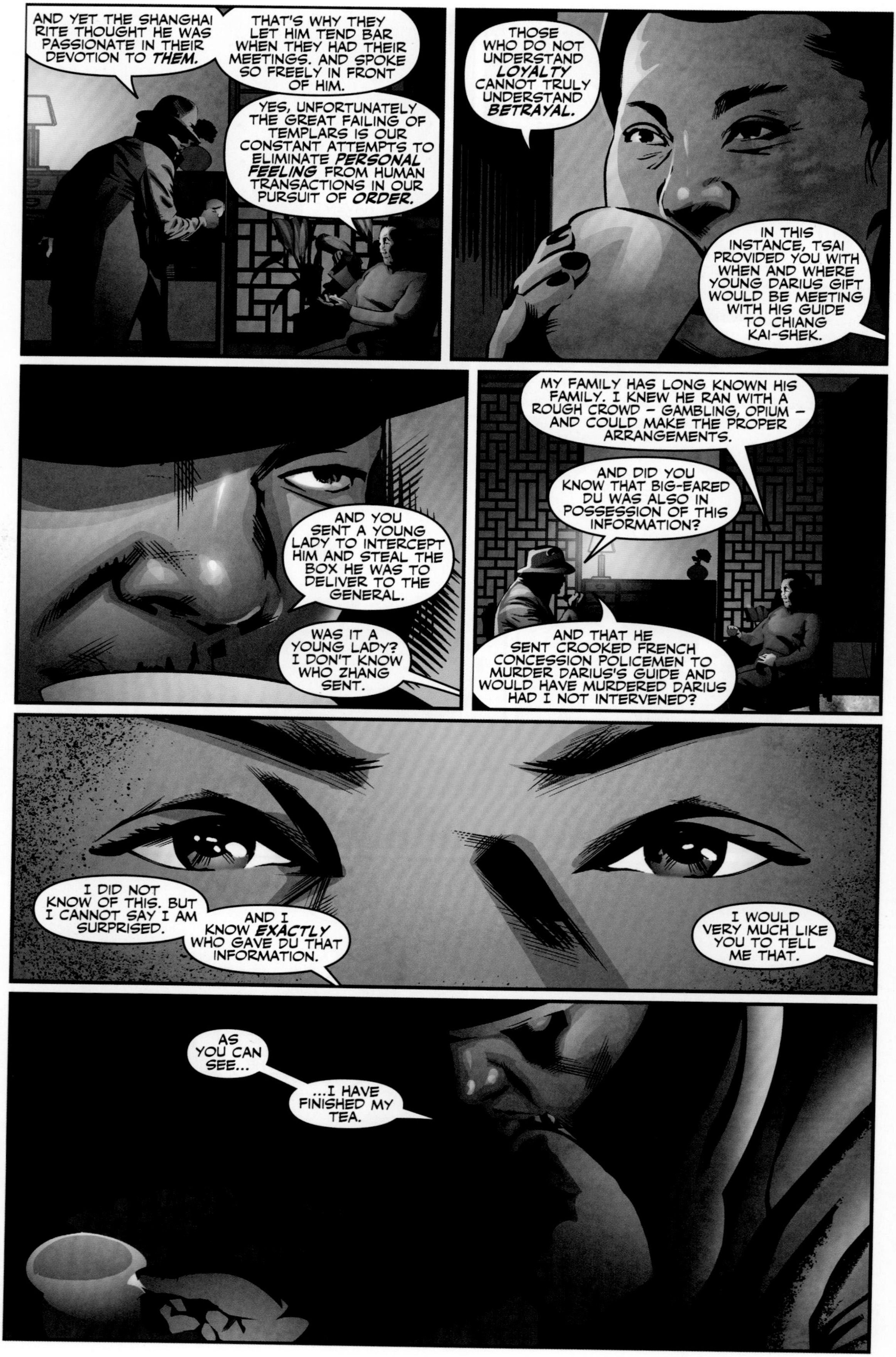
AND YET THE SHANGHAI RITE THOUGHT HE WAS PASSIONATE IN THEIR DEVOTION TO *THEM.*
THAT'S WHY THEY LET HIM TEND BAR WHEN THEY HAD THEIR MEETINGS. AND SPOKE SO FREELY IN FRONT OF HIM.
YES, UNFORTUNATELY THE GREAT FAILING OF TEMPLARS IS OUR CONSTANT ATTEMPTS TO ELIMINATE *PERSONAL FEELING* FROM HUMAN TRANSACTIONS IN OUR PURSUIT OF *ORDER.*
THOSE WHO DO NOT UNDERSTAND *LOYALTY* CANNOT TRULY UNDERSTAND *BETRAYAL.*
IN THIS INSTANCE, TSAI PROVIDED YOU WITH WHEN AND WHERE YOUNG DARIUS GIFT WOULD BE MEETING WITH HIS GUIDE TO CHIANG KAI-SHEK.
AND YOU SENT A YOUNG LADY TO INTERCEPT HIM AND STEAL THE BOX HE WAS TO DELIVER TO THE GENERAL.
WAS IT A YOUNG LADY? I DON'T KNOW WHO ZHANG SENT.
MY FAMILY HAS LONG KNOWN HIS FAMILY. I KNEW HE RAN WITH A ROUGH CROWD – GAMBLING, OPIUM – AND COULD MAKE THE PROPER ARRANGEMENTS.
AND DID YOU KNOW THAT BIG-EARED DU WAS ALSO IN POSSESSION OF THIS INFORMATION?
AND THAT HE SENT CROOKED FRENCH CONCESSION POLICEMEN TO MURDER DARIUS'S GUIDE AND WOULD HAVE MURDERED DARIUS HAD I NOT INTERVENED?
I DID NOT KNOW OF THIS. BUT I CANNOT SAY I AM SURPRISED.
AND I KNOW *EXACTLY* WHO GAVE DU THAT INFORMATION.
I WOULD VERY MUCH LIKE YOU TO TELL ME THAT.
AS YOU CAN SEE...
...I HAVE FINISHED MY TEA.

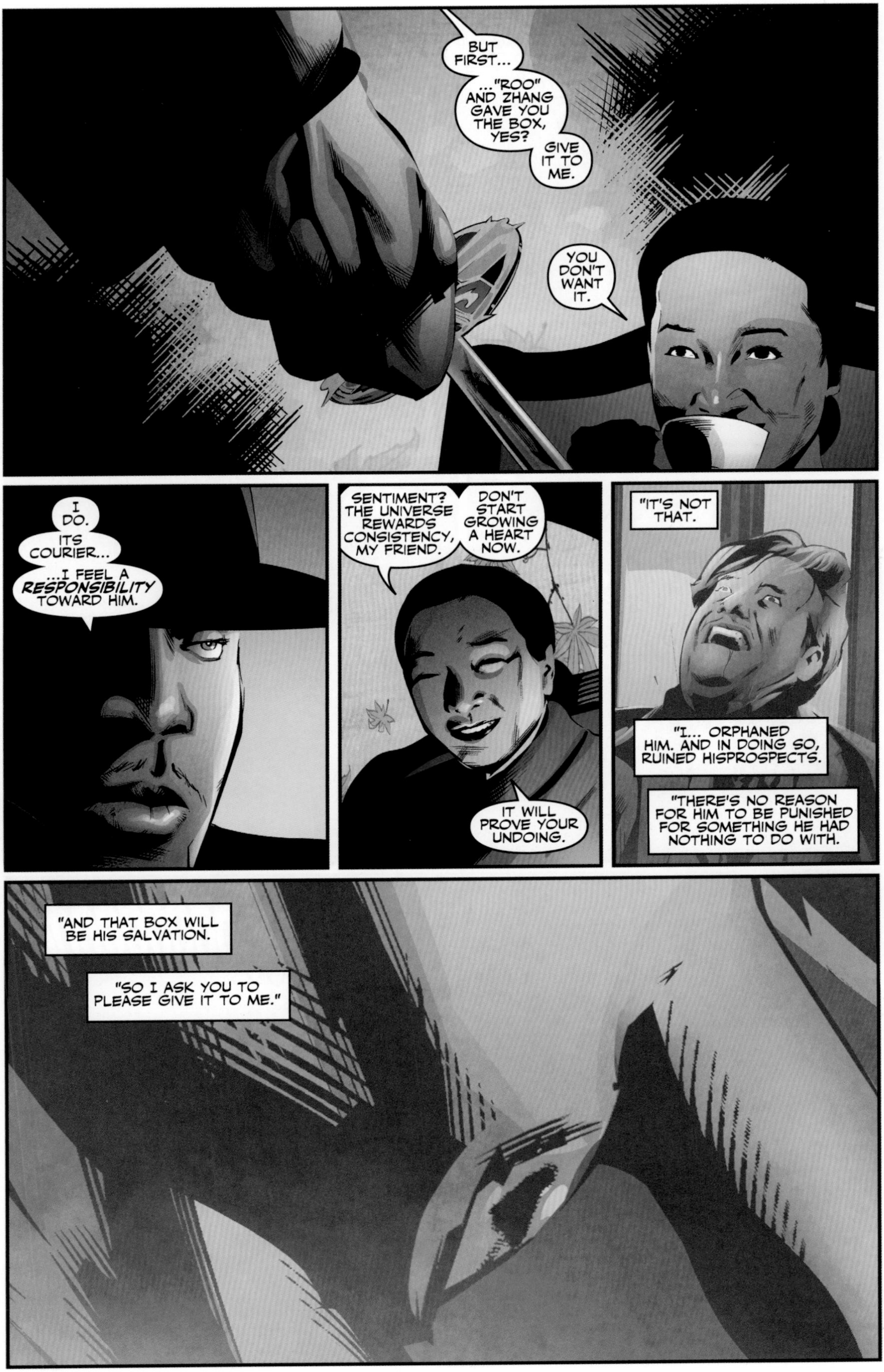
BUT FIRST...
..."ROO" AND ZHANG GAVE YOU THE BOX, YES?
GIVE IT TO ME.
YOU DON'T WANT IT.
I DO.
ITS COURIER...
...I FEEL A RESPONSIBILITY TOWARD HIM.
SENTIMENT? THE UNIVERSE REWARDS CONSISTENCY, MY FRIEND.
DON'T START GROWING A HEART NOW.
IT WILL PROVE YOUR UNDOING.
"IT'S NOT THAT.
"I... ORPHANED HIM. AND IN DOING SO, RUINED HISPROSPECTS.
"THERE'S NO REASON FOR HIM TO BE PUNISHED FOR SOMETHING HE HAD NOTHING TO DO WITH.
"AND THAT BOX WILL BE HIS SALVATION.
"SO I ASK YOU TO PLEASE GIVE IT TO ME."

I WOULD GIVE *ANYONE* THE BOX... EXCEPT FOR WHOM IT IS *INTENDED*.

BUT I'M AFRAID, AS YOU CAN SEE...

...IT IS NO *GOOD* TO ANYONE LIKE THIS.

≷SIGH.≷

EMPTY.

ARRROOOOOOOOOOOOOOOOOO

MY WORD! WHAT...?

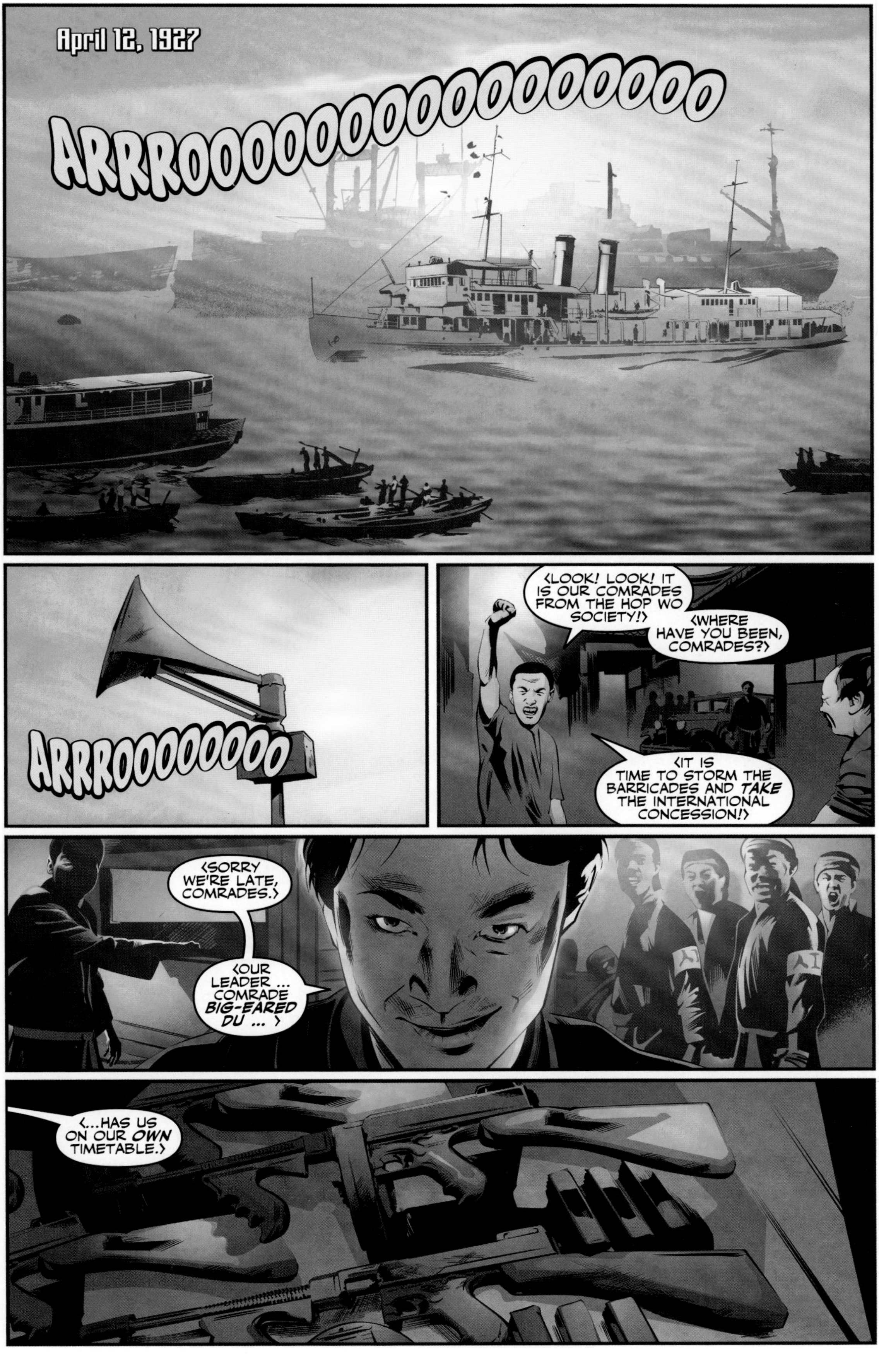
April 12, 1927
ARRROOOOOOOOOOOOOOOOOO
ARRROOOOOOOO
‹LOOK! LOOK! IT IS OUR COMRADES FROM THE HOP WO SOCIETY!›
‹WHERE HAVE YOU BEEN, COMRADES?›
‹IT IS TIME TO STORM THE BARRICADES AND TAKE THE INTERNATIONAL CONCESSION!›
‹SORRY WE'RE LATE, COMRADES.›
‹OUR LEADER ... COMRADE BIG-EARED DU ... ›
‹...HAS US ON OUR OWN TIMETABLE.›

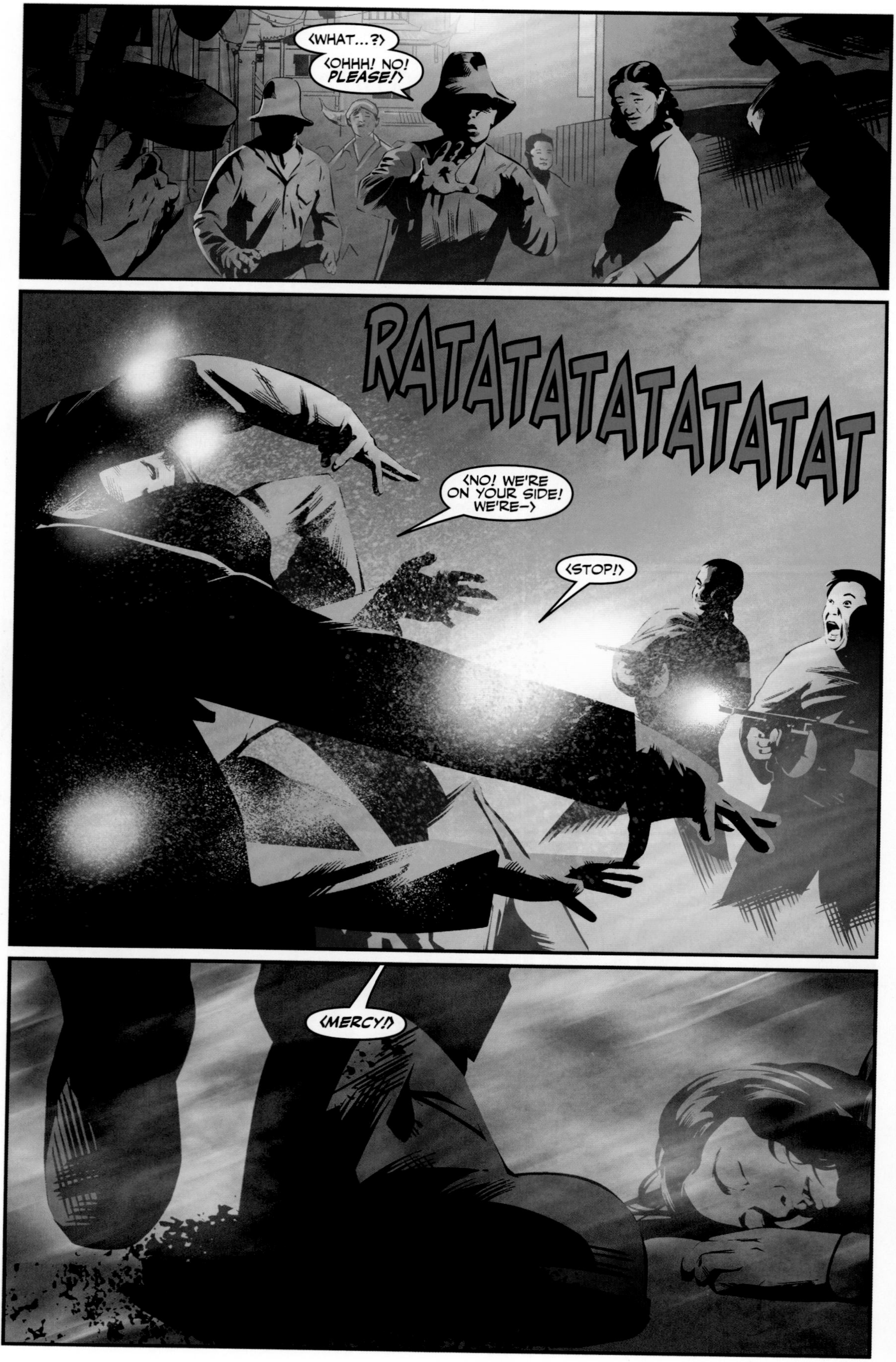
‹WHAT...?›
‹OHHH! NO! PLEASE!›
RATATATATATATAT
‹NO! WE'RE ON YOUR SIDE! WE'RE–›
‹STOP!›
‹MERCY!›

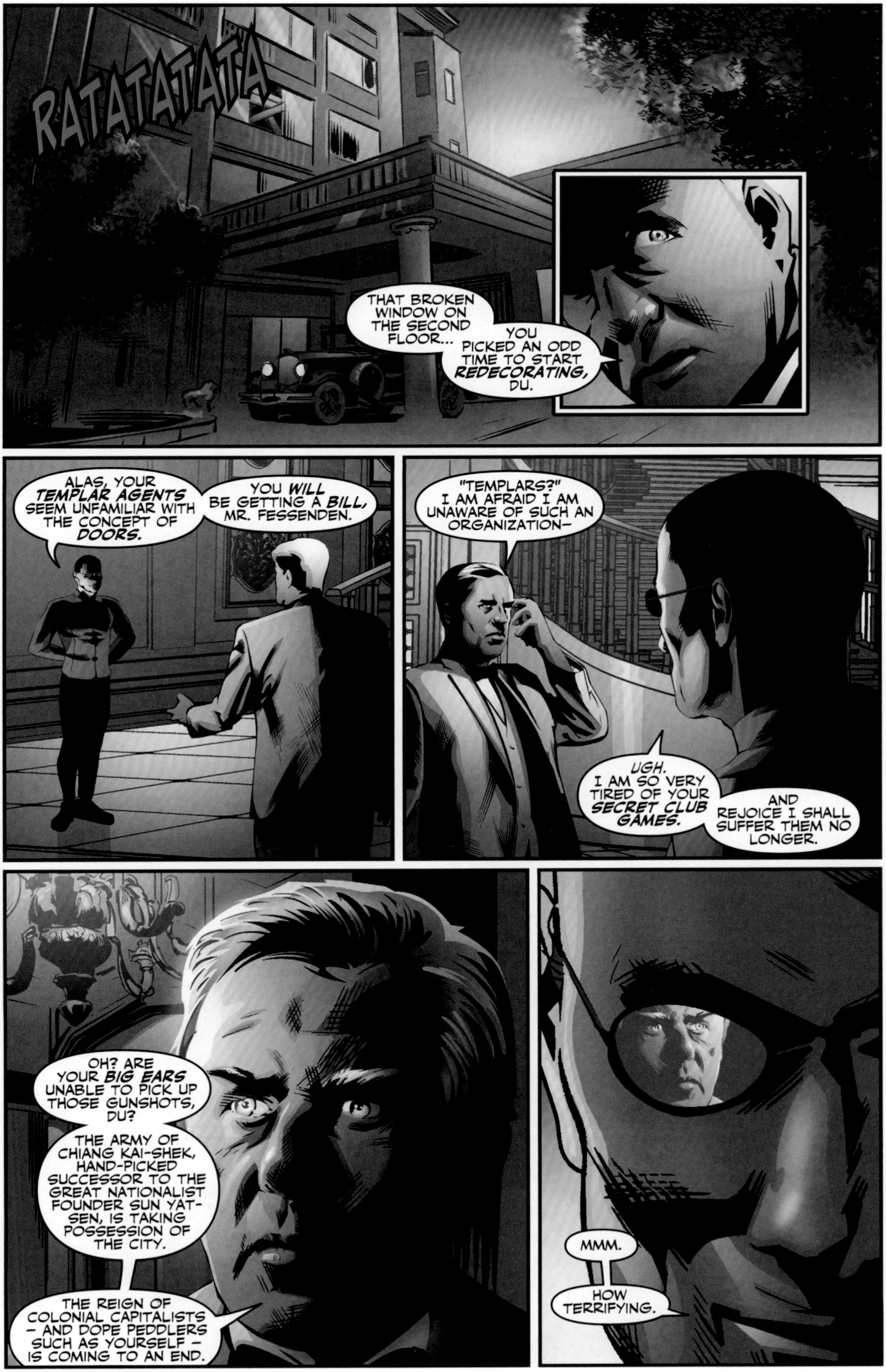
RATATATATA
THAT BROKEN WINDOW ON THE SECOND FLOOR...
YOU PICKED AN ODD TIME TO START REDECORATING, DU.
ALAS, YOUR TEMPLAR AGENTS SEEM UNFAMILIAR WITH THE CONCEPT OF DOORS.
YOU WILL BE GETTING A BILL, MR. FESSENDEN.
"TEMPLARS?" I AM AFRAID I AM UNAWARE OF SUCH AN ORGANIZATION–
UGH. I AM SO VERY TIRED OF YOUR SECRET CLUB GAMES.
AND REJOICE I SHALL SUFFER THEM NO LONGER.
OH? ARE YOUR BIG EARS UNABLE TO PICK UP THOSE GUNSHOTS, DU?
THE ARMY OF CHIANG KAI-SHEK, HAND-PICKED SUCCESSOR TO THE GREAT NATIONALIST FOUNDER SUN YAT-SEN, IS TAKING POSSESSION OF THE CITY.
THE REIGN OF COLONIAL CAPITALISTS – AND DOPE PEDDLERS SUCH AS YOURSELF – IS COMING TO AN END.
MMM.
HOW TERRIFYING.

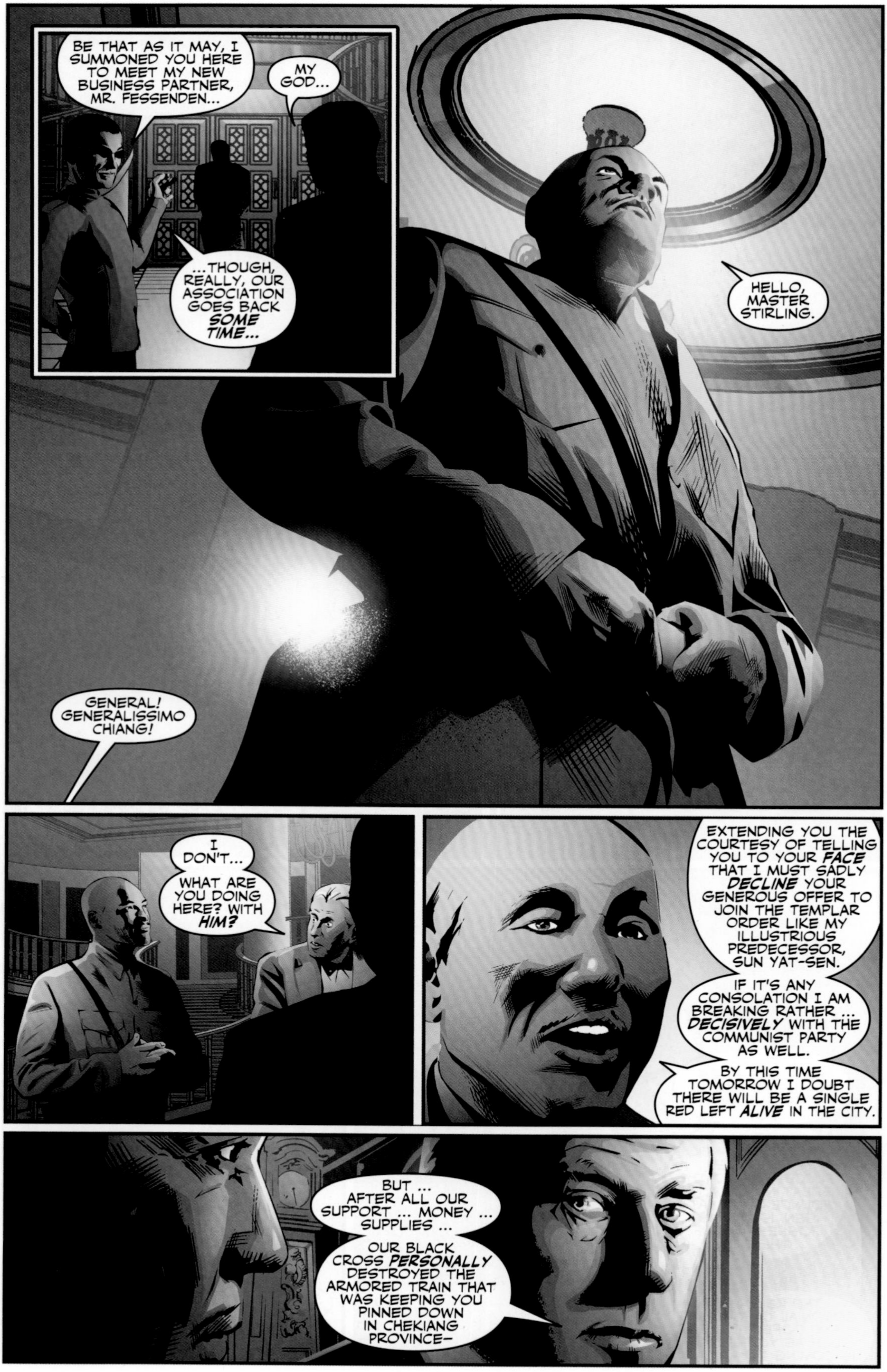
BE THAT AS IT MAY, I SUMMONED YOU HERE TO MEET MY NEW BUSINESS PARTNER, MR. FESSENDEN...
MY GOD...
...THOUGH, REALLY, OUR ASSOCIATION GOES BACK SOME TIME...
HELLO, MASTER STIRLING.
GENERAL! GENERALISSIMO CHIANG!
I DON'T...
WHAT ARE YOU DOING HERE? WITH HIM?
EXTENDING YOU THE COURTESY OF TELLING YOU TO YOUR FACE THAT I MUST SADLY DECLINE YOUR GENEROUS OFFER TO JOIN THE TEMPLAR ORDER LIKE MY ILLUSTRIOUS PREDECESSOR, SUN YAT-SEN.
IF IT'S ANY CONSOLATION I AM BREAKING RATHER ... DECISIVELY WITH THE COMMUNIST PARTY AS WELL.
BY THIS TIME TOMORROW I DOUBT THERE WILL BE A SINGLE RED LEFT ALIVE IN THE CITY.
BUT ... AFTER ALL OUR SUPPORT ... MONEY ... SUPPLIES ...
OUR BLACK CROSS PERSONALLY DESTROYED THE ARMORED TRAIN THAT WAS KEEPING YOU PINNED DOWN IN CHEKIANG PROVINCE–

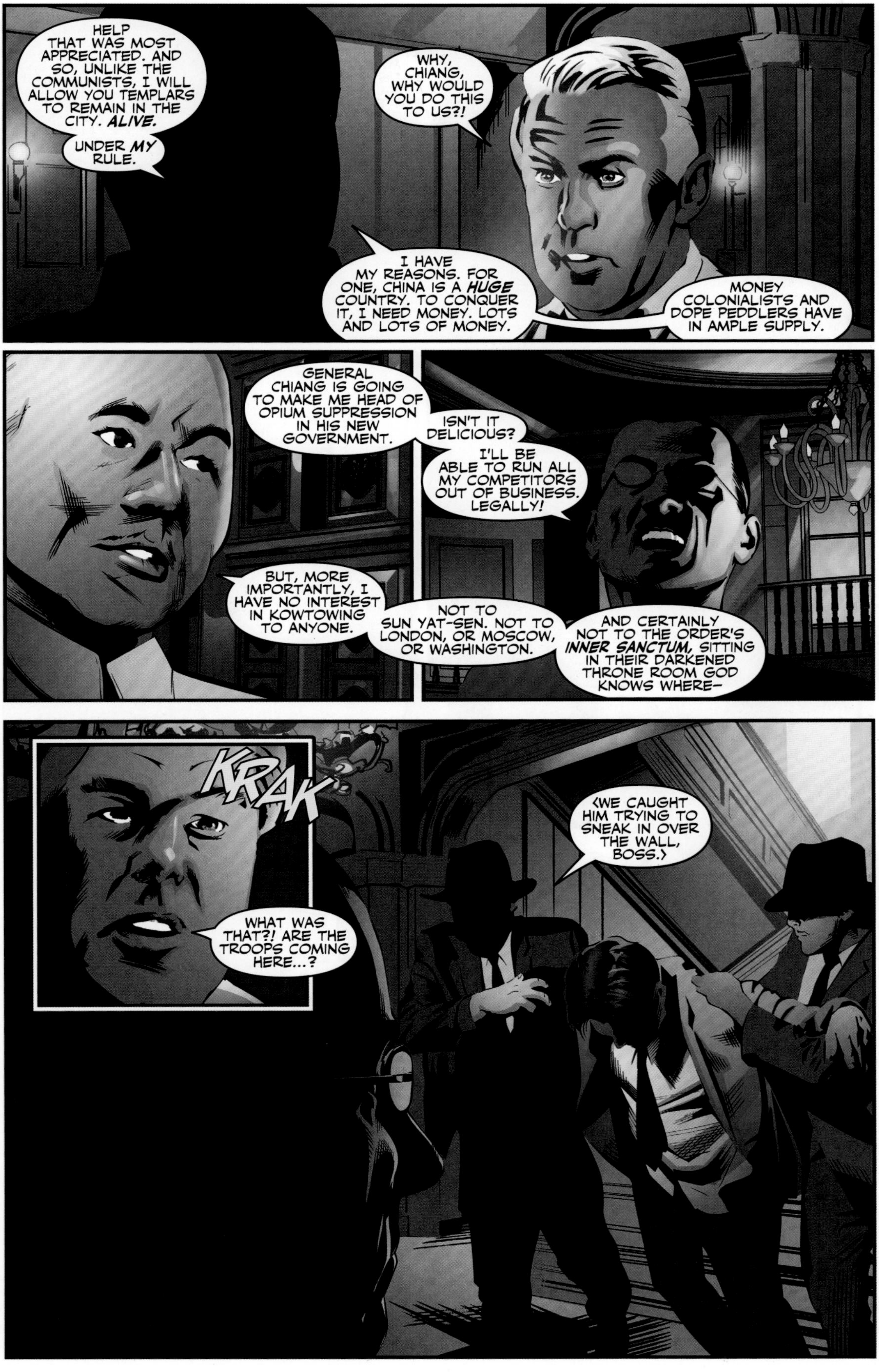
HELP THAT WAS MOST APPRECIATED. AND SO, UNLIKE THE COMMUNISTS, I WILL ALLOW YOU TEMPLARS TO REMAIN IN THE CITY. *ALIVE.*
UNDER *MY* RULE.
WHY, CHIANG, WHY WOULD YOU DO THIS TO US?!
I HAVE MY REASONS. FOR ONE, CHINA IS A *HUGE* COUNTRY. TO CONQUER IT, I NEED MONEY. LOTS AND LOTS OF MONEY.
MONEY COLONIALISTS AND DOPE PEDDLERS HAVE IN AMPLE SUPPLY.
GENERAL CHIANG IS GOING TO MAKE ME HEAD OF OPIUM SUPPRESSION IN HIS NEW GOVERNMENT.
ISN'T IT DELICIOUS?
I'LL BE ABLE TO RUN ALL MY COMPETITORS OUT OF BUSINESS. LEGALLY!
BUT, MORE IMPORTANTLY, I HAVE NO INTEREST IN KOWTOWING TO ANYONE.
NOT TO SUN YAT-SEN. NOT TO LONDON, OR MOSCOW, OR WASHINGTON.
AND CERTAINLY NOT TO THE ORDER'S *INNER SANCTUM,* SITTING IN THEIR DARKENED THRONE ROOM GOD KNOWS WHERE–
KRAK
WHAT WAS THAT?! ARE THE TROOPS COMING HERE...?
<WE CAUGHT HIM TRYING TO SNEAK IN OVER THE WALL, BOSS.>

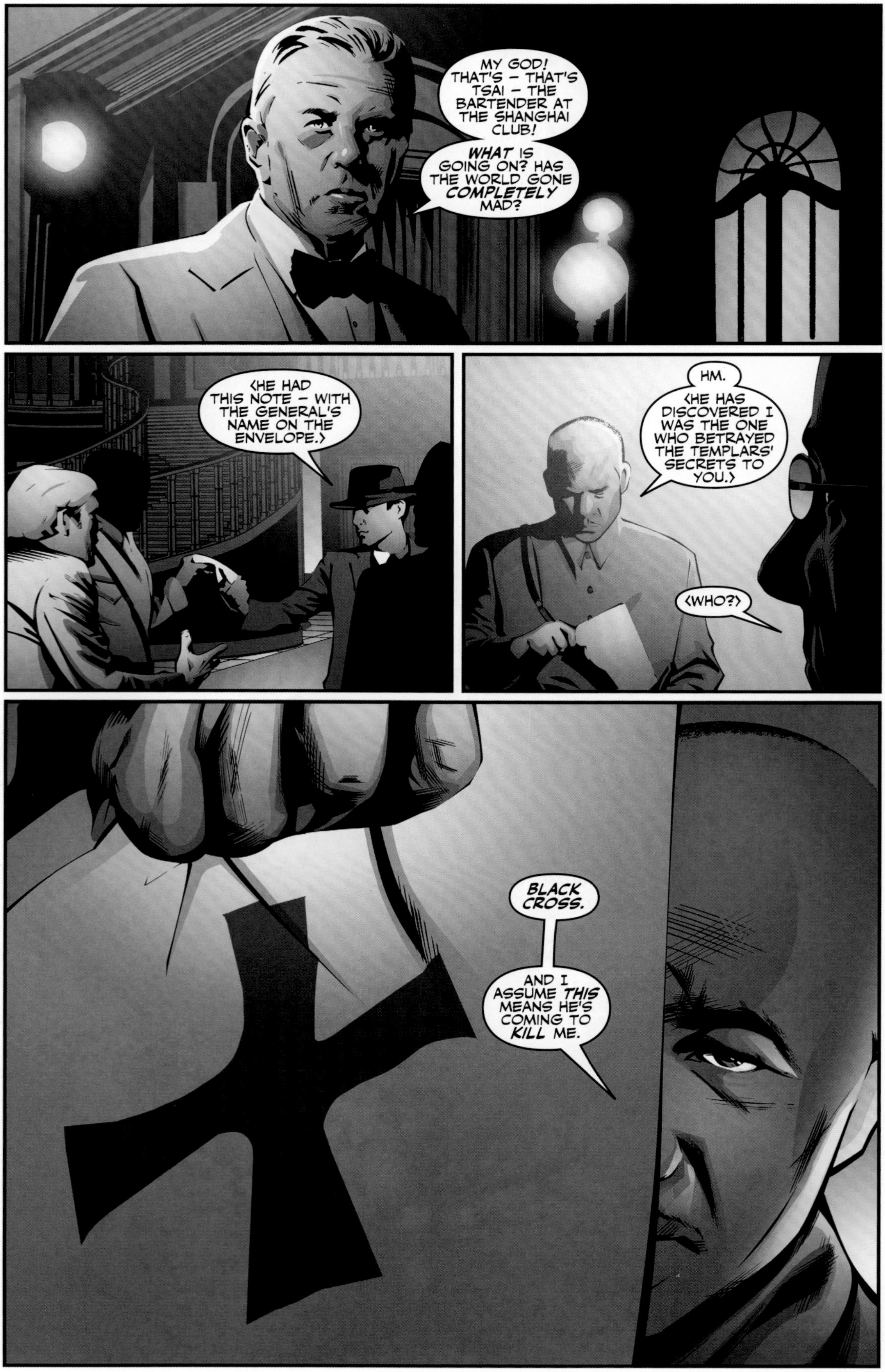
MY GOD! THAT'S – THAT'S TSAI – THE BARTENDER AT THE SHANGHAI CLUB!
WHAT IS GOING ON? HAS THE WORLD GONE COMPLETELY MAD?
<HE HAD THIS NOTE – WITH THE GENERAL'S NAME ON THE ENVELOPE.>
HM.
<HE HAS DISCOVERED I WAS THE ONE WHO BETRAYED THE TEMPLARS' SECRETS TO YOU.>
<WHO?>
BLACK CROSS.
AND I ASSUME THIS MEANS HE'S COMING TO KILL ME.

CHAPTER FIVE

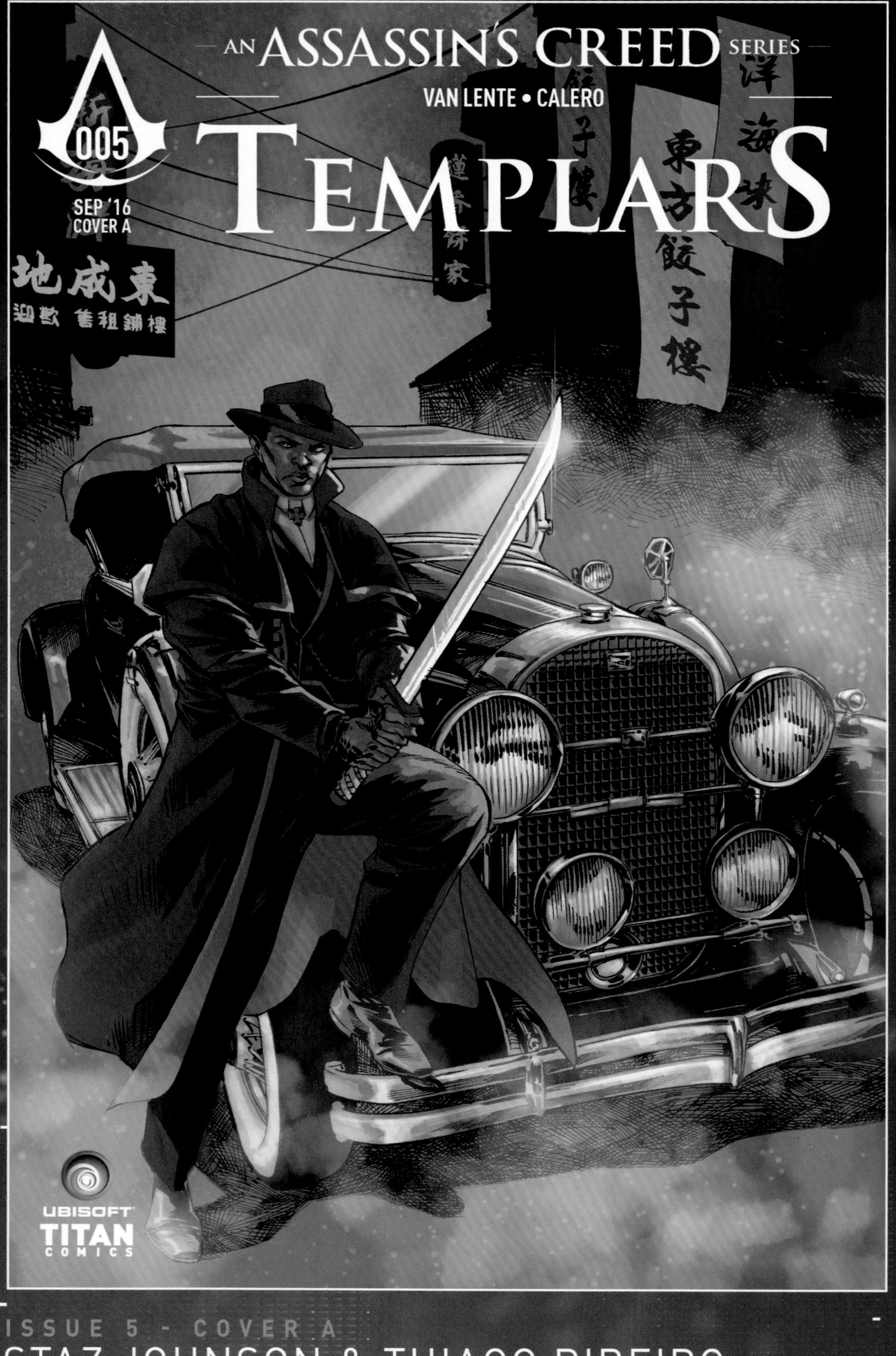
AN ASSASSIN'S CREED SERIES
VAN LENTE • CALERO
005
TEMPLARS
SEP '16
COVER A
東方餃子樓
UBISOFT
TITAN COMICS

ISSUE 5 - COVER A
STAZ JOHNSON & THIAGO RIBEIRO

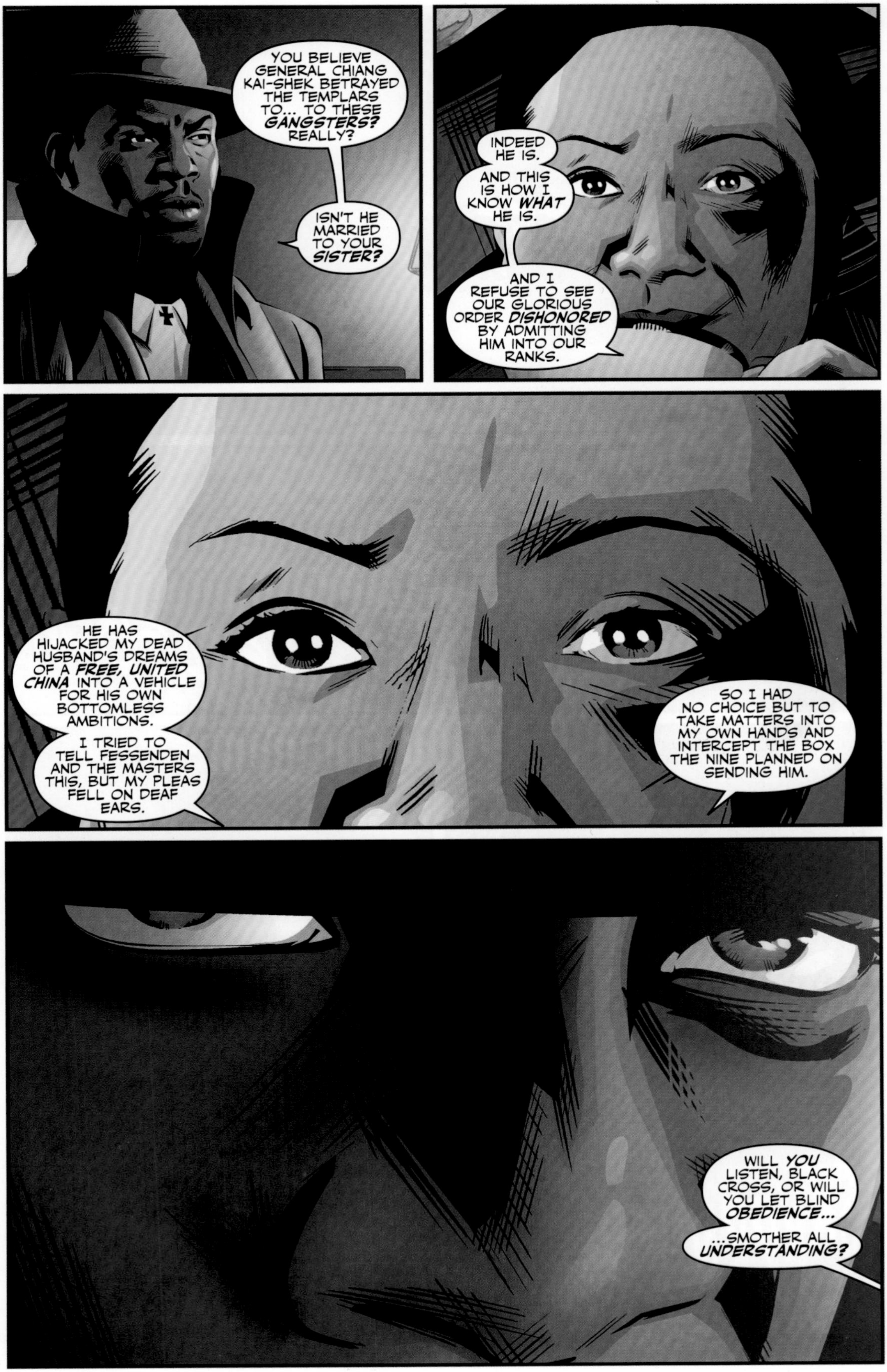
YOU BELIEVE GENERAL CHIANG KAI-SHEK BETRAYED THE TEMPLARS TO... TO THESE *GANGSTERS?* REALLY?
ISN'T HE MARRIED TO YOUR *SISTER?*
INDEED HE IS.
AND THIS IS HOW I KNOW *WHAT* HE IS.
AND I REFUSE TO SEE OUR GLORIOUS ORDER *DISHONORED* BY ADMITTING HIM INTO OUR RANKS.
HE HAS HIJACKED MY DEAD HUSBAND'S DREAMS OF A *FREE, UNITED CHINA* INTO A VEHICLE FOR HIS OWN BOTTOMLESS AMBITIONS.
I TRIED TO TELL FESSENDEN AND THE MASTERS THIS, BUT MY PLEAS FELL ON DEAF EARS.
SO I HAD NO CHOICE BUT TO TAKE MATTERS INTO MY OWN HANDS AND INTERCEPT THE BOX THE NINE PLANNED ON SENDING HIM.
WILL *YOU* LISTEN, BLACK CROSS, OR WILL YOU LET BLIND *OBEDIENCE...*
...SMOTHER ALL *UNDERSTANDING?*

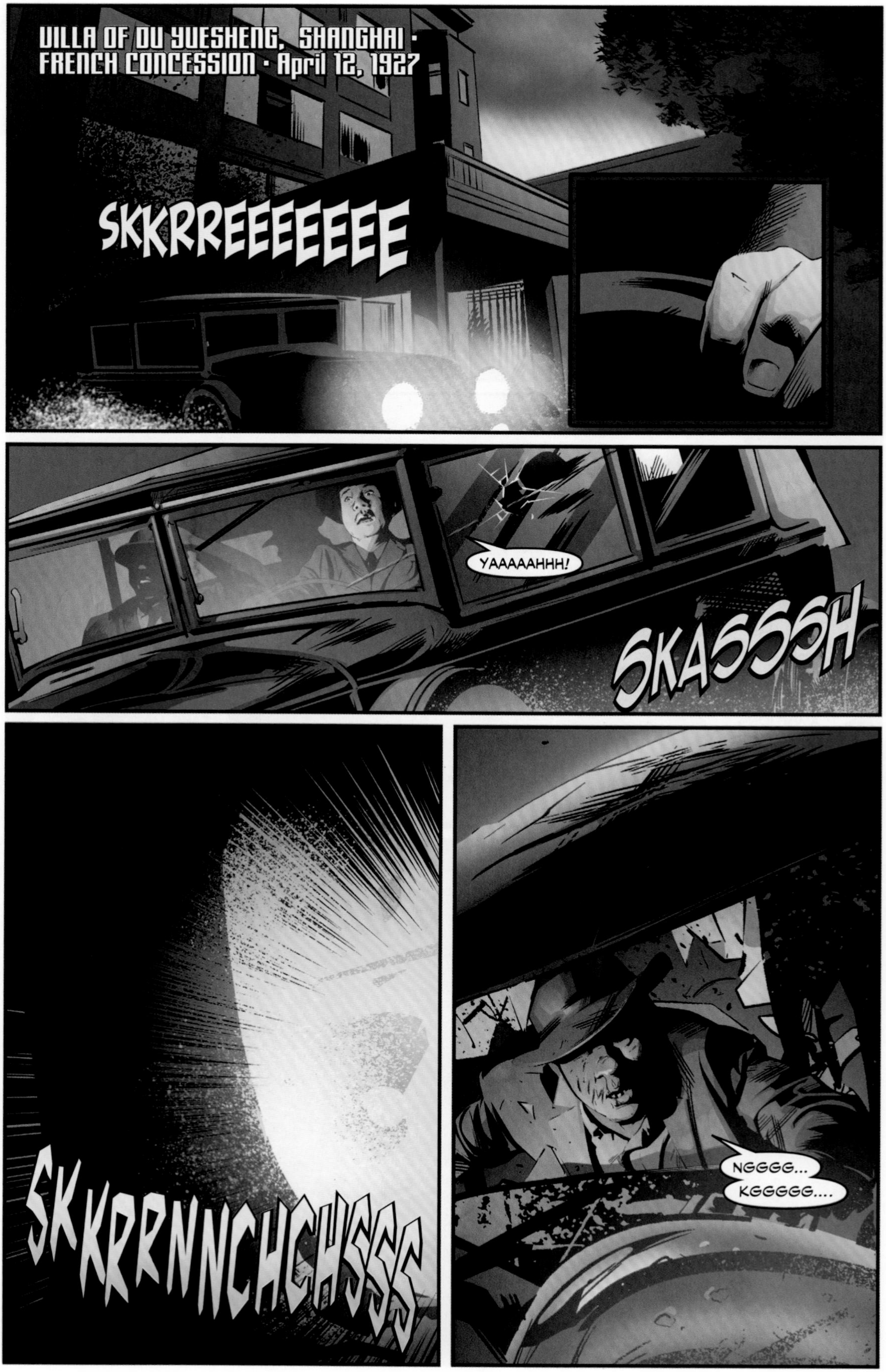
VILLA OF DU YUESHENG, SHANGHAI · FRENCH CONCESSION · April 12, 1927
SKKRREEEEEEE
YAAAAAHHH!
SKASSSH
SKKRRNNCHCHSSSS
NGGGG...
KGGGGG....

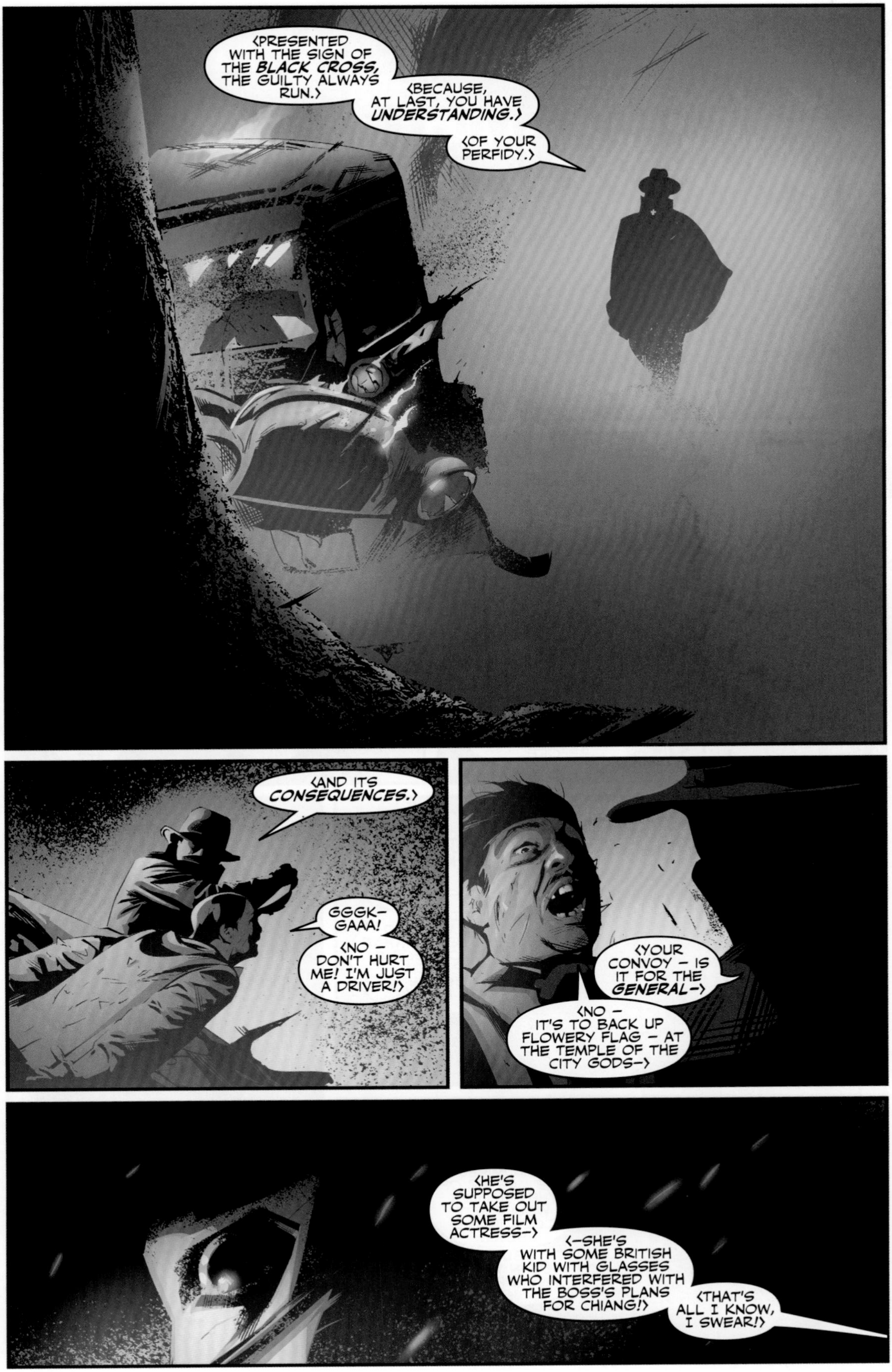

<PRESENTED WITH THE SIGN OF THE *BLACK CROSS,* THE GUILTY ALWAYS RUN.>
<BECAUSE, AT LAST, YOU HAVE *UNDERSTANDING.*>
<OF YOUR PERFIDY.>
<AND ITS *CONSEQUENCES.*>
GGGK-GAAA!
<NO – DON'T HURT ME! I'M JUST A DRIVER!>
<YOUR CONVOY – IS IT FOR THE *GENERAL*–>
<NO – IT'S TO BACK UP FLOWERY FLAG – AT THE TEMPLE OF THE CITY GODS–>
<HE'S SUPPOSED TO TAKE OUT SOME FILM ACTRESS–>
<–SHE'S WITH SOME BRITISH KID WITH GLASSES WHO INTERFERED WITH THE BOSS'S PLANS FOR CHIANG!>
<THAT'S ALL I KNOW, I SWEAR!>

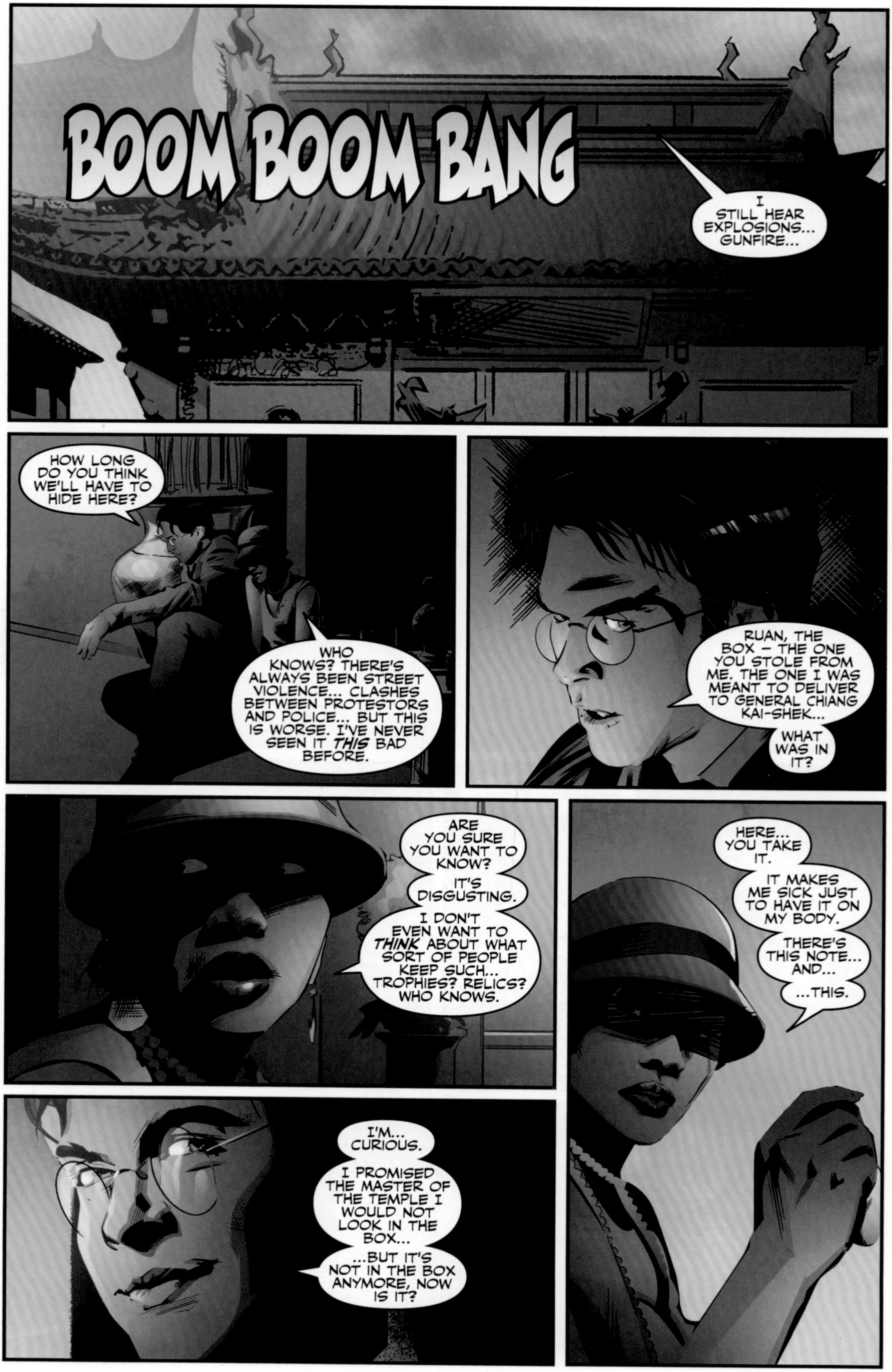

BOOM BOOM BANG
I STILL HEAR EXPLOSIONS... GUNFIRE...
HOW LONG DO YOU THINK WE'LL HAVE TO HIDE HERE?
WHO KNOWS? THERE'S ALWAYS BEEN STREET VIOLENCE... CLASHES BETWEEN PROTESTORS AND POLICE... BUT THIS IS WORSE. I'VE NEVER SEEN IT *THIS* BAD BEFORE.
RUAN, THE BOX – THE ONE YOU STOLE FROM ME. THE ONE I WAS MEANT TO DELIVER TO GENERAL CHIANG KAI-SHEK...
WHAT WAS IN IT?
ARE YOU SURE YOU WANT TO KNOW?
IT'S DISGUSTING.
I DON'T EVEN WANT TO *THINK* ABOUT WHAT SORT OF PEOPLE KEEP SUCH... TROPHIES? RELICS? WHO KNOWS.
HERE... YOU TAKE IT.
IT MAKES ME SICK JUST TO HAVE IT ON MY BODY.
THERE'S THIS NOTE... AND...
...THIS.
I'M... CURIOUS.
I PROMISED THE MASTER OF THE TEMPLE I WOULD NOT LOOK IN THE BOX...
...BUT IT'S NOT IN THE BOX ANYMORE, NOW IS IT?

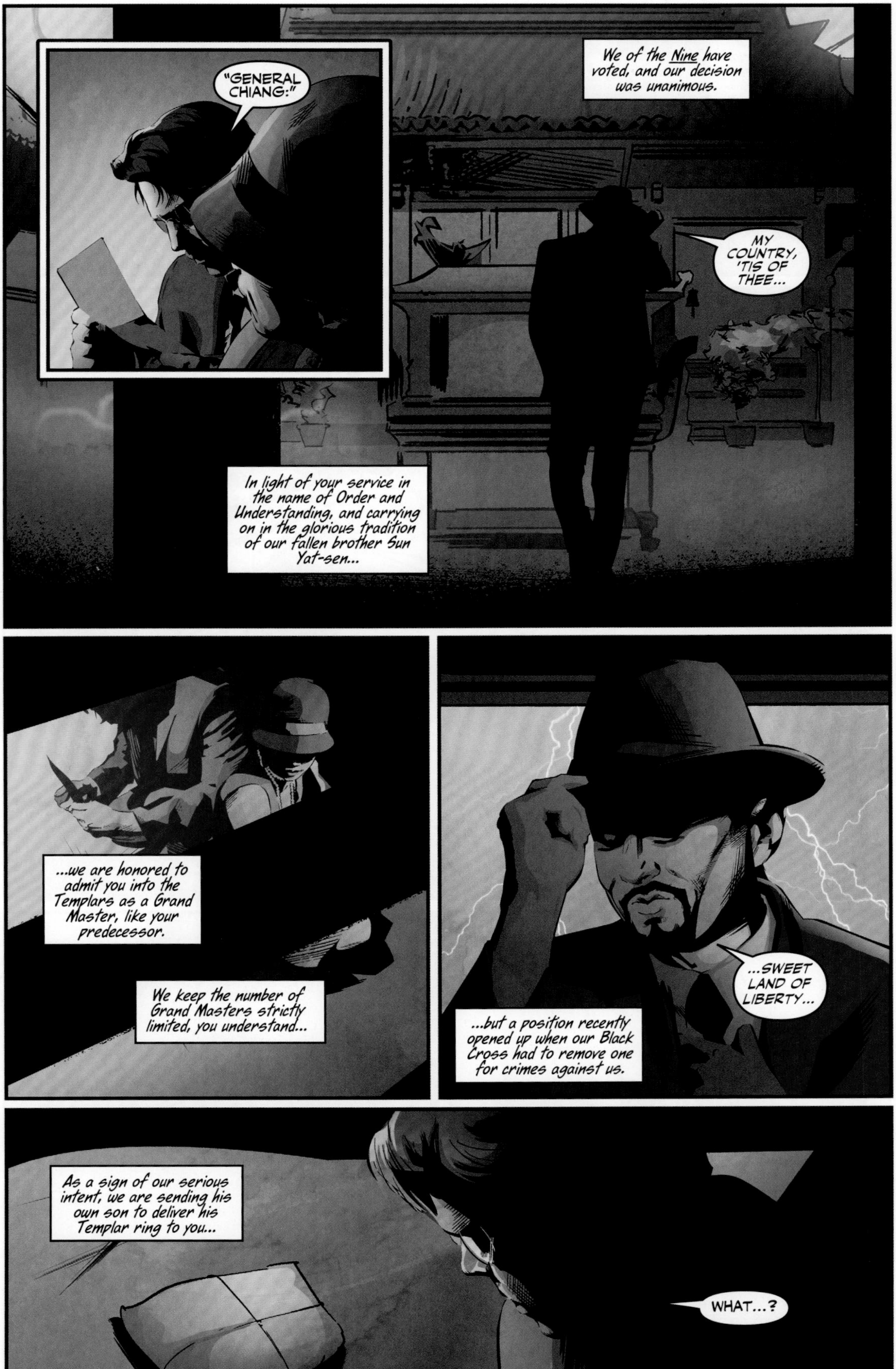
"GENERAL CHIANG:"
We of the Nine have voted, and our decision was unanimous.
MY COUNTRY, 'TIS OF THEE...
In light of your service in the name of Order and Understanding, and carrying on in the glorious tradition of our fallen brother Sun Yat-sen...
...we are honored to admit you into the Templars as a Grand Master, like your predecessor.
We keep the number of Grand Masters strictly limited, you understand...
...SWEET LAND OF LIBERTY...
...but a position recently opened up when our Black Cross had to remove one for crimes against us.
As a sign of our serious intent, we are sending his own son to deliver his Templar ring to you...
WHAT...?

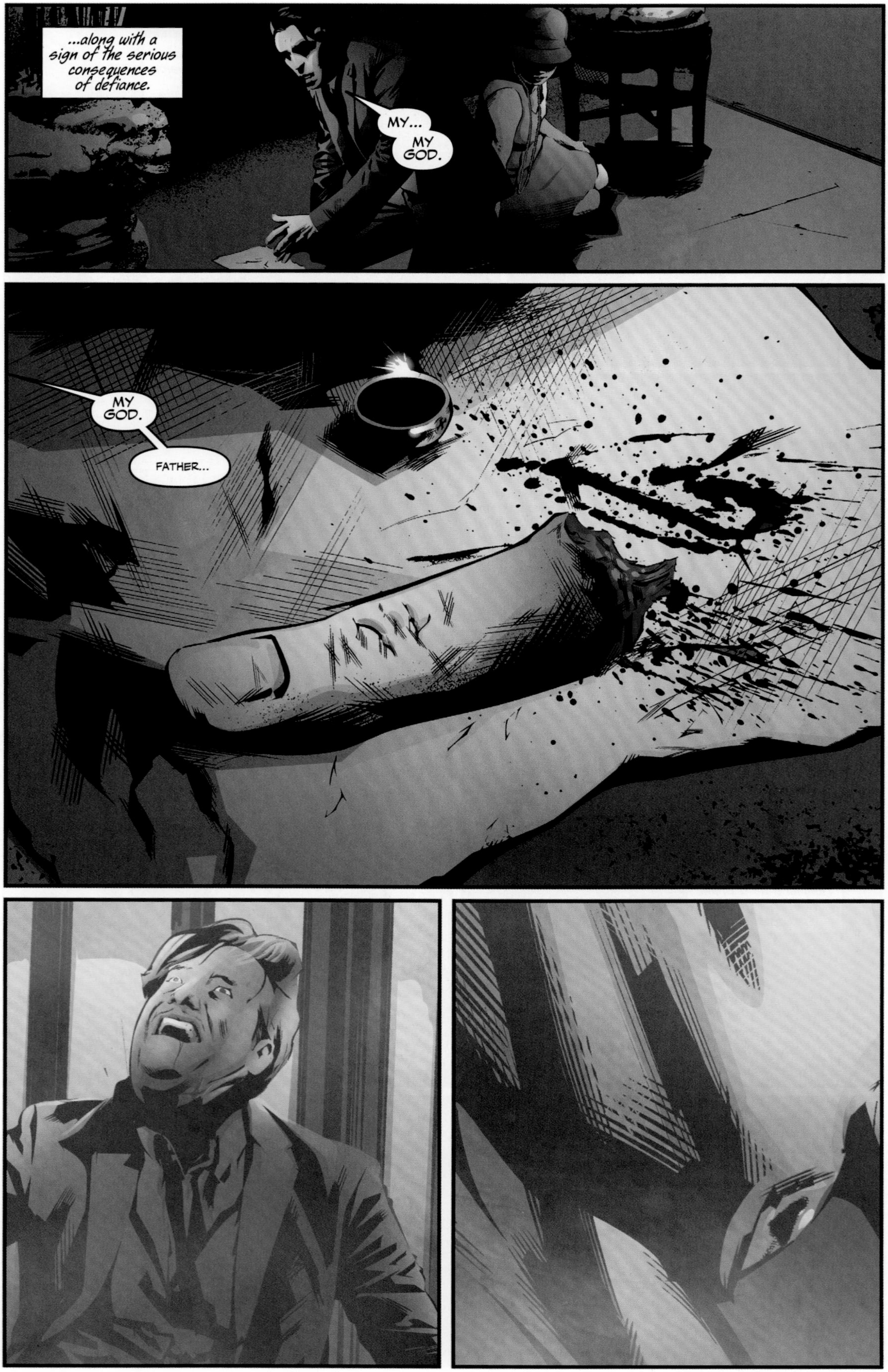
...along with a sign of the serious consequences of defiance.
MY... MY GOD.
MY GOD.
FATHER...

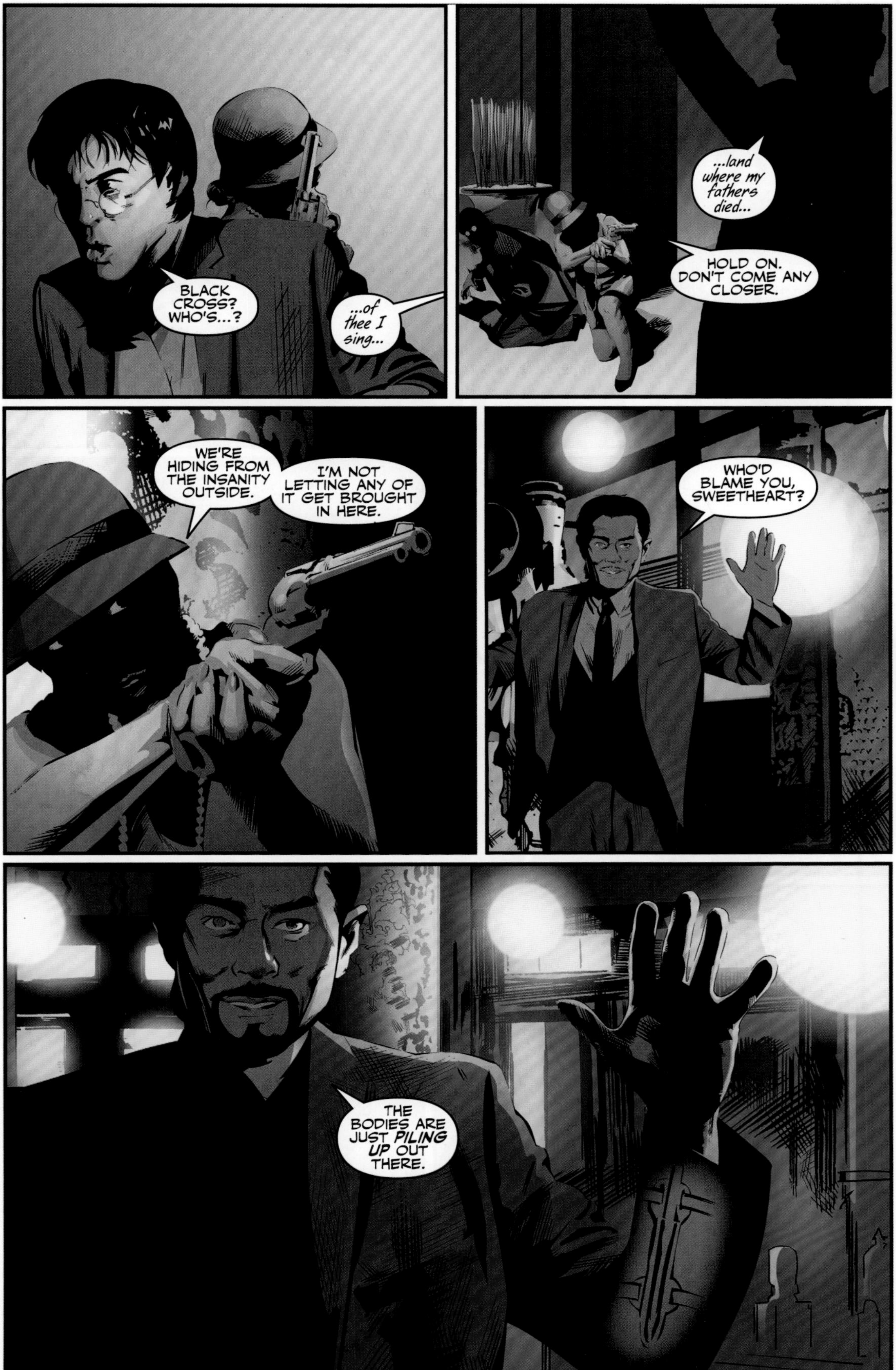

BLACK CROSS? WHO'S...?
...of thee I sing...
...land where my fathers died...
HOLD ON. DON'T COME ANY CLOSER.
WE'RE HIDING FROM THE INSANITY OUTSIDE.
I'M NOT LETTING ANY OF IT GET BROUGHT IN HERE.
WHO'D BLAME YOU, SWEETHEART?
THE BODIES ARE JUST *PILING UP* OUT THERE.

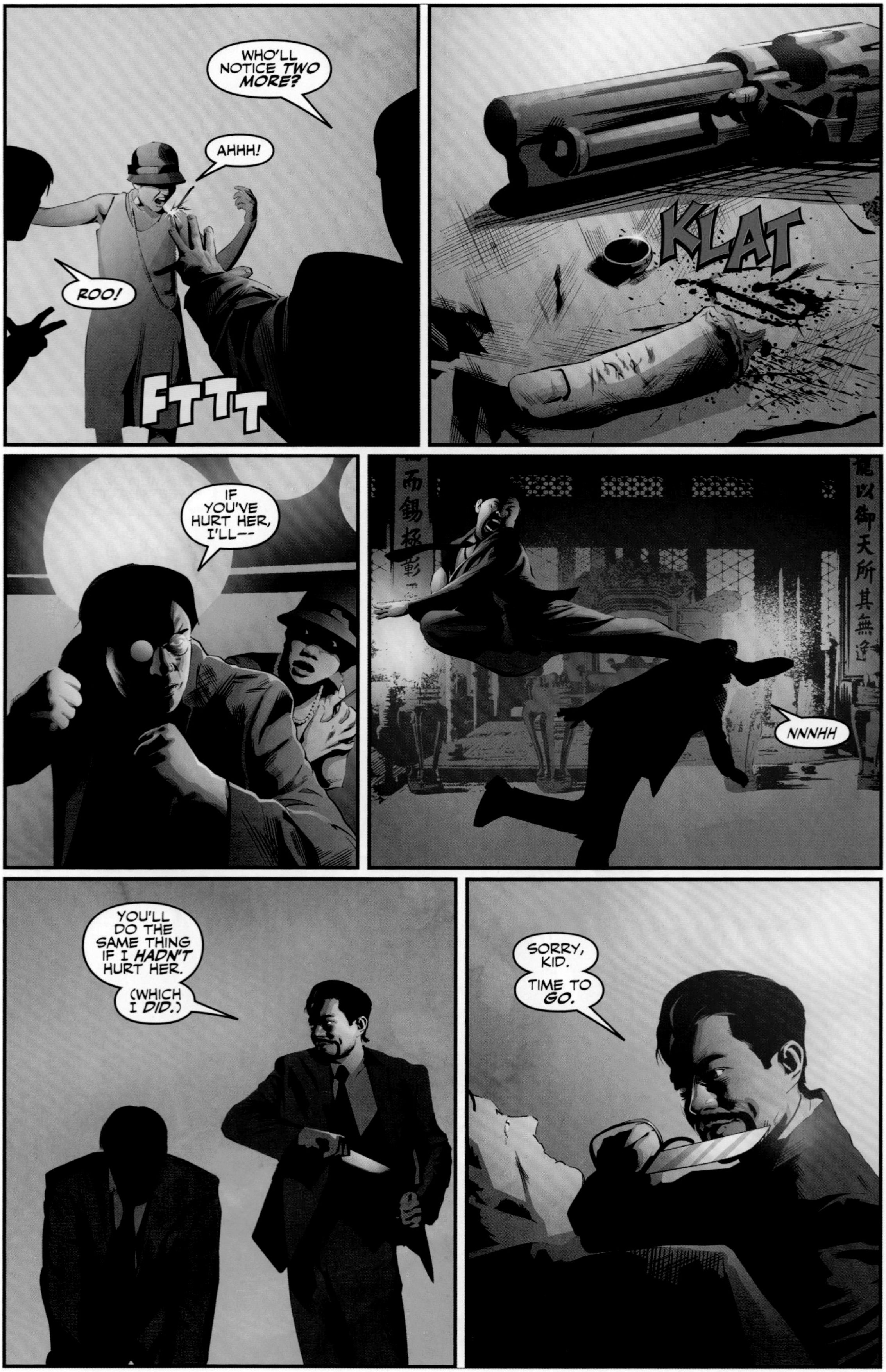
WHO'LL NOTICE *TWO MORE?*
AHHH!
ROO!
FTTT
KLAT
IF YOU'VE HURT HER, I'LL--
NNNHH
YOU'LL DO THE SAME THING IF I *HADN'T* HURT HER.
(WHICH I *DID.*)
SORRY, KID.
TIME TO *GO.*

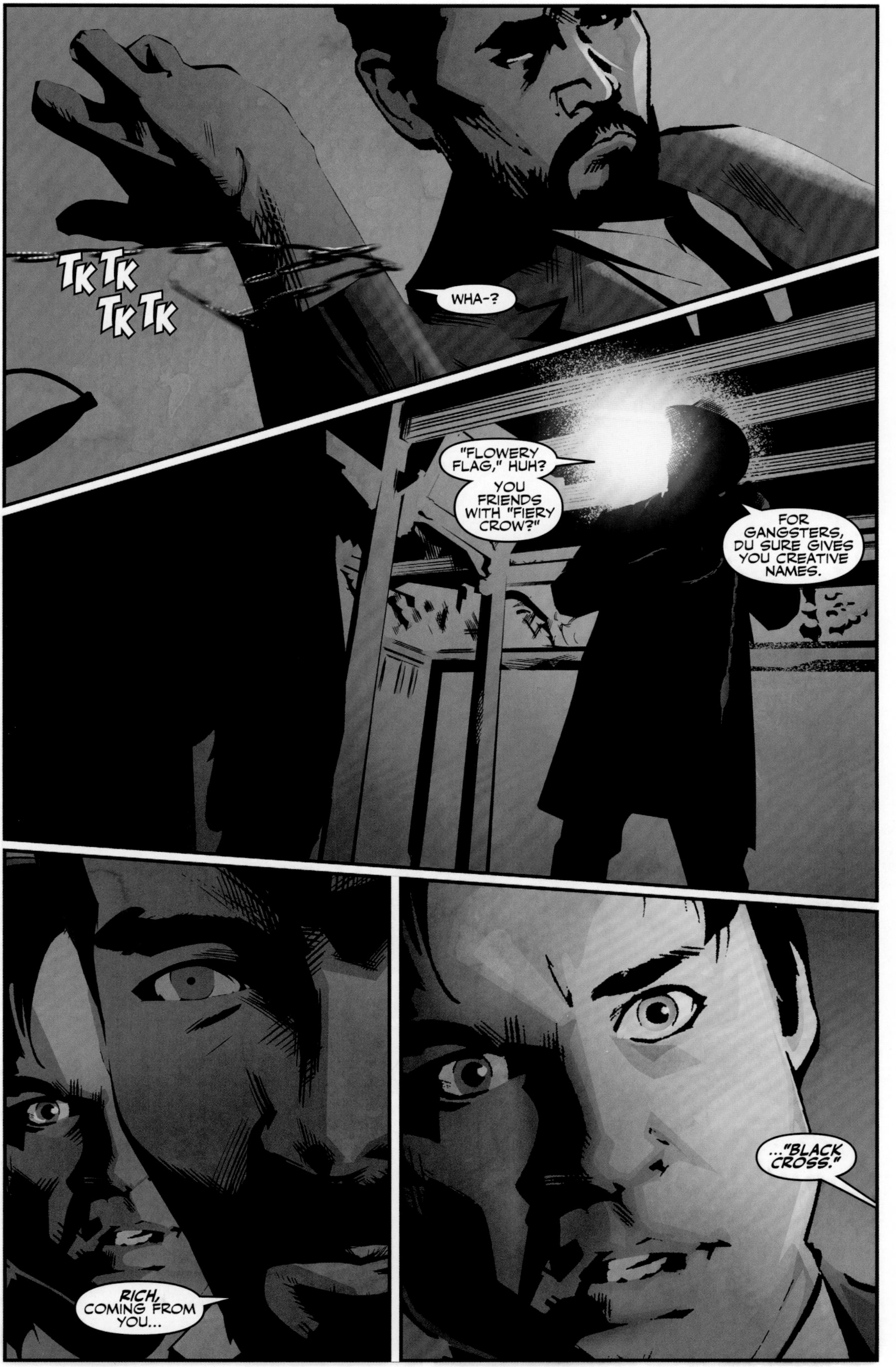
TK TK
TK TK
WHA-?
"FLOWERY FLAG," HUH?
YOU FRIENDS WITH "FIERY CROW?"
FOR GANGSTERS, DU SURE GIVES YOU CREATIVE NAMES.
RICH, COMING FROM YOU...
..."BLACK CROSS."

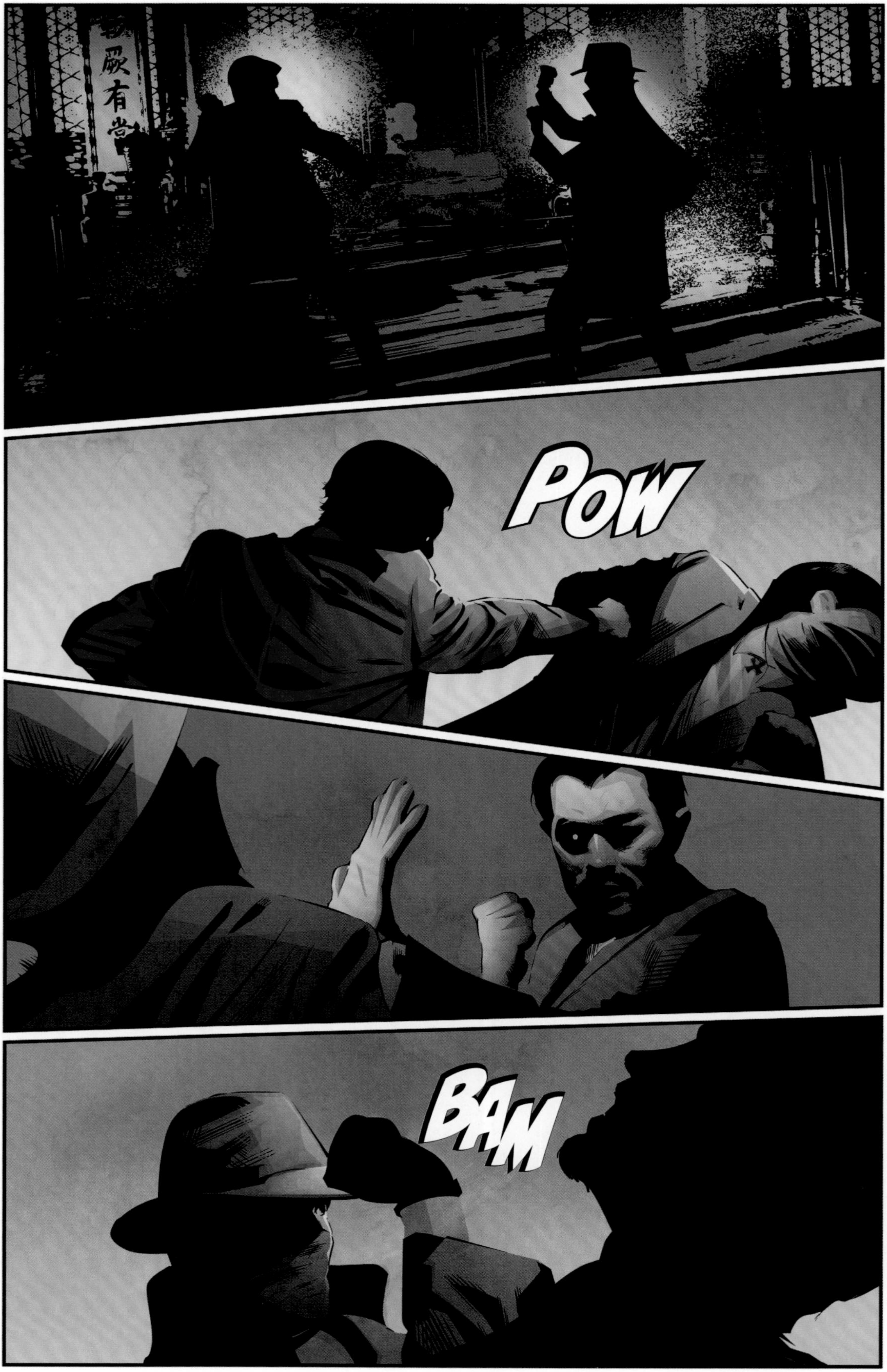
POW
BAM

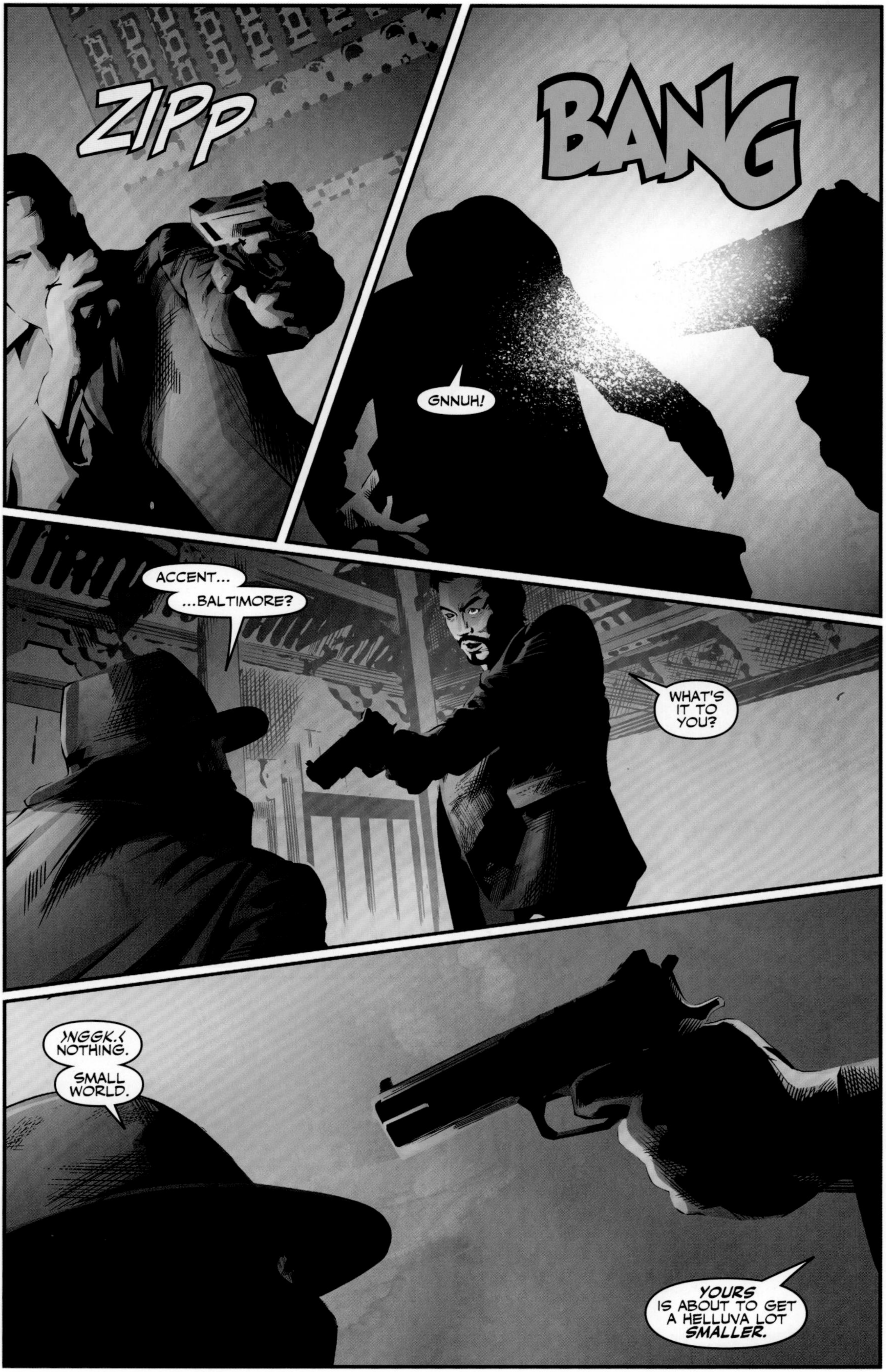
ZIPP
BANG
GNNUH!
ACCENT...
...BALTIMORE?
WHAT'S IT TO YOU?
›NGGK.‹ NOTHING.
SMALL WORLD.
YOURS IS ABOUT TO GET A HELLUVA LOT SMALLER.

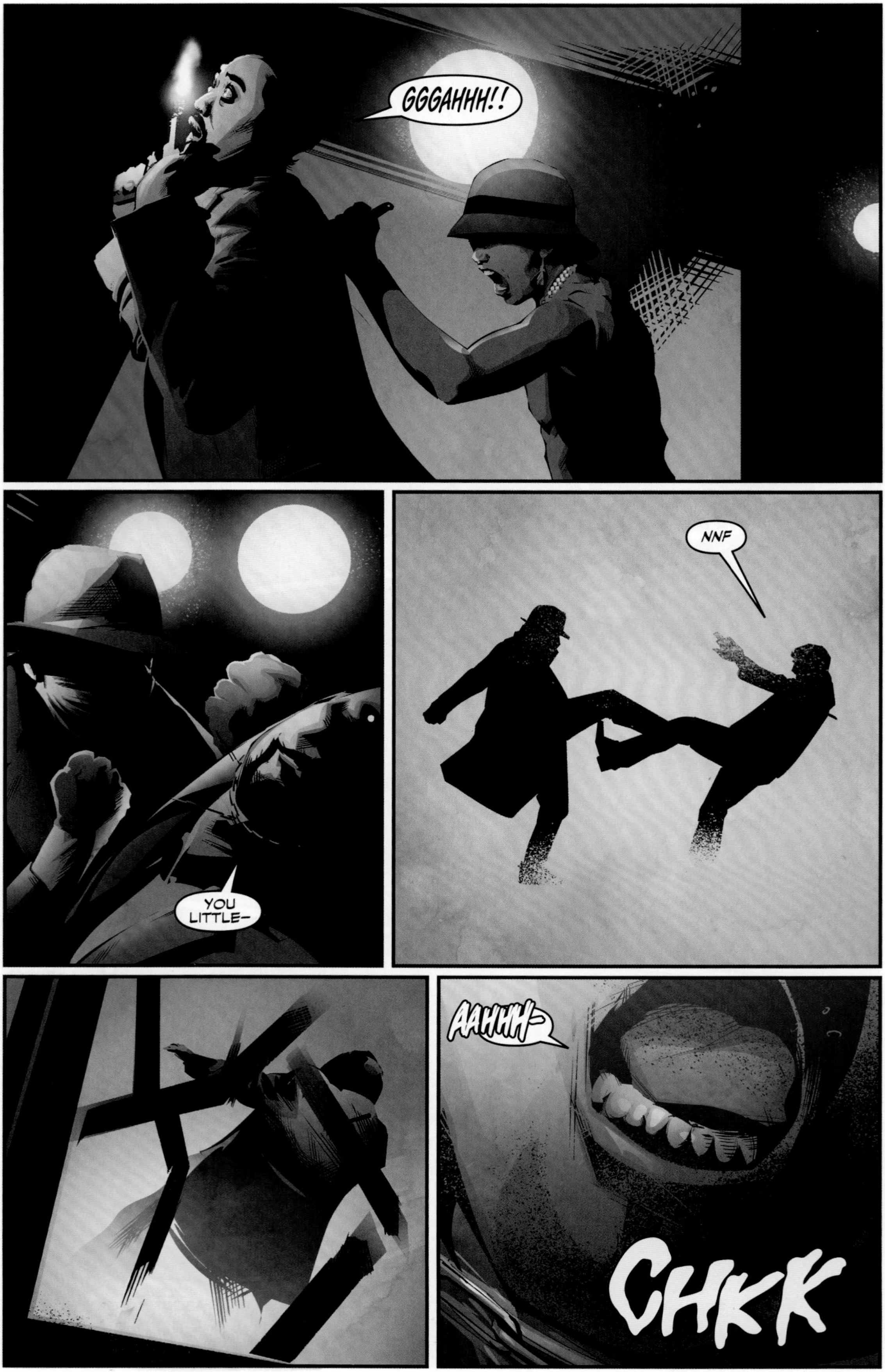
GGGAHHH!!
YOU LITTLE-
NNF
AAHHH-
CHKK

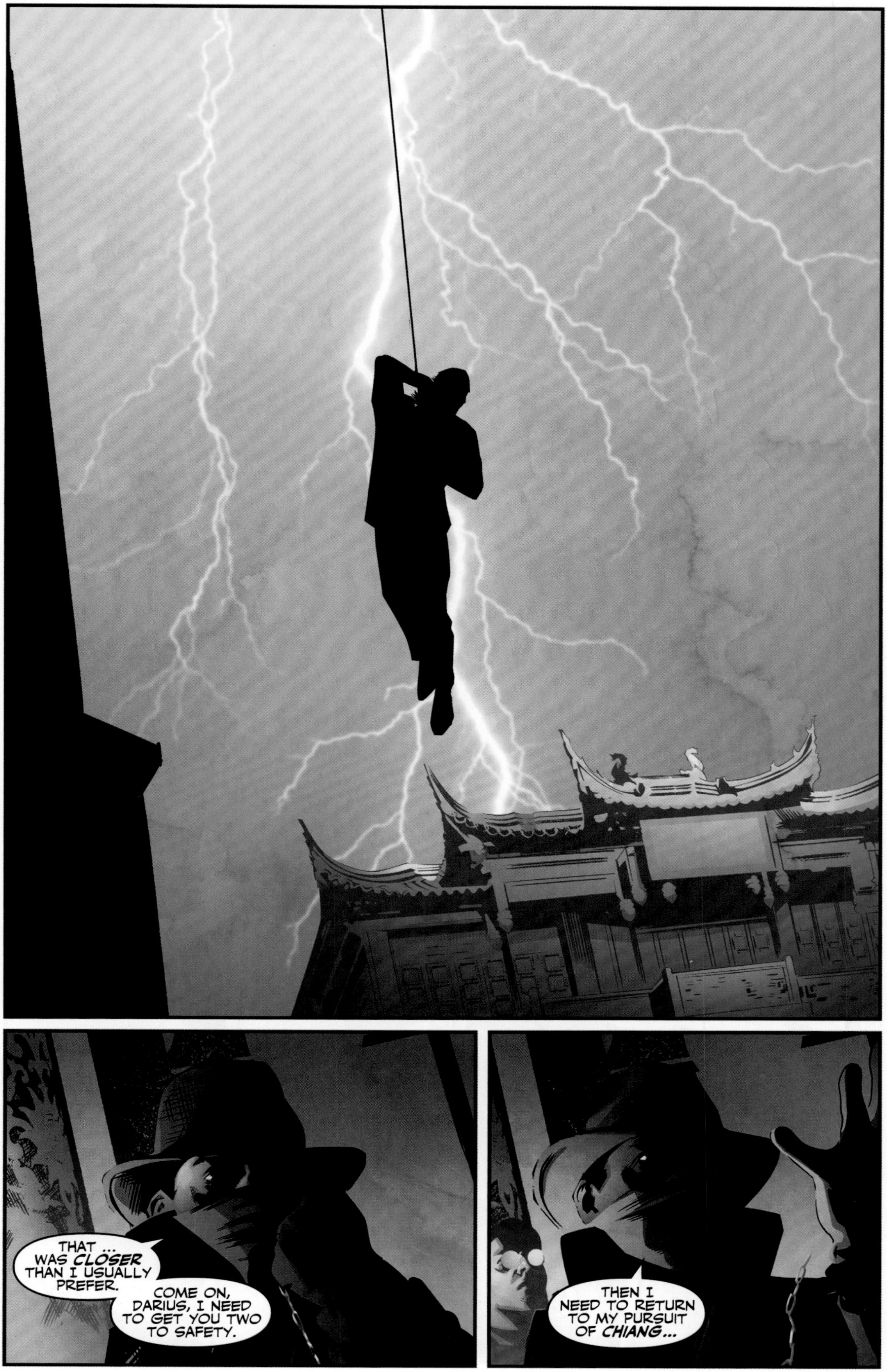
THAT ... WAS *CLOSER* THAN I USUALLY PREFER.
COME ON, DARIUS, I NEED TO GET YOU TWO TO SAFETY.
THEN I NEED TO RETURN TO MY PURSUIT OF *CHIANG*...

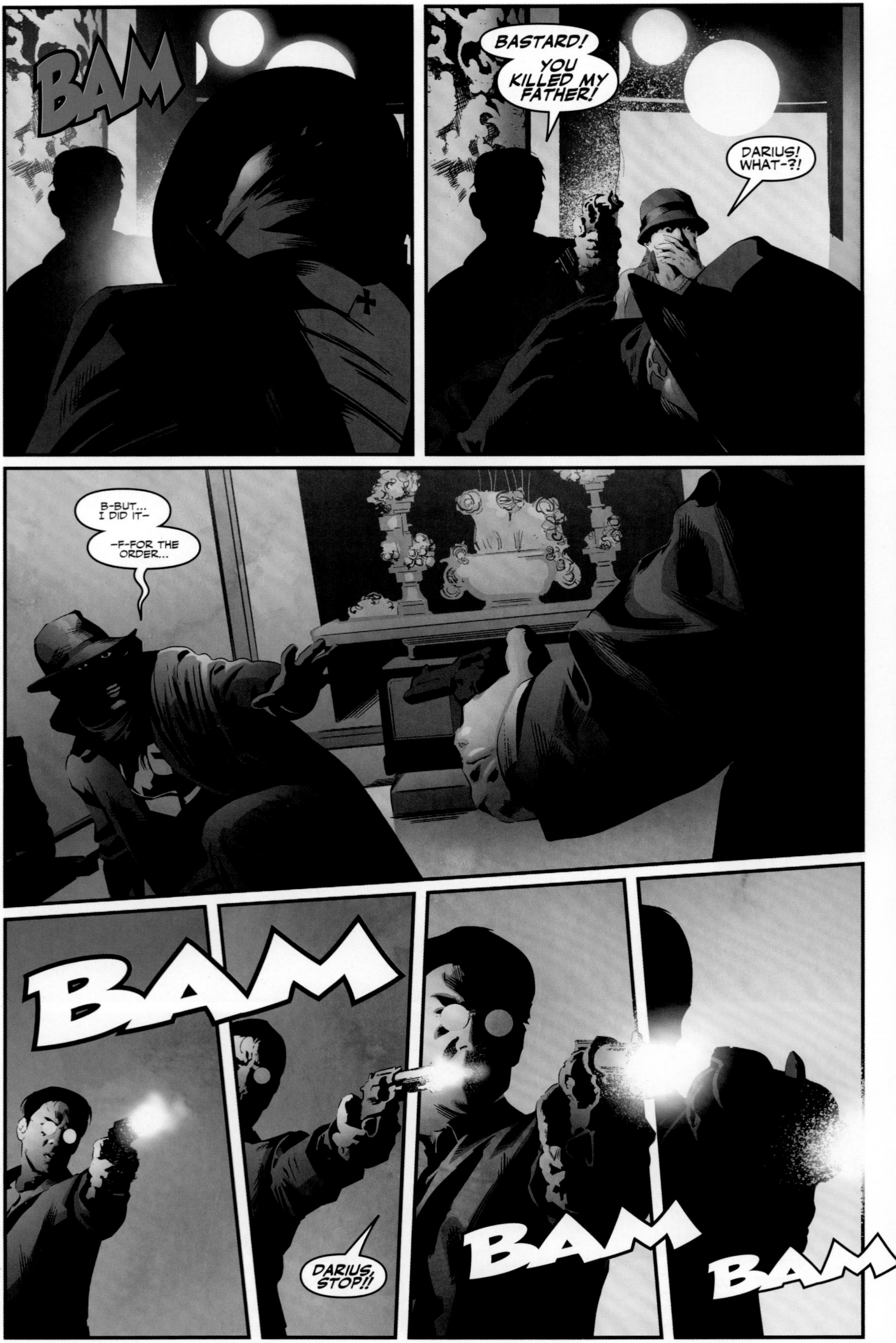
BAM
BASTARD! YOU KILLED MY FATHER!
DARIUS! WHAT-?!
B-BUT... I DID IT-
-F-FOR THE ORDER...
BAM
DARIUS, STOP!!
BAM
BAM

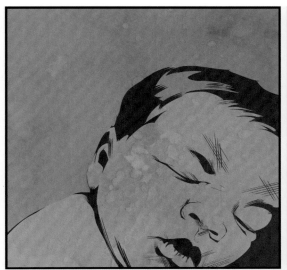

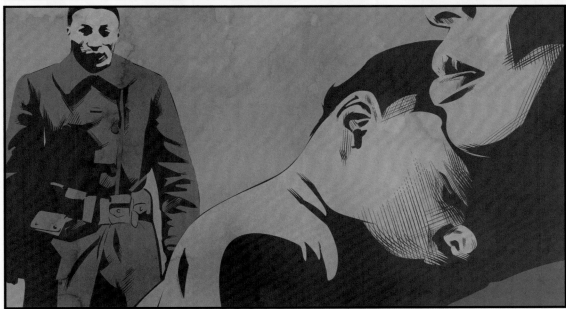

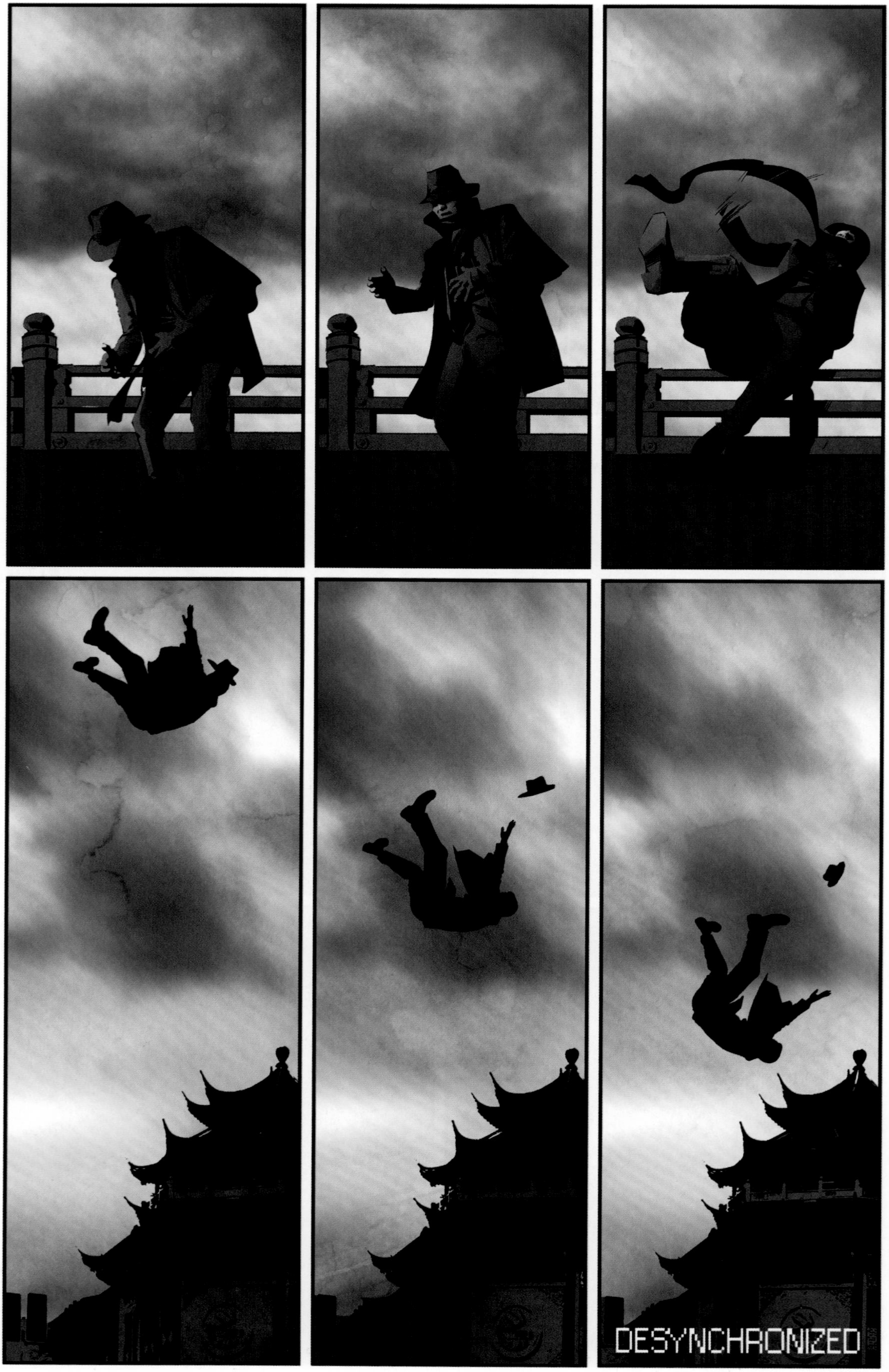
DESYNCHRONIZED

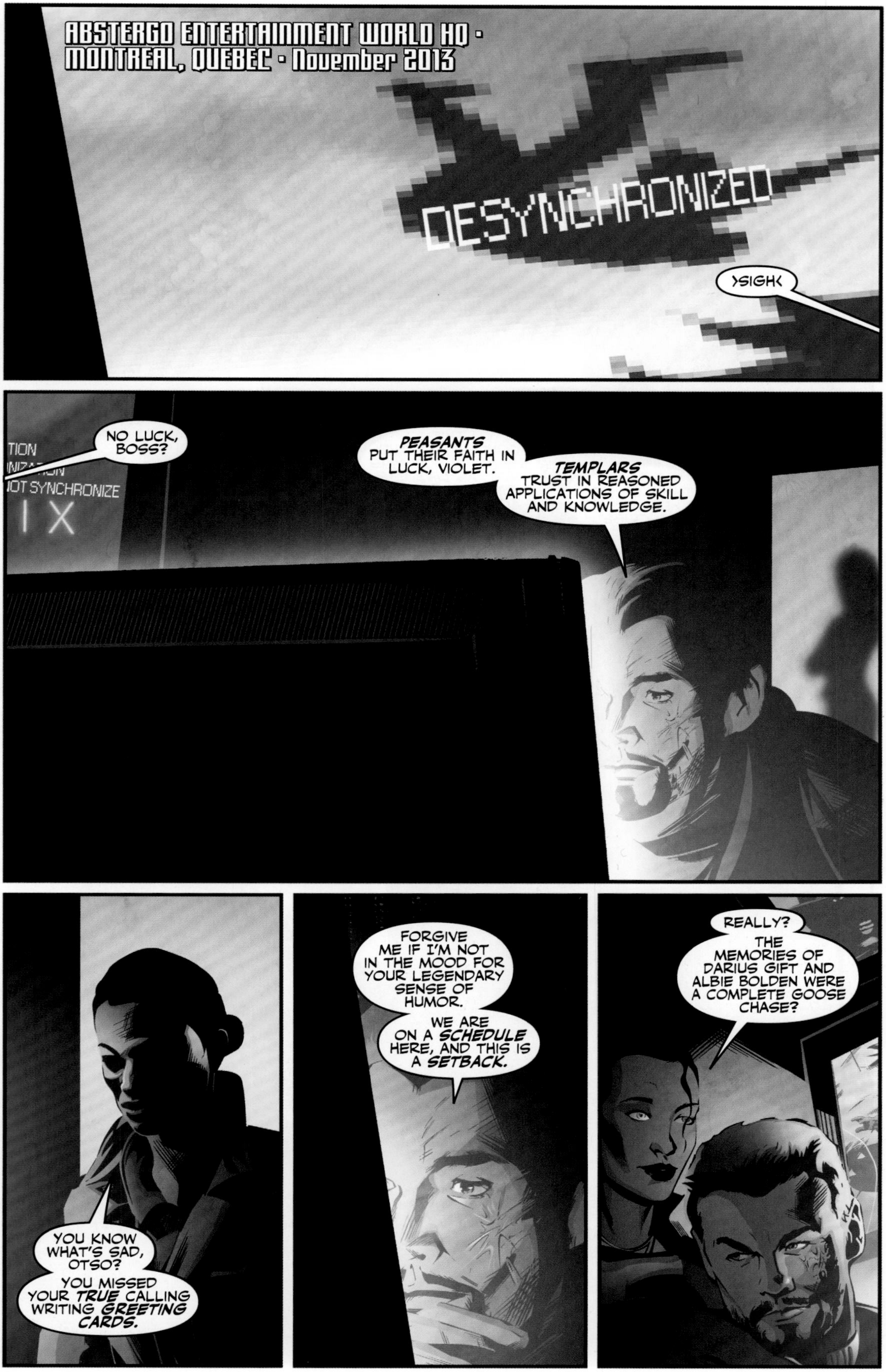
ABSTERGO ENTERTAINMENT WORLD HQ · MONTREAL, QUEBEC · November 2013
DESYNCHRONIZED
>SIGH<
NO LUCK, BOSS?
PEASANTS PUT THEIR FAITH IN LUCK, VIOLET.
TEMPLARS TRUST IN REASONED APPLICATIONS OF SKILL AND KNOWLEDGE.
YOU KNOW WHAT'S SAD, OTSO?
YOU MISSED YOUR TRUE CALLING WRITING GREETING CARDS.
FORGIVE ME IF I'M NOT IN THE MOOD FOR YOUR LEGENDARY SENSE OF HUMOR.
WE ARE ON A SCHEDULE HERE, AND THIS IS A SETBACK.
REALLY?
THE MEMORIES OF DARIUS GIFT AND ALBIE BOLDEN WERE A COMPLETE GOOSE CHASE?

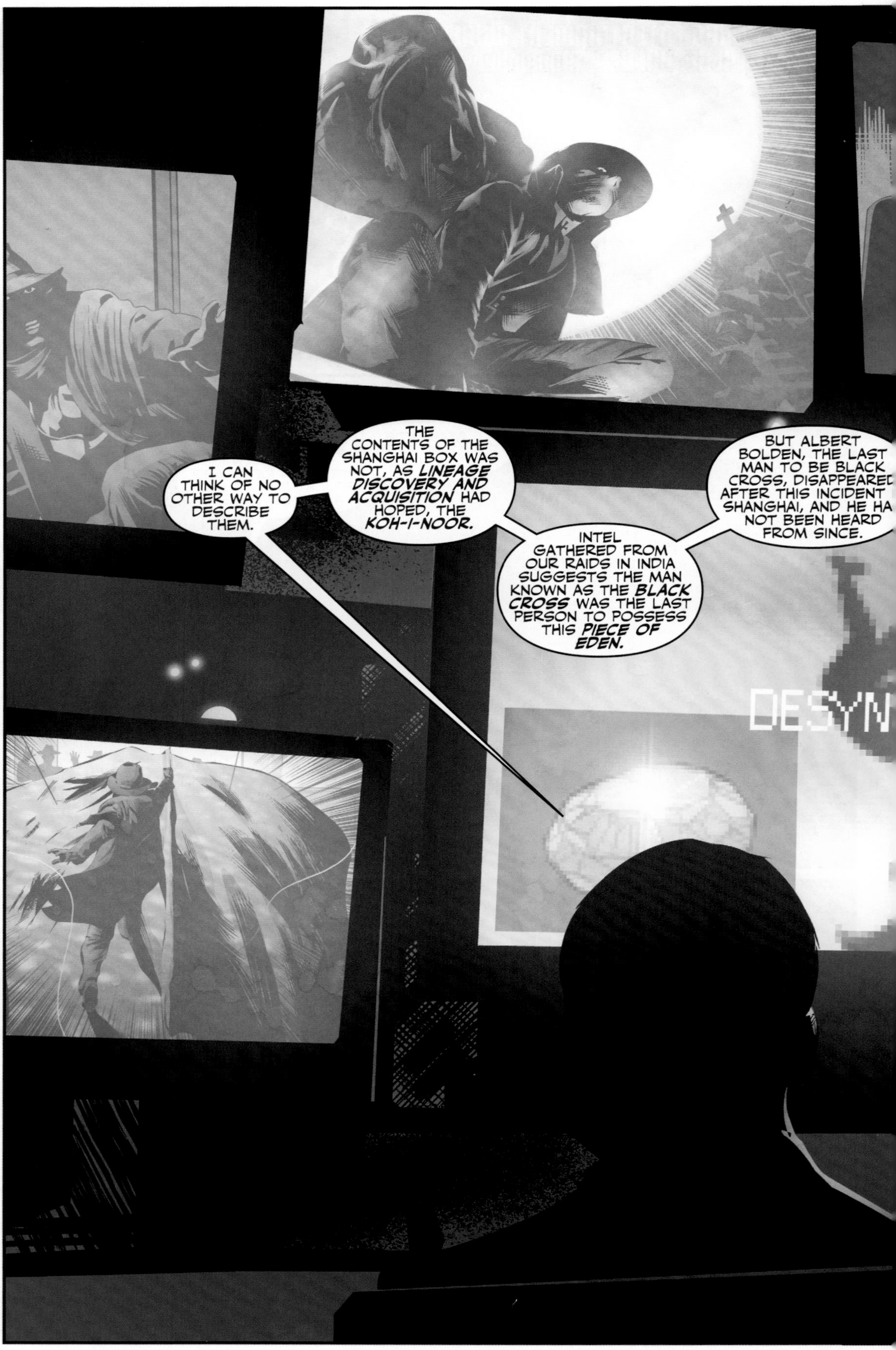
I CAN THINK OF NO OTHER WAY TO DESCRIBE THEM.
THE CONTENTS OF THE SHANGHAI BOX WAS NOT, AS *LINEAGE DISCOVERY AND ACQUISITION* HAD HOPED, THE *KOH-I-NOOR.*
INTEL GATHERED FROM OUR RAIDS IN INDIA SUGGESTS THE MAN KNOWN AS THE *BLACK CROSS* WAS THE LAST PERSON TO POSSESS THIS *PIECE OF EDEN.*
BUT ALBERT BOLDEN, THE LAST MAN TO BE BLACK CROSS, DISAPPEARED AFTER THIS INCIDENT SHANGHAI, AND HE HA NOT BEEN HEARD FROM SINCE.
DESYN

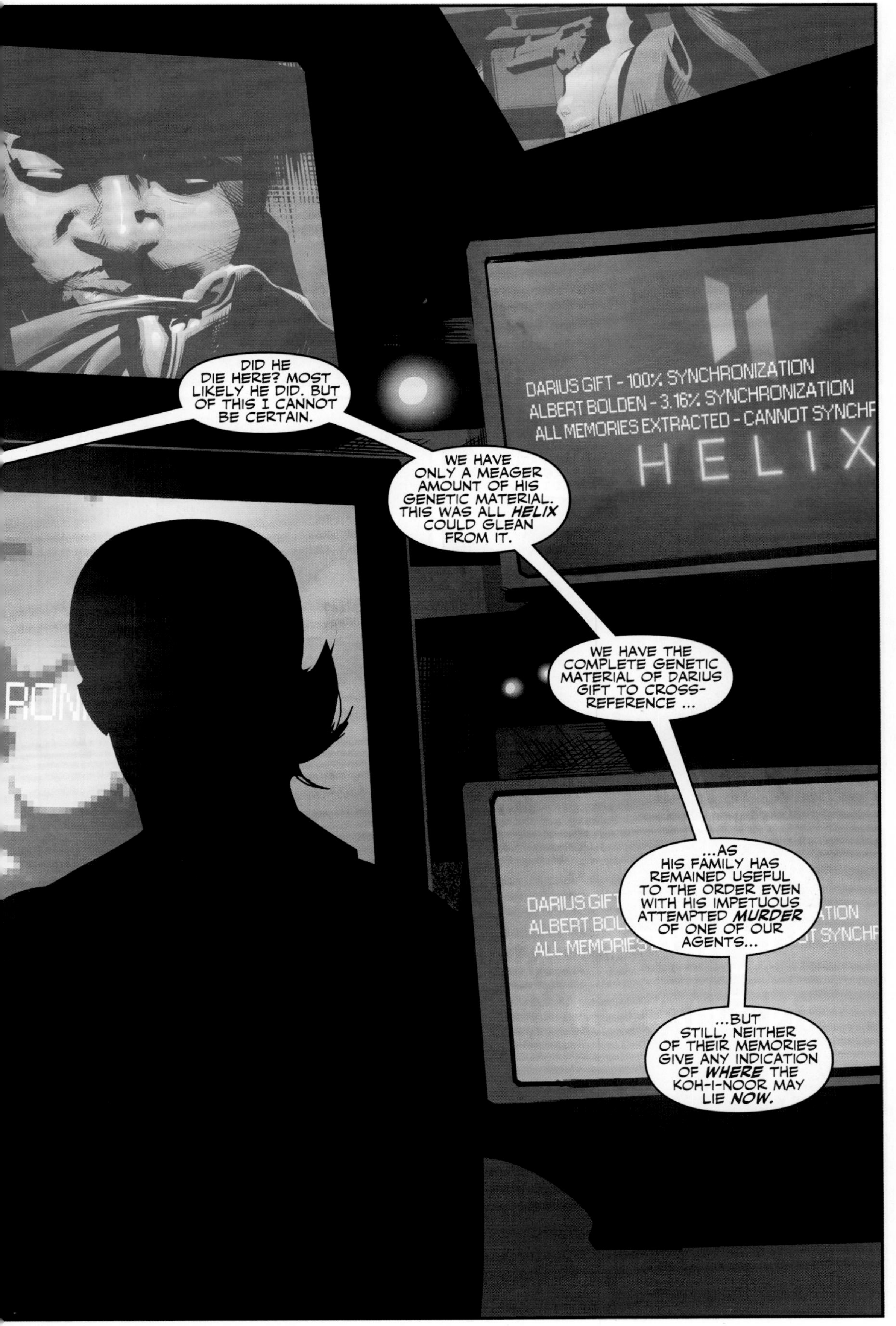
DID HE DIE HERE? MOST LIKELY HE DID. BUT OF THIS I CANNOT BE CERTAIN.
DARIUS GIFT - 100% SYNCHRONIZATION
ALBERT BOLDEN - 3.16% SYNCHRONIZATION
ALL MEMORIES EXTRACTED - CANNOT SYNCHR
HELIX
WE HAVE ONLY A MEAGER AMOUNT OF HIS GENETIC MATERIAL. THIS WAS ALL *HELIX* COULD GLEAN FROM IT.
WE HAVE THE COMPLETE GENETIC MATERIAL OF DARIUS GIFT TO CROSS-REFERENCE ...
...AS HIS FAMILY HAS REMAINED USEFUL TO THE ORDER EVEN WITH HIS IMPETUOUS ATTEMPTED *MURDER* OF ONE OF OUR AGENTS...
...BUT STILL, NEITHER OF THEIR MEMORIES GIVE ANY INDICATION OF *WHERE* THE KOH-I-NOOR MAY LIE *NOW.*

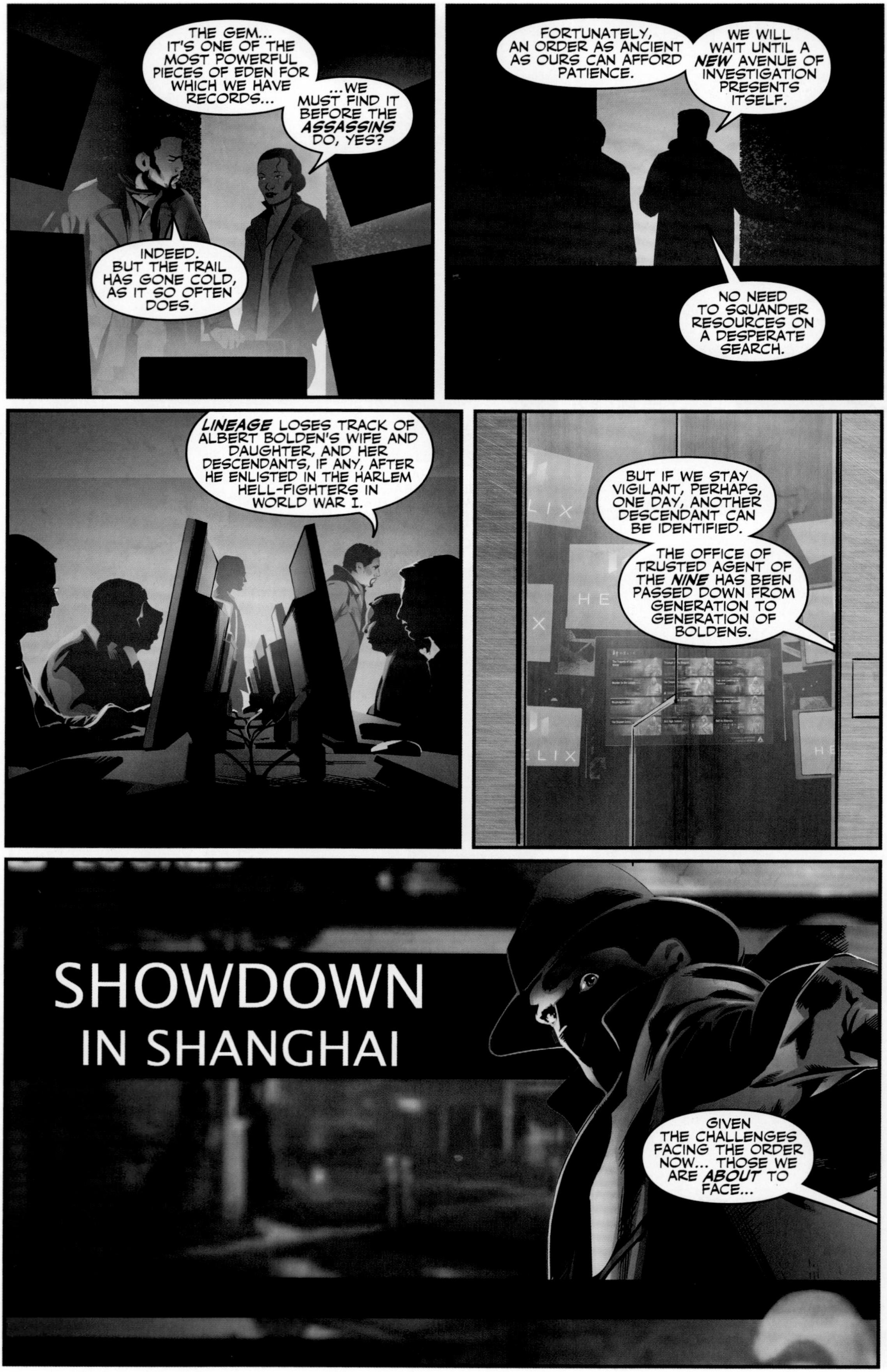
THE GEM... IT'S ONE OF THE MOST POWERFUL PIECES OF EDEN FOR WHICH WE HAVE RECORDS...
...WE MUST FIND IT BEFORE THE ASSASSINS DO, YES?
INDEED. BUT THE TRAIL HAS GONE COLD, AS IT SO OFTEN DOES.
FORTUNATELY, AN ORDER AS ANCIENT AS OURS CAN AFFORD PATIENCE.
WE WILL WAIT UNTIL A NEW AVENUE OF INVESTIGATION PRESENTS ITSELF.
NO NEED TO SQUANDER RESOURCES ON A DESPERATE SEARCH.
LINEAGE LOSES TRACK OF ALBERT BOLDEN'S WIFE AND DAUGHTER, AND HER DESCENDANTS, IF ANY, AFTER HE ENLISTED IN THE HARLEM HELL-FIGHTERS IN WORLD WAR I.
BUT IF WE STAY VIGILANT, PERHAPS, ONE DAY, ANOTHER DESCENDANT CAN BE IDENTIFIED.
THE OFFICE OF TRUSTED AGENT OF THE NINE HAS BEEN PASSED DOWN FROM GENERATION TO GENERATION OF BOLDENS.
SHOWDOWN IN SHANGHAI
GIVEN THE CHALLENGES FACING THE ORDER NOW... THOSE WE ARE ABOUT TO FACE...

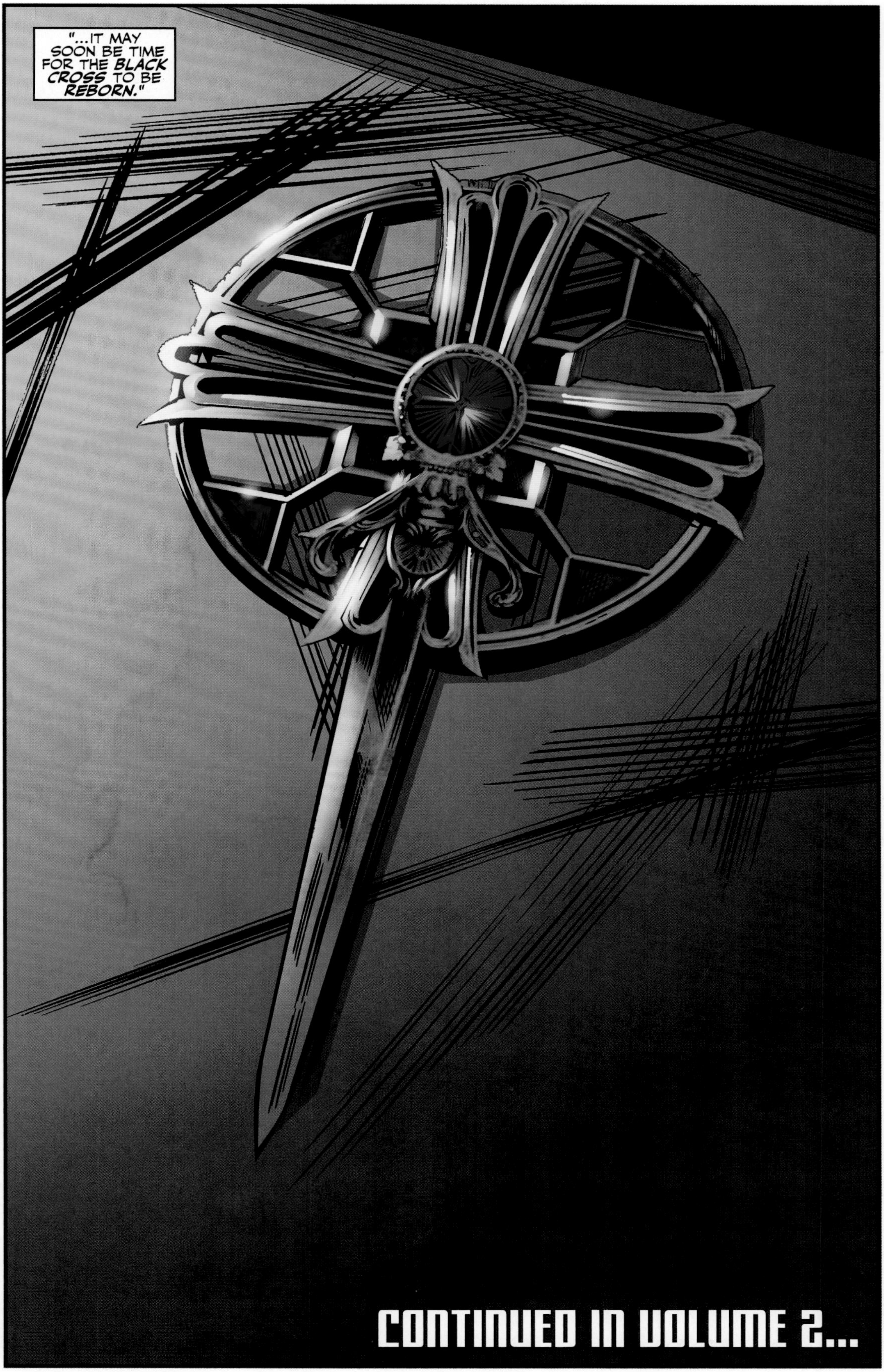
"...IT MAY SOON BE TIME FOR THE BLACK CROSS TO BE REBORN."
CONTINUED IN VOLUME 2...

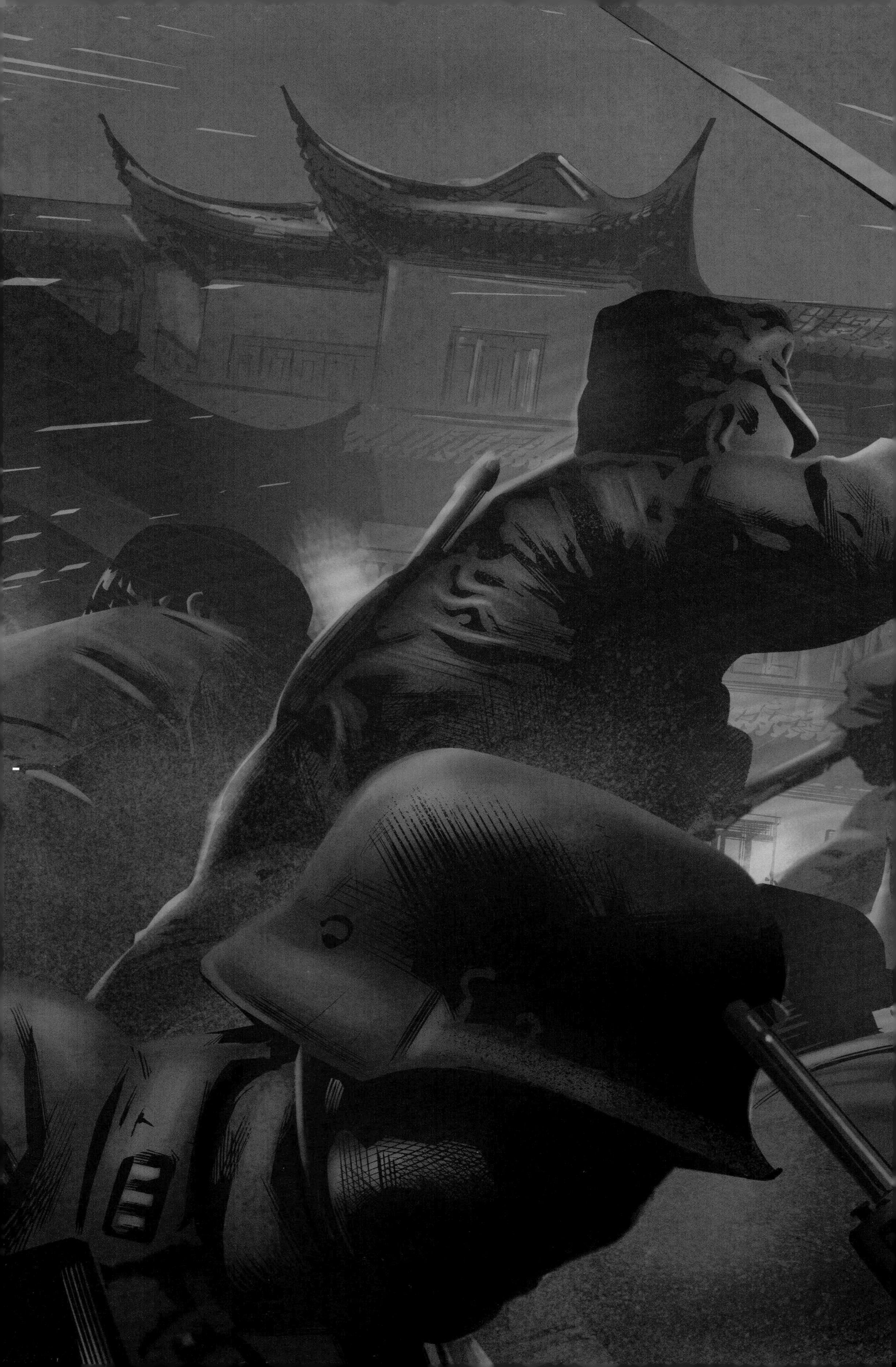

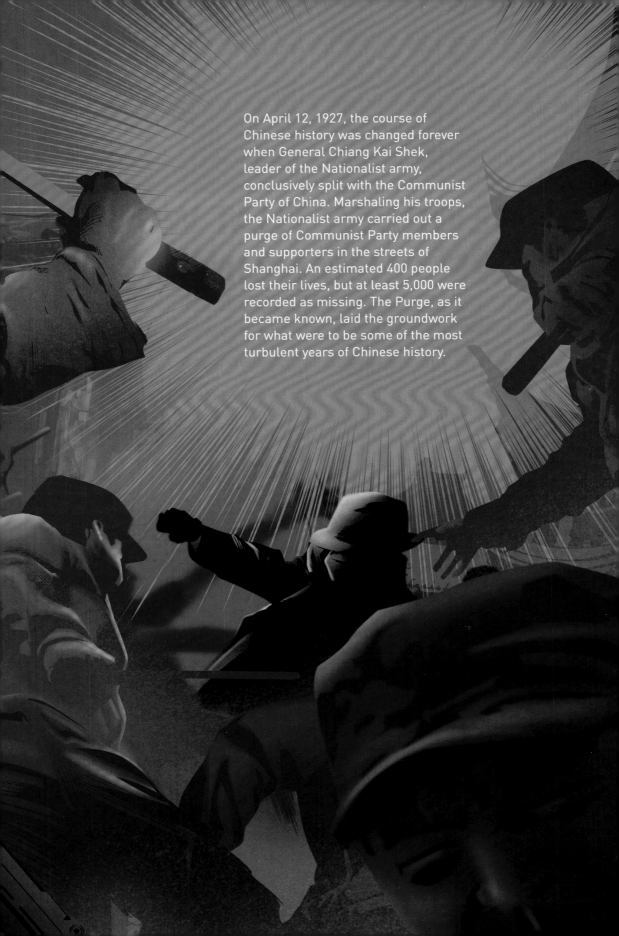

On April 12, 1927, the course of Chinese history was changed forever when General Chiang Kai Shek, leader of the Nationalist army, conclusively split with the Communist Party of China. Marshaling his troops, the Nationalist army carried out a purge of Communist Party members and supporters in the streets of Shanghai. An estimated 400 people lost their lives, but at least 5,000 were recorded as missing. The Purge, as it became known, laid the groundwork for what were to be some of the most turbulent years of Chinese history.

ASSASSIN'S CREED
TEMPLARS

THE ORDER THAT WOULD SAVE HUMANKIND...

The Order of the Knights Templar is a secret organization that has operated globally for millennia. While the story of the Order's origin has been lost to the sands of time, it is believed to have taken an active role in the shaping of humanity since it freed itself from enslavement to the mysterious progenitor race known as The Ones Who Came Before.

The Templars have worked tirelessly towards a better future for humanity, and have been instrumental in bringing about significant change and progress in the world. However, it is this very desire for a better world, and the methods by which the Templars believe it will be attained, that puts them in direct opposition to the Assassin Brotherhood.

The Templars believe that it is though control and guidance that humankind will achieve perfection – in essence, freedom through control – whereas the Assassins believe it is though individual self-expression and open access to all knowledge that humankind will reach its full potential. These two ideologies have a similar goal; it is the method by which they intend to reach it that differs, and has caused centuries of bloodshed.

The Templars' ideology has attracted some of the greatest minds of all ages to their cause, the most remarkable and successful of which have often been men and women of science, and they have suffered greatly for their beliefs. As visionaries, the ideas they championed were usually significantly before their time, which left them vulnerable to attack and censorship. Never was this more true than during the Dark Ages in Europe, when countless brilliant minds were silenced and made to suffer for their foresight.

In the 12th century, the leading Templars were able to align themselves with the Church, and so were able to pursue their agendas free from persecution. However, their main goal, the betterment of humanity though scientific and technical knowledge, was never made public, and remained a closely guarded secret. For almost two hundred years, the Templars were able to steer a course for humankind that would bring about great advances in medicine, the military, even in basic living conditions. They were influencers, advising kings and emperors on how best to rule.

They were also under attack. Their numbers were being systematically depleted by the Assassin Brotherhood. The issue came to a head in the 13th century when the Templars were denounced as heretics, and forced to disband. This decision was taken by the last publicly recognized Grand Master of the Order of the Knights Templar, Jaques de Molay. Making the ultimate sacrifice, he was burned at the stake, letting everyone think that the Templar Order would die with him. Unbeknownst to them, however, de Molay had selected nine trusted members of the Order to go forth into the world and spread the Templars philosophy, armed with their knowledge of The Ones Who Came Before. In doing this, de Molay ensured that the Order would live on, and could continue to work towards their ultimate goal.

The Order entered what they now consider to be a dark age. Despondency and corruption were rife, with leadership coming from those who had little respect for the original altruistic philosophy. Despite this, the Templars were still at the vanguard of scientific development during this time, and loyal members worked tirelessly toward their ultimate goal. The European colonization of the New World gave the Templars the opportunity to recover and rebuild, and the chance to retaliate and turn the tables on their foe, wiping out much of the Brotherhood leadership, and destroying any Assassin influence in the region.

The Templar Order's goals have evolved over time, with the dawning of the 20th century marking a turning point for the organization.

Following decades of innovation and invention, culminating in the astounding technological and scientific advancements seen during the Industrial Revolution, the Templars recognized that continued progress at that rate could lead them to their goal faster and more successfully than they had ever dreamed. Capitalism would be the tool that would allow the leaps in development that the Templars knew were within their reach.

In the uncertain days before the Second World War, Abstergo Industries was formed. For the second time in its history, the Templars had a public face, although the true aims of the Order, and the very existence of the Order itself, remained a secret. Only a few employed by Abstergo were Templars. Through the work of its many divisions, Abstergo would provide the means by which the Templars' notion of a perfectly functioning capitalist society could be brought about. As a multinational corporation with concerns spanning all areas of modern life, Abstergo was the perfect front for the Templar Order to pursue their agenda.

While their methods and goals have evolved, at its root the Templar Order believes in the betterment of humanity through technological and scientific advancement. For centuries uncounted, the search for relics left by The Ones Who Came Before, called Pieces of Eden, has occupied the Order. Significant resources have been devoted to acquiring as many of these unique artifacts as possible, in order that the technology they possess is harnessed and can be used for the greater good of humanity. ♦

Abstergo▲

ISSUE_ONE

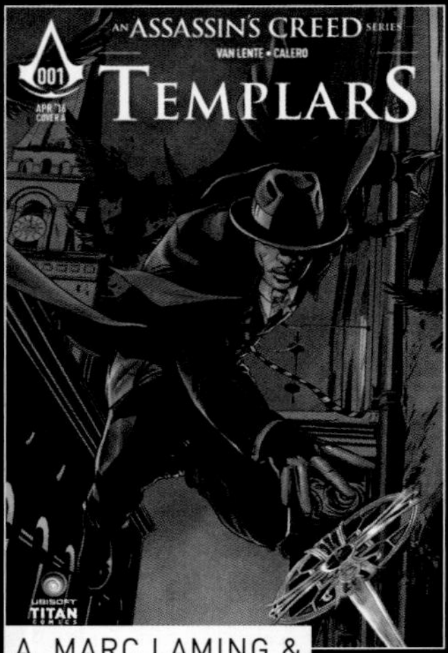
AN ASSASSIN'S CREED SERIES
VAN LENTE • CALERO
TEMPLARS
001
APR '16
COVER A
UBISOFT
TITAN COMICS

A_MARC LAMING & LARA MARGARIDA

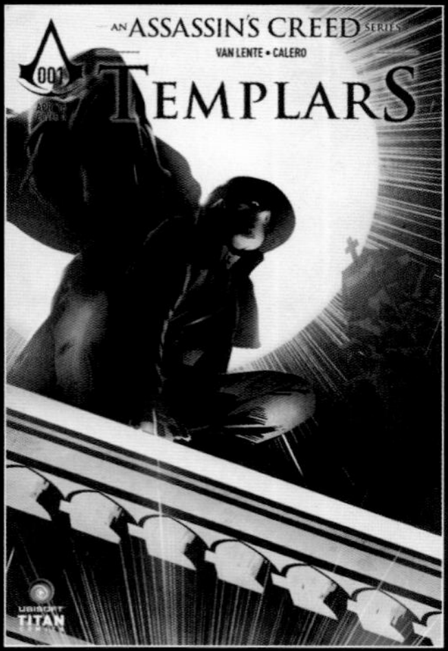
AN ASSASSIN'S CREED SERIES
VAN LENTE • CALERO
TEMPLARS
001
UBISOFT
TITAN COMICS

D_DENNIS CALERO

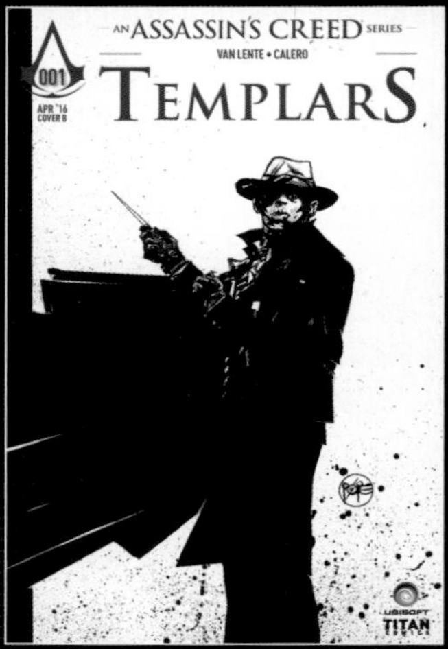
AN ASSASSIN'S CREED SERIES
VAN LENTE • CALERO
TEMPLARS
001
APR '16
COVER B
UBISOFT
TITAN COMICS

B_PAUL POPE

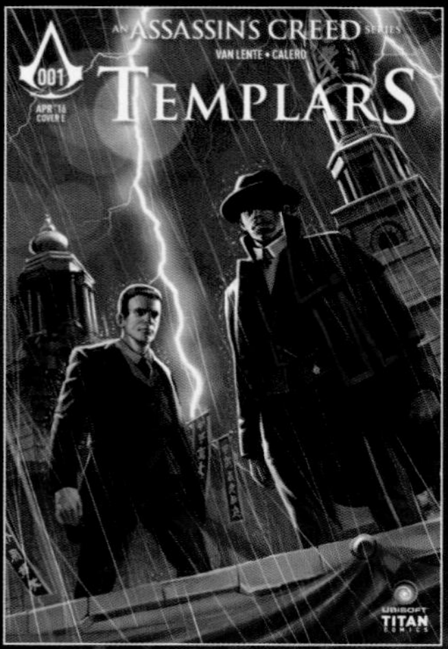
AN ASSASSIN'S CREED SERIES
VAN LENTE • CALERO
TEMPLARS
001
APR '16
COVER E
UBISOFT
TITAN COMICS

E_MARIANO LACLAUSTRA

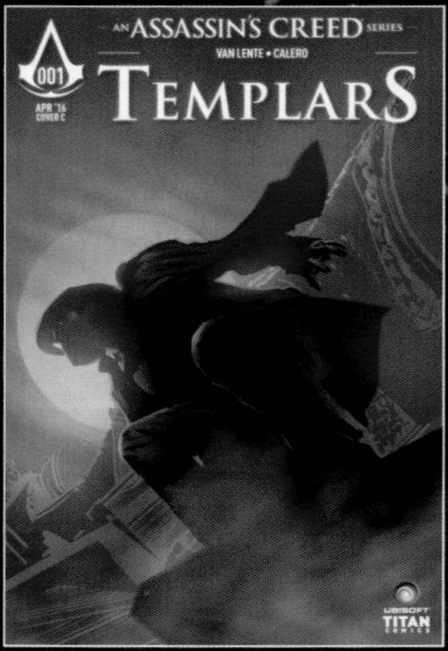
AN ASSASSIN'S CREED SERIES
VAN LENTE • CALERO
TEMPLARS
001
APR '16
COVER C
UBISOFT
TITAN COMICS

C_DENNIS CALERO

ISSUE_TWO

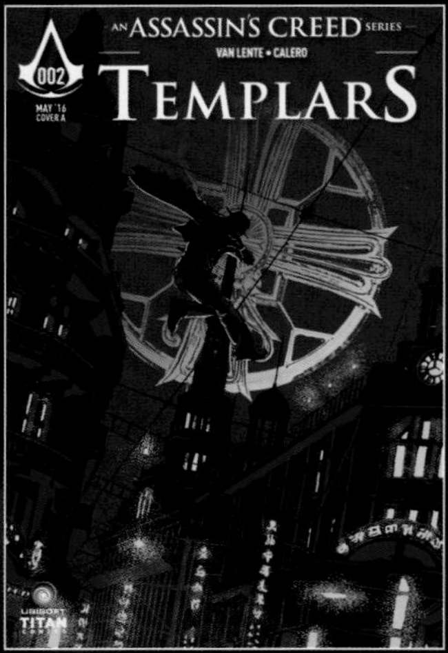
AN ASSASSIN'S CREED SERIES
VAN LENTE • CALERO
TEMPLARS
002
MAY '16
COVER A
UBISOFT
TITAN COMICS

A_CHRIS THORNLEY

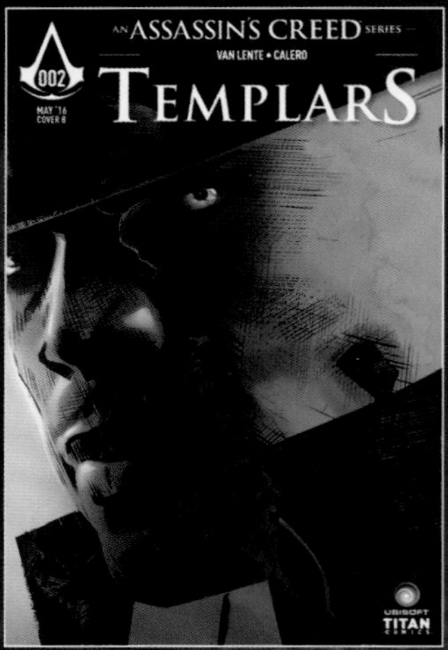
AN ASSASSIN'S CREED SERIES
VAN LENTE • CALERO
TEMPLARS
002
MAY '16
COVER B
UBISOFT
TITAN COMICS

B_DENNIS CALERO

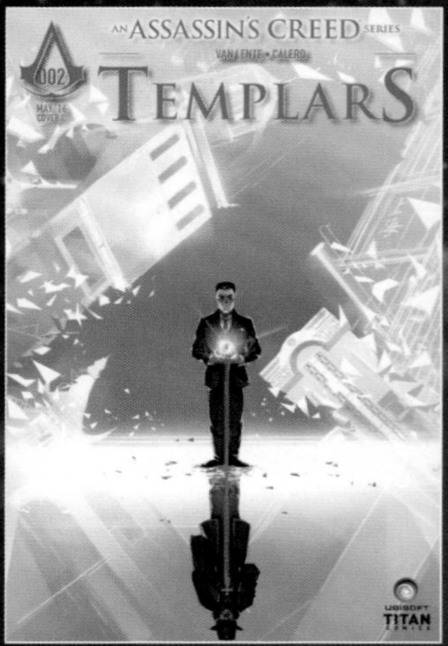
AN ASSASSIN'S CREED SERIES
VAN LENTE • CALERO
TEMPLARS
002
UBISOFT
TITAN COMICS

C_VERITY GLASS

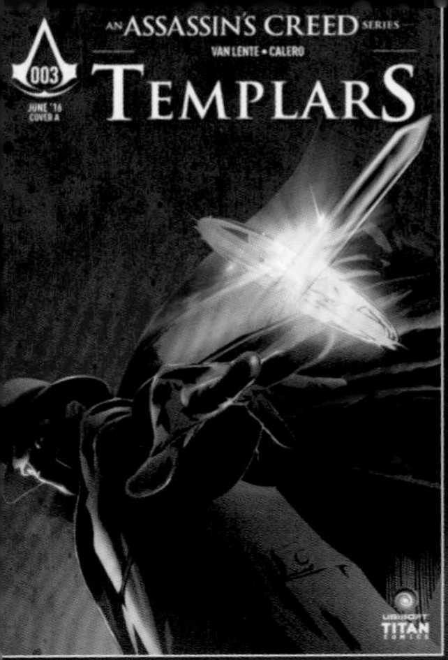
AN ASSASSIN'S CREED SERIES
VAN LENTE • CALERO
003
TEMPLARS
JUNE '16
COVER A
UBISOFT
TITAN COMICS

A_DENNIS CALERO

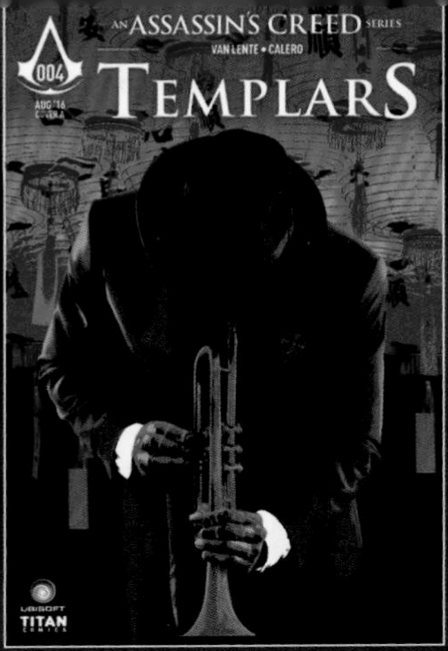
AN ASSASSIN'S CREED SERIES
VAN LENTE • CALERO
004
TEMPLARS
AUG '16
COVER A
UBISOFT
TITAN COMICS

A_MATT TAYLOR

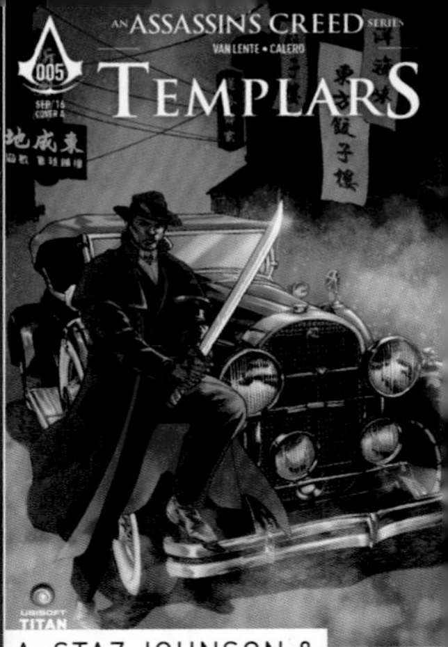
AN ASSASSIN'S CREED SERIES
VAN LENTE • CALERO
005
TEMPLARS
SEP '16
COVER A
UBISOFT
TITAN

A_STAZ JOHNSON & THIAGO RIBEIRO

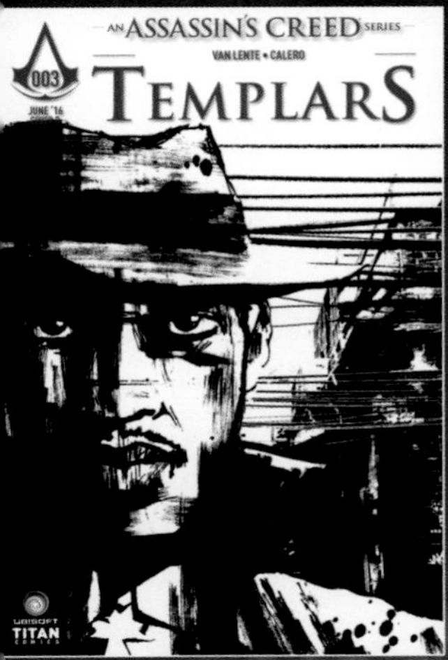
AN ASSASSIN'S CREED SERIES
VAN LENTE • CALERO
003
TEMPLARS
JUNE '16
UBISOFT
TITAN COMICS

B_JAKE

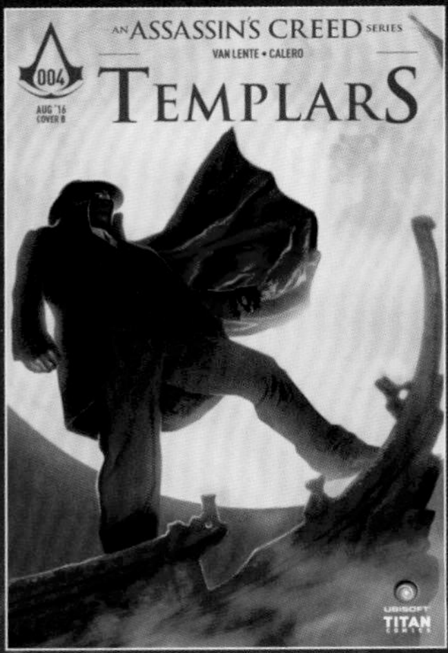
AN ASSASSIN'S CREED SERIES
VAN LENTE • CALERO
004
TEMPLARS
AUG '16
COVER B
UBISOFT
TITAN COMICS

B_DENNIS CALERO

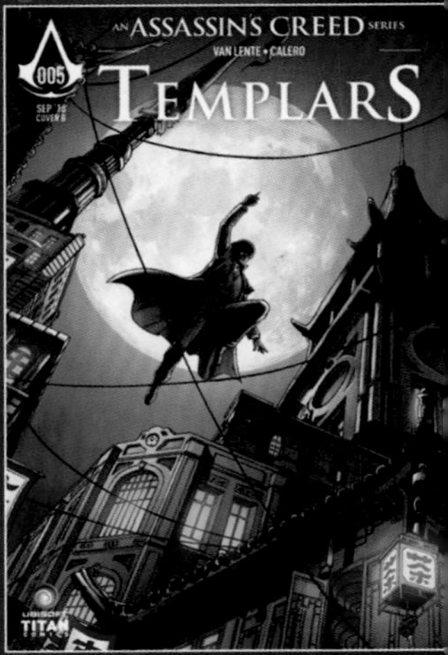
AN ASSASSIN'S CREED SERIES
VAN LENTE • CALERO
005
TEMPLARS
SEP '16
COVER B
UBISOFT
TITAN

B_MARIANO LACLAUSTRA

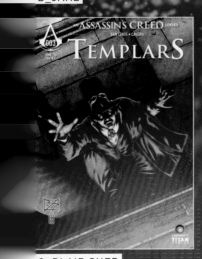

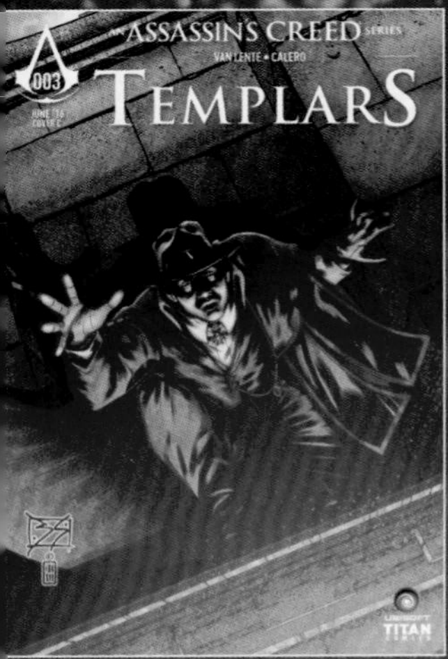
AN ASSASSIN'S CREED SERIES
VAN LENTE • CALERO
003
TEMPLARS
JUNE '16
COVER C
UBISOFT
TITAN COMICS

C_BLAIR SHED

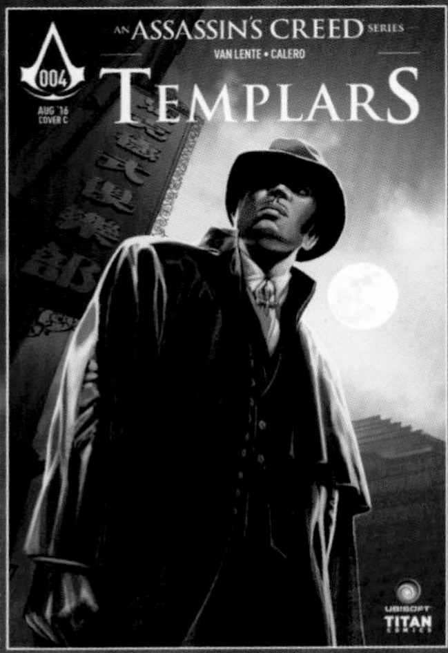
AN ASSASSIN'S CREED SERIES
VAN LENTE • CALERO
004
TEMPLARS
AUG '16
COVER C
UBISOFT
TITAN COMICS

C_ASHLEY MARIE WITTER

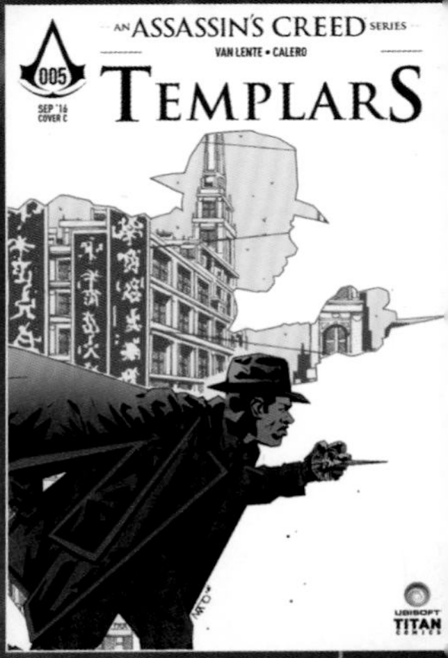
AN ASSASSIN'S CREED SERIES
VAN LENTE • CALERO
005
TEMPLARS
SEP '16
COVER C
UBISOFT
TITAN COMICS

C_ANTONIO FUSO

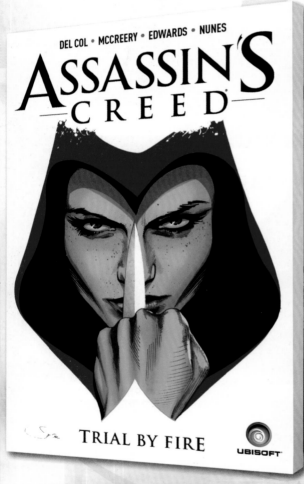
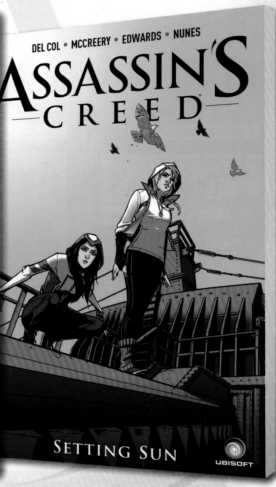